A poetic journey into the life of a genius journalist. Compelling and inspiring.

— Nik Wallenda, extreme funambulist,
wire walker of Niagara Falls,
seventh generation daredevil of the Flying Wallendas

Jack Perkins is the kind of storyteller who shows us things we might miss even standing next to him. Enjoy!

— Bob Dotson, national correspondent, NBC's *Today* show

Jack Perkins is a poet, and that means enjoyment for the reader. Jack's mastery of the English language provides pleasure aplenty. You will want to pass this book along to your friends. But before you do, you may want to read it again yourself. Jack is on to something; you can sense it. He moves past the apparent to the truth, to God. About this journey he is passionate, but as a poet he must keep his passion on a leash, out of respect for the reader, who needs room to make his or her own journey. So no packaged conclusions here, no coercion here, no grand claims to have walked all the way around God and taken pictures. The poet knows that truth comes suggestively, not dogmatically. The poet pauses over hints and coincidences, not with doubt's hesitation but with reverence for the God who came veiled in flesh.

— Fred B. Craddock, Bandy Distinguished Professor
of Preaching and New Testament, Emeritus,
Candler School of Theology, Emory University

Finding Moosewood, Finding God is wonderful. My memories of our trip across Africa are both rich and painful. I looked to Jack as our spiritual leader and our practical and loving guide. I hope people will avail themselves of the wisdom, humor, and insight in this book. I thank him for so many things, including helping me, too, find Moosewood.

— Patty Duke (Anna Pearce), actress

Jack Perkins's book transcends the common boundaries of a biography, perhaps because it was written by an uncommon man who is among the rarest of national treasures: an original American voice. *Finding Moosewood, Finding God* is, in itself, a literary gem, an inspired primer on how to live one's life with passion, kindness, humor, and a fierce devotion to the secret voice inside us all that steers us (if we allow it) to our hearts' own destiny.

— Randy Wayne White, author of the Doc Ford novels

FINDING
MOOSEWOOD,
FINDING
GOD

JACK PERKINS

What Happened When a TV Newsman Abandoned His Career *for* Life on an Island

FINDING MOOSEWOOD, FINDING GOD

ZONDERVAN®

ZONDERVAN

Finding Moosewood, Finding God
Copyright © 2013 by Jack Perkins

This title is also available as a Zondervan ebook.
Visit www.zondervan.com/ebooks.

This title is also available in a Zondervan audio edition.
Visit www.zondervan.fm.

Requests for information should be addressed to:

Zondervan, *Grand Rapids, Michigan 49530*

This edition: ISBN 978-0-310-31870-5 (softcover)

Library of Congress Cataloging-in-Publication Data

Perkins, Jack, 1933–
    Finding Moosewood, finding God : what happened when a TV newsman
abandoned his career for life on an island / Jack Perkins.
          p.   cm.
    ISBN 978-0-310-31825-5 (hardcover, jacketed)
    1. Perkins, Jack, 1933– 2. Television journalists—United States—Biography.
3. Television personalities—United States—Biography. I. Title.
PN4874.P4355A3 2013
070.92—dc23   [B] 2012027190

Cover design: Gearbox
Cover photography: Mary E Eaton / National Geographic Society / Corbis
Interior illustration: Mary Jo Perkins
Interior design: Katherine Lloyd, The DESK

Printed in the United States of America

14 15 16 17 18 19 20 /DCI/ 22 21 20 19 18 17 16 15 14 13 12 11 10 9 8 7 6 5 4 3 2 1

For God, our Creator

For God, my Re-creator

And for Mary Jo,
without whom Moosewoodn't

CONTENTS

FOREWORD

J ack Perkins wasn't always a person whose presence could fill a room just with the sound of his deep James Earl Jones voice. That would come.

When we first met at NBC Washington back in the '60s (that would be the 1960s, not the 1860s, for you ageists), Jack's official job description was to be a writer for the nationally known broadcast journalist David Brinkley. Being a writer for Brinkley was like being a hitting coach for Ted Williams. Brinkley wrote virtually all of his own stuff in a unique style. Jack covered the doings of government and oversaw the editing of the film Brinkley wanted to use on the show that night. After some of that, he was sent out into the field to cover the story of the day: the Civil Rights Movement across the South. I, through all of this, was a lowly copyboy at NBC News in Washington, but Jack and I both saw ourselves as "in the door" at this great journalistic institution.

Like all of humanity, we were searching for the meaning of life, but didn't know it at the time. In journalism, one can quickly become cynical because we see so many tragedies and so many political phonies and religious hypocrites who fail to live up to promises they make or to practice what they preach. And so even if one decides to search for objective truth, one can often wind up lost by focusing on things below, rather than things above.

After leaving NBC in Washington, Jack was dispatched to Saigon to cover the emerging Vietnam War. Three years later, he was back in the States, posted (along with broadcasters Tom Snyder and Tom Brokaw) to NBC in Los Angeles, which served as a kind of farm team for up and coming talent.

On both the *NBC Nightly News* and *Today*, Jack was widely seen reporting on offbeat stories that set him apart from many other journalists. He became successful, and earned and appreciated a certain celebrity. What he did not realize, though, was that his real journey, the nonprofessional one, was leading him to a place he had not sought and in a way that surprised even him.

Abruptly retiring from NBC, Jack and his wife, Mary Jo, moved to a little island off the Maine Coast. They were the only residents, living in a small cabin surrounded by Acadia National Park. Inspired by a TV visit he had made with the great master Ansel Adams, Jack took up photography. He also began to write poetry, a discipline that has eluded some of the best writers in other fields. Jack discovered not only that he was good at both photography and poetry but that these pursuits led him to a new place. Ultimately, his commanding presence found an outlet on the A&E cable network, where, along with actor Peter Graves, Jack hosted the popular *Biography* series, which probed the backgrounds of celebrities and other people of interest.

When one wishes to see the stars clearly at night, astronomers advise to get away from the bright lights of a big city so they might be seen clearly and in their splendor. It took moving away from the bright political lights of Washington and the brighter celebrity lights of Los Angeles for Jack to see clearly and to recognize the splendor of the One who wanted his attention and, much more, his life.

In this book, Jack Perkins takes us on his personal journey, which led him to Jesus of Nazareth and to a new life with more purpose and power than anything Washington can offer or Hollywood can deliver. The problem with so many of us is that we never begin the journey, and thus we never know that what is waiting for us is so much more — "exceedingly, abundantly, above all we ask or think," as Scripture puts it — than the petty, unimportant, and disposable things in which we place so much of our puny faith.

Jack's faith in Christ is real because he has processed it — worked it out, as Paul the apostle of Jesus commanded. *Finding Moosewood, Finding God* is as unique as Jack is. It avoids the cliches of contemporary evangelicalism and introduces us to what seems like an exciting life interviewing celebrities, only to present a much more purposeful life after Jack meets the Creator of all.

It is said that God has his people everywhere — seemingly less so in journalism and in the arts, perhaps because of the view that these professions contaminate any follower of Jesus who enters them. But microphones and cameras carry only what people put through them, and failing to engage culture guarantees its remaining a "vast wasteland," as former FCC Commissioner Newton Minow called it fifty years ago in a far more innocent age. It is true that it seems one must either hide or downplay one's faith in order to rise through the ranks, but it is not impossible if we are determined to honor God.

Maybe that's one of the many reasons I love Jack Perkins. He and I have been saved not to leave the world but to serve God in the worlds of writing, broadcasting, poetry, and photography. Perhaps there are others who, after reading Jack's book, will be inspired to follow Jesus, and then us as well.

— Cal Thomas, former NBC News copyboy
and current syndicated and USA Today *columnist*

INTRODUCTION

Later, things would be different. By the time I found myself hosting A&E's *Biography* series, doing essays for *The MacNeil Newshour*, broadcasting Fourth of July concerts of the Boston Pops in front of a third of a million people on the Esplanade plus millions more on TV, reporting documentaries across various PBS stations — by that time many things would be different.

I would be different. And, significantly, TV news would be different, more as we find it today — a crazed kaleidoscope of crises and crimes, disputes and incitements, pointless polls and arguing experts talking too much about what matters little, too little of what matters most. So seems news today.

But there was a time, back in the early days of TV news, a time I knew well. For three momentous decades, I labored and learned as a TV newsman, traveling that decidedly secular world, encountering many remarkable people who offered by word or deed lessons for a hungry heart to hoard. I reflected on those, absorbed some, but never plumbed the belief, the faith that oft underlay them.

Nor, for the longest time, did I plumb my own. I never doubted the existence of God. I just didn't care. I was doing fine living a life unexamined. Serendipitous flukes, coincidences, and lucky breaks seemed to guide my life just where I wanted to go. I had success, recognition, and enough acclaim to coddle the ego. There was no room in my life for God. For a journalist, the coin of the realm is fact, hard fact. Not speculation. And certainly not unprovable belief.

And yet, and yet ...

Though there was no room in my life for God, there *was* room in God for my life.

The epiphany, when it came, came not by flukes, coincidences, or breaks but by more powerful guidance than those. At the height of my career, I made the drastic and transforming decision to retreat with my wife to an island-for-two off the coast of Maine. After years of telling other people's lives, it was time to start living my own, time to understand and acknowledge the godly guidance that made it possible.

And that would be the greatest story this newsman could ever report.

1

WHY
THOREAU
IT ALL AWAY?

"Commentator Jack Perkins Leaving NBC for an Island"
— *Los Angeles Herald-Examiner,* front page headline

After 25 years as a TV correspondent, anchorman and commentator, Jack Perkins said Friday he plans to retire from broadcast journalism next month to move to a small island off the coast of Maine.
— *Los Angeles Times,* p. 12

"Jack Perkins Leaves for Maine after Leaving His Mark." Jack started doing TV when TV started doing news. He is one of the founding fathers of TV journalism. He helped give it direction and purpose. TV news is important in our society because people like Jack covered news as if it were important and as if we viewers were able to understand and learn from it.
— *Burbank Leader*

"Newsman Perkins Ankling in June"
— *Variety*

The day those stories appeared, five questions tickled. (1) Why did the *Herald-Examiner* think the story deserved front page? (2) Why *didn't* the *LA Times* think it deserved front page? (3) Why was the *Leader* so embarrassingly effusive? (4) Why did *Variety* talk that way? And (5) just plain *why?*

Why, in the midst of a successful and satisfying television career, was I chucking it — trading West Coast for East; megalopolis of eight million for island, population two; airline schedules for tide table; *TV Guide* for *Peterson Field Guides*; Saks for L. L. Bean; fourteen local TV stations and eighty-two local radio stations for none of either; three newspapers delivered to the front gate each morning and three more waiting at work, for a trip across the bay to Sherman's to buy the local weekly; smog for fog; mockingbirds for loons; new BMW for used Jeep; convenient public utilities for woodstove and solar power; monthly bills and paychecks for monthly bills; sounds of sounds for sounds of quiet; and freeways for free ways? Why?

For a quarter century, I had been a swimmer in the magic aquarium, an electronic image that flickered and fled. Correspondent/commentator/anchorman for NBC News is how I described myself.

"Noted actor/reporter," mocked a non-TV colleague, in envy, I assumed.

"That *blankety-blank* Jack Perkins," muttered a certain president of the United States, not in envy, I assumed.

Chaser of big doings, teller of grand tales, dweller among great cities, I not only loved my job but loved myself for having it. So what happened? Didn't I still enjoy the recognition? When approached on the street by a stranger to whom — I could tell from the knowing glint in his eyes — I was not a stranger but a familiar somebody from somewhere to whom he had to say *something*, that wasn't unpleasant, was it?

Even better was being recognized by someone who really was a somebody. Like approaching Bob Newhart at a party to tell him how much I admired his work, only to find him approaching me to tell me how much he admired mine; or when someone on the phone told me his friends had been praising a commentary I'd delivered on the air that day, and those friends were Elizabeth Taylor, Gregory Peck, and Cary Grant, and the someone on the phone was Frank Sinatra. Why would I choose to "ankle" away from moments like those and become a certifiable nobody?

Beyond its superficial satisfaction, TV reporting offered joys of substance — the pleasure of a story well told, a persuasive commentary. A reporter had the rare and enviable power to shine light into the dark corners where land developers readied blueprints for urban blight, where con men schemed "Christian book sales" to separate the gullible from their nest eggs, where malingerers feigned disabilities to bilk taxpayers, the shadowy back rooms where frauds, quacks, and never-rich-enough billionaires plotted and conspired. That flickering blue light in a distant window really could dispel darkness. In an ephemeral medium, you actually could do lasting good.

Why abandon that? Why would an ego fed on fame decide to diet? Why the introvert, dependent on recognition to grease social ways, withdraw to anonymity? Having persuaded himself that the spotlight shining on him really did make him brighter, why, while that light still shone, would the actor, midplay, exit grinning and head for a deserted island?

Or as pastor Dr. Robert Schuller, a man who loved wordplay,

asked us in California one day, "Jack, Mary Jo, with all you have here, why do you want to Thoreau it away?"

Clever line, which at that moment I couldn't answer. I didn't know.

Thinking about it today, I realize that while I certainly enjoyed the touch of celebrity back then, something inside me, yet unacknowledged, was nagging: *You're known, Big Guy. Hooray. But is that enough? Is it enough to have recognition if you don't use it? And how should you use it? Well, think of it this way, TV Man: Where did everything come from; who allowed you to enjoy such recognition? Might it have been the grace of a holy God, giving you gifts not just to have but also to use? You've sung the hymn "To God Be the Glory." Might that be a purpose for what you have?*

Again, these were thoughts I should have been thinking years back, but at least at a conscious level was not. In those golden-ego days, dazzled by the spotlight of celebrity, vanity, and self-satisfaction, I was lost in the dark of my own illumination. Never did it occur to me that the flukes, impulses, and happenstances that seemed to be directing my life were, in fact, the guidance of a generous hand — indeed, the guidance of the Holy Spirit. I didn't know and wouldn't know for a while, the ultimate acknowledgment coming only slowly, a reluctant revelation.

I've heard people ask, often sourly after a painful ordeal, "Where was God all this time?" My times had been far from painful, and I didn't ask that question back then. My answer today, with the clear eyes of retrospection, would be, He was there, always there, patiently waiting for me to know it.

I beg the reader, then, to be patient as I recount happenings without seeming at first to appreciate their profound, hidden meaning.

A reporter learns early that behind every small headline lurks a long story, perhaps a sequence of stories and sometimes unconscious decisions that only in the floodlight of a headline appear to be the product of forethought.

As a teenager, you accept an undefined job and decades later realize that at that moment, your career was chosen. You flirt with a stranger and later realize you were meeting your soul mate. One day you go for a walk in the woods with no destination, and on another, very distant day you look back over your footsteps and notice they led to your destiny. You call in sick one time — a little fib — and before you know it, you're emptying your desk, your awards for past work and notes for future work, into a cardboard box and setting out for the horizon.

A good newsman can't resist digging into that chain of little stories, those coincidences and offhand decisions, in pursuit of the why. That's what this book is about.

The day the first reports of our departing LA hit the headlines was also the day of the Emmy Awards. I was nominated for Best Commentary because of a piece that I had written in anger, disregarding the likelihood that it also might anger my own bosses. I wasn't sure they would let it be aired, but I was determined to try.

The explosion in illegal drugs was one of the greatest problems our society faced while trying not to face it. The media, I believed, were morally culpable for condoning drug use through the snickering humor of movies and late-night TV, rock songs, and rock star behavior. Wouldn't John Belushi's recent death by overdose be a lesson to NBC, my employer, which for years had profited from his and his buddies' stoner humor on *Saturday Night Live*? One hoped. I hoped.

But as *SNL* began its new season, what was its very first skit?

A skit cynically joking about cast members taking drug tests. The scene was an office with a table full of specimen cups. And who presided over this urinous moment, making a cameo appearance in the skit? None other than the president of NBC Entertainment, Brandon Tartikoff. I thought it reprehensible and felt compelled to say so in my nightly TV commentary on the network's flagship station, KNBC. My commentaries were broadcast from NBC Burbank, Tartikoff's home base, but when I turned in my copy, to the credit of network and station, there were some gulps and hesitations, but not a single person censored or softened a word.

Tartikoff heard it. A few days later, he issued a public apology and announced a new policy: NBC Entertainment would no longer treat drug abuse as a laughing matter. And somebody — I don't know who — nominated that commentary for an Emmy.

Dressed for the awards banquet in cerise silk overblouse and white silk trousers, Jo was hardly the backwoods recluse the morning papers had our friends expecting to see. In a hall of a thousand industry insiders, there was an eveningful of astonishment to be expressed (or feigned), congratulations sincerely offered, and, of course, genuine puzzlement as to why we were leaving all this behind. Not that our colleagues and friends in tuxes and evening gowns wouldn't want to do it themselves, many of them said.

So why don't you? we asked.

It was as hard for them to explain why they *weren't* going to run away and live in a cabin in the woods as it was for us to say why we were.

Idaho — We'd met the real thing once, a genuine back-to-basics hermit. He and his story were engaging and, in a twisted way, even inspiring. He lived in the northern Idaho wilderness and was called Buckskin Bill.

Once, decades earlier, he had carried another name, Sylvan Ambrose, and had been an eager young man with an engineering degree from Cornell whose family tradition was that each boy-child, completing college, went to the wilderness to survive by himself for a year — nature's graduate school. The difference with Sylvan was that he never went back.

He met us at the end of the narrow, swaying suspension bridge he had engineered across a roaring tributary. Everything about him smelled of the bear grease he used for hair tonic, salve, and boot oil. A short man, his belly was ample, his face weathered to leather. His mouth was small, as if, living alone with no one to talk to, he had little use for it. His eyes were large, overworked in a wilderness paradise with so much to see.

We spent a day with him, walking his proud empire and constantly wondering what kept him here. Was it a twisted religious fervor? Did this man worship nature? Reporters often ran across religious zealots whose eccentricities encouraged the biases many journalists already held against religion. Reporters tended to think the only things that matter are those that are known, not vaguely believed. Accordingly, most journalists I knew were agnostics, if not atheists. So was I.

It was late in the afternoon, sitting out on the riverbank, when I finally got around to asking him, "Don't you miss a lot you left behind?"

"What should I miss?" he countered, not brushing me off but genuinely interested in hearing something he hadn't considered.

Knowing he'd been raised amid culture, I said, "Theater, art, the symphony —"

"Let me tell ya about that," he jumped in, eyes a-twinkle. He pointed toward the craggy cliff across the river. "Up there's the stage, see? Goats, Dall sheep, hawks, eagles, sometimes a bear shamblin' along. Those are the players, and they put on a heck of a show. Different ever' day, ever' night. Never the same twice." He swept his hand back toward the meadow beside his garden. It was spattered with tiny milfoil waving in the breeze. Overhead darted a mountain bluebird. "There's all the art gallery I need. Ya understand?"

I understood.

"And, hey, far as sym-phony," pronouncing it like the synonym for fraud, "who wants to sit there listening to folks up on some platform goin' tweedle-tweedle and oompah-oompah? I figger if he's worth anythin' at all, a man's gotta make his own oompahs."

I knew at the time I could never adopt Buckskin Bill's lifestyle, but I understood what he was saying. And I remembered. When finally, after more than thirty years of reporting other people's stories and I found myself ready to live my own, that's how I thought of it: I was going to make my own oompahs!

Emmy night was a poignant time of camaraderie, love, and farewells. It was also a long night, since every recipient of every award, betraying his or her professional responsibility to put the interests of the audience first, blathered on until it was near midnight when the prize for commentaries finally came up.

The professional thing is to have an acceptance speech prepared, timed and trimmed, with allowance for the obligatory claim of incredulity. I had not prepared. I had so much in my heart, overflowing gratitudes and fond recollections all overlaid with excited anticipation, I never could have written them in a speech.

The five nominees were called to the stage, and I stood there among them looking out over that dressy crowd and feeling curiously disembodied, there but not there. Through the vast hall were mirrored columns, and in one of them I could see us, five tuxed-up monkeys with spotlights shining on us. I stood up *here* looking at me standing out *there* and knew something no one else knew: that fellow out there in the mirror wasn't I. It couldn't be. Not puffed up like that, swilling with the swells. At the least, that guy out there, I knew for certain, was not who I wanted to be. That was the person I was leaving behind, that was Jack "Perkins of NBC." Applause. Raucous yelling from the table down front where my colleagues were looking up at me. Jo beaming up, that beautiful face.

I stepped forward, shook hands with someone, received the statuette from someone else, walked to a podium, took a deep breath, and, looking out across the faces of friends and colleagues, acquaintances and competitors, companions of the last twenty-five years, I spoke just five words. The shortest speech of the night, maybe the shortest Emmy acceptance on record.

"Thanks," I said, pausing to savor the delicious moment that would have to last a long while. "But we're still going."

2

HORRIBLE MAN, SMALL TOWNS, AND A STORYTELLER MAKES IT TO TV

Center Lovell, Maine — I was on my way to meet a horrible man — and, unwittingly, taking the first step on a path that would lead to an island, a new life, and God.

Getting to Horrible Man wasn't easy. Maine isn't on the way from any *here* to any *there*. You don't happen upon it on the way to someplace else. You have to seek it out, travel intentionally. For me, from Los Angeles, it was as far as I could go without crossing an international border or an ocean. For most people, that kind of remoteness is a pain; for Mainers, it's a blessing.

Horrid, horrendous, horrible — the adjectives were all warranted. As any bookseller and millions of book readers could attest, even back then, there was no one as horrific ("causing horror"), horrendous ("fitted to excite horror"), and horrible ("exciting horror") as young Stephen King of Bangor and Center Lovell, Maine.

His Center Lovell summer home was on Kezar Lake, a true *Golden Pond* where the movie of that play would have been shot but for the lack of accommodations and services. (Instead, the film about a pond in Maine was shot in New Hampshire.) Getting to Kezar Lake required traveling from city airport to freeway to highway to winding two-lane road past general store to rutted dirt track through deep woods until finally, vectoring on hope and the glints of sunlight from a calm face of water, the TV crew and I found an aging but proud compound of gray-shingled buildings with forest green shutters: our first destination, the lodge called Westways.

Stepping from the car, smelling the piney perfume and listening to the lake lapping on the shore, I was smitten. This wasn't a place of pretense; the buildings were neat, the rooms clean but simple, natural. Last hotel I'd been in was a gaudy excess in Miami Beach, where a card was placed on your evening pillow instructing you how much to tip. There was no card on the pillow at Westways.

The inn was run by Stephen's friends Don and Barbara Tripp, who had their own fascinating story. Don had been an executive with General Motors in Michigan until he and Barbara decided, suddenly in midlife, they needed a change. So they overturned their lives and started anew. Don enjoyed handiwork; Barbara liked cooking. Their seven children were game for anything. So the family moved here to Maine to manage this inn in the woods. The joy of their transformation was still infectious years later.

Then, too, just a half mile up a trail through birch and fir were Stephen and Tabitha King with their kids and welcoming warmth. He was horrid to see, but this time in the *Oxford English Dictionary*'s first sense of the word: "bristling, shaggy, rough," the bulky, black-bearded roughness not of some monster-creature he might have conjured but of a gentled Maine black bear. Disarmingly, this young fellow, thirty-two at the time, seemed almost cuddly. He was not yet the mega-success he was to become; the film of *The Shining* had just been released, and Jack Nicholson's leering mug — "Here's Johnny!" — was just beginning to become a cultural icon. Stephen had not yet appeared in *Creepshow*, he hadn't computer-coauthored *The Talisman*, published *It*, acknowledged the pseudonymously written Bachman books, produced any of his numerous screenplays, been on the cover of *Time*, or become such a central figure in American culture that Moscow correspondent Nicholas Daniloff had been arrested by the KGB for subversion simply because he gave a Russian friend a copy of a new Stephen King book. This was before all that, and before Stephen's personal finances had grown to rival the state of Maine's. Still, he was known and had early wealth; he did not need whatever publicity our report might produce, but there was never, in all that week, any indication that it mattered to him. He acceded to whatever the producer and cameraman asked, not out of a desire for fame but because they seemed like decent folks, and helping decent folks is why we live. That was the feeling we got as we followed him to his writing studio in the early morning, a small, separate building in which his desk and keyboard were carefully turned away from the stunning lake-scape through the picture window, because even a man of his irrepressible creativity could not face that view and ignore it. Then, in late morning, he hopped into the Blazer to reward himself for a good day's work with a bouncing romp up the dirt road to the post office for mail and to the general store for gossip. Then back home for lunch on the deck with Tabby and the kids, the whole tribe casually brainstorming ideas that one day, perhaps, would find their way into bestsellers.

After lunch with them one day, I returned to Westways to lounge on the deck of the boathouse and reflect on why the Kings' unaffected lifestyle seemed so comforting and familiar, yet also surprising. Stephen and Tabby were small-towners by choice as well as birth and upbringing, and to someone like me who still accepted freeways and airports, deadlines and headlines, and the constant buzz of electronic media as nonnegotiable facts of life, there was something extraordinary about that. At what point in my life, I began to wonder, had I given up my own small-townness?

Wooster, Ohio — When I was growing up there, Wooster was a town of ten thousand. It had a public square in the center of town, where Dad used to take my brother, Jim, and me every other weekend to Dick Morrison's barbershop to get haircuts and listen to men telling tales of their lives and their town. I loved hearing those hometown storytellers. From the barbershop, it was a short walk to the bank on the west side of the square, where Jim and I would each make a small deposit, getting a handwritten record of it in our precious passbooks, or we'd buy some war stamps to paste into government-issued albums. That was one of the rituals of life Dad taught us: whatever a man earns, he goes to the bank and puts some of it away for the future.

The town had a small Presbyterian college where many of my buddies' fathers taught. I wouldn't attend the College of Wooster or its church. My family was not much for churchgoing. When we did attend, the church was chosen not for its theology or denomination but for how interesting was the preacher and who else did or didn't attend. For a while, when our church of choice was the

Lutheran, I got into a youth group. I recall that in one of our Bible studies, we read Jesus' parable of the spreading of seeds. I didn't know it then, but today, looking back, I see how appropriate those verses were. I find myself in that parable — several times. At first, as Jesus told his disciples, some of the seed the farmer spread fell onto the road where the soil was packed down hard, no chance for the seed to take root. The seed represented God's Word, and in our family, the soil was packed hard. There was always a Bible on the shelf in our home, but it was *on the shelf*. When it seemed necessary that grace be said before a special meal, it was usually one of those hackneyed bits of prayer-doggerel taught to kids: "God is great; God is good; let us thank him for this food." Neither good verse nor meaningful prayer. If my parents held any fervent religious beliefs, they neither spoke of nor modeled them. Accordingly, neither did I. I was too busy, as kids can be. Every day, I rode my bike through the college campus to get from our house to the high school, and I spent many evenings in the college library, a great stone edifice where I could wander the stacks and explore the microfiche archives, researching topics for debate or news analyses for "Extemp" (Extemporaneous Speaking), my favorite event in the speech tournaments that were consuming more and more of my after-school hours.

I won a lot of ribbons and trophies at those tournaments. They decorated my room at home. Moreover, at one of those events, I won the best prize of all, a prize I hadn't sought or immediately appreciated, and never would have won if it hadn't been for a bad break that proved to be a very good break.

Four of us on a Boy Scout winter camping trip at a place called Pee Wee Hollow learned that a toboggan cannot be steered around a fast-approaching oak tree. I don't remember the moment of crash. With all the bundling clothes, I didn't hear the crack of my right tibia and fibula being broken, nor did I immediately feel the pain shoot up my leg. But by the time we had humbled ourselves before our exasperated scoutmaster and he had driven me back into town to the doctor, I could feel the break all too well.

I spent the next six weeks in bed with a plaster cast on my leg and without much to do.

Our speech coach discovered, early in the competition season, that he had a gap in the team he needed to fill: Original Oratory. He'd seen me plunge recklessly into Humorous Reading, Debate, and Extemporaneous Speaking, and there was the evidence of that plaster cast, so he realized he'd found the perfect candidate. Would I be interested in a challenge, he proposed, using my recuperative weeks to compose something original to present? I figured, Why not?

I began doing what little research I could from my bedroom, a significant challenge in those days before broadband access, Google, and Wikipedia. Today I'm willing to confess that, though the category was Original Oratory, it could be argued my speech was not wholly original — that, in fact, my ten-minute oration might, to the discerning eye, have had some striking similarities to a piece in *Parade* magazine, the ubiquitous Sunday supplement carried by the *Cleveland Plain Dealer* that was delivered to our front porch.

Plagiarism!

Mea culpa. But at this point, who cares? If the most blatant, it was also the most fortuitous bit of cheating in a long career.

March 2, 1951 — (You bet I don't forget the date!) The tournament was at Canton McKinley High. I was wearing a bright red sport coat, a white shirt, blue tie ("Patriotism and You" was the title of my cribbed oration), and was still on crutches, milking sympathy. I won my event that Saturday; that I recall. But the most vivid memory is not of the moments at a podium making the same speech over and over to different panels of judges, or of the announcement of the winners. Little of that remains. The most vivid memory is of what happened between sessions.

During the breaks, the kids from a dozen schools milled around, chatting both to make new friends and to dispel nervousness. I joined one group gathered on a broad staircase; a deck of cards appeared, and we started playing. I couldn't tell you what game. What matters is the pretty face (no makeup; she didn't need it) of the girl who had supplied the cards, a freshman from Orrville, a tiny burg half the size of Wooster. I tried not to lord my urban sophistication over this kid from Hicksville. She was competing in Dramatic Reading, performing from the play *Our Town*. She played Emily, a sweet and gentle small town girl from Grover's Corner. It was typecasting. I tried not to appear boastful when I informed her that the play's author had come to Wooster to perform it. That's right, the famous playwright Thornton Wilder came and performed in *my* hometown. But Orrville also has its claim to fame, I pointed out in a kindly, generous way. Apple butter. The J. M. Smucker Company, makers of jams and jellies, was headquartered in Orrville.

She could have told me, "Yes, I know. My dad is sales manager of Smucker's," but she didn't. She wasn't the type for dismissive remarks. Rather, she gave me what I took as the awed look befitting a freshman learning from a big-town senior.

After the card game, we all went off to our separate competitions. I kept winning. So (I eventually found out) did little Miss Orrville. But I barely saw her again that day and probably never would have seen her again had it not been for another "accident."

When I got home and hung up my red sport coat, I found in my pocket the deck of cards we'd been playing with. I must have inadvertently stuck it in there when the bell had summoned us to our next competition. The gentlemanly thing to do would be to call the girl up and offer to return it.

If you've already guessed that little Miss Orrville had planted the cards in my pocket so I'd be obliged to call her, you're brighter than I was in those days.

Nowadays when I see players from the NFL gathering each year in Canton, Ohio, to be enshrined in the Football Hall of Fame, I can't help but think they're getting cheated. When *I* was in the NFL — the National Forensic League — I went to Canton and received not just a yellow jacket and a plaque but a love for the rest of my life.

Not long after the speech tournament at Canton McKinley, while still on crutches, I won another tournament, this one cosponsored by Western Reserve University and Cleveland radio station WGAR. The prize was a full, four-year scholarship to the university in whose hospital I had been born seventeen years earlier, and also a job at the radio station, a fifty-thousand-watt CBS affiliate.

My parents were proud and pleased (they'd not have to bear college expenses), and I was ecstatic. Finally, the speechifying of the past few years was paying off!

It was an amazingly generous prize, although, curiously, in the eight years the university and the station had been hosting the tournament, no winner had ever accepted it. They had other colleges lined up or had no interest in working in radio. For the tournament sponsors, it was a great deal, getting credit for generosity while never having to deliver.

This time, however, a gangly, six-foot-three, 152-pound kid from Wooster hobbled into the radio station to claim his reward.

What were the WGAR bosses to do? I can only imagine their head-scratching until the station's news director, Charlie Day, rescued the moment. (I give thanks that Stan Gee or Manny Eisner didn't suggest the kid be brought into their sales department.) Charlie said, "I could use the kid. Maybe he can change paper in the machines." Wire service teletype machines were always running, always consuming paper or ribbon or both. WGAR had six of them.

As the months passed, I watched as the regulars in the newsroom did their jobs: checking sources with police and fire departments, following up on phoned-in tips and earlier stories of the day, going through the wire copy, rewriting scripts, dashing — always dashing, never two seconds to spare — to the studio before airtime.

I watched and learned, until the day Charlie told me he wanted me to take over the weekend newscasts. WGAR had just signed a new sponsor, the flower growers Jackson and Perkins, whose name made my presence on those shows a natural.

And then came another string of those random accidents (as they still seemed to the spiritually myopic) that can define a person's destiny. WGAR's prime evening newscaster, Jack Dooley, accidentally shot himself in the arm while cleaning a handgun.

Unable to type a script, he couldn't work; the station offered him an unpaid leave of absence and offered me his position and salary until he returned. I accepted on the condition that the station continue paying him the salary. He had a wife and children; I was a college kid, unencumbered, didn't need the money. I figured the opportunity to do some real reporting every day and polish my new craft was of greater value to me. As it turned out, even my youthful optimism vastly underestimated the opportunity I'd fallen into. Soon I was experiencing the absolute heights and depths of journalism.

I had watched Dooley working his police sources enough to know what to do on a Sunday morning, July 4, 1954, when a startling police call came in: there'd been a murder out in the western Cleveland suburb of Bay Village. A woman named Marilyn Sheppard had been found bloodily beaten to death in her bed. Her husband, a respected neurosurgeon, was found lying unconscious downstairs. Dr. Sam Sheppard claimed their home had been invaded by a man he had chased to the beach below their home, where the man had turned on him and beaten him senseless. It was this "bushy-haired man" who had killed his wife, Sam Sheppard insisted, a claim few of the hardened cops on the scene believed. (In the TV series, and later in the movie, inspired by the case, the killer was a one-armed man.)

I started scribbling notes for my broadcast, the first news coverage of what would come to be called the Trial of the Century. It was O. J. before O. J.

It was also one of the most shameful episodes in modern American journalism. Often the coverage was nothing more than sensational speculation and hysteria posing as news. "Why Isn't Sam Sheppard in Jail?" screamed the headline across the front page of the *Cleveland Press* as the investigation began. And that was just the start of what the US Supreme Court, reversing Sam Sheppard's conviction years later, described as the "carnival atmosphere" that denied him due process.

The trial began in the fall of 1954, by which time I was one of the most knowledgeable radio reporters covering the story. Big guns came rolling into town — Theo Wilson, the top crime reporter for the *New York Daily News*, the nation's biggest-selling newspaper; the renowned journalist Bob Considine; some famous detective from Scotland Yard whose name I don't recall. The courtroom was packed every day, the papers rushing to publish every tidbit they could uncover or manufacture. A chain of downstate Ohio newspapers signed me to write daily features, while I was also doing a nightly radio newscast and attending college full-time. Supposedly.

When, on December 21, the guilty verdict finally came in, as other reporters scrambled for pay phones (in that era before cell phones), I dashed from the courtroom, ran down the hall, and squeezed into a janitor's closet the wily WGAR team had clandestinely fitted with a live mike. Within seconds, I was on the air ad-libbing my scoop, with a bit of heart-thumping, heavy breathing coloring my delivery.

Next day, a local paper remarked on my "beat," noting in particular that one of the competing newsmen I'd scooped was Warren Guthrie, one of my professors at Western Reserve. Wouldn't help my grades, the columnist joked.

If he'd seen my grades, he would have known I had nothing to lose. By the end of that fall semester, my grades were three F's, a D, and a W (withdrawn). I'd been so consumed by the Sheppard case that I'd hardly been attending class. Although during that time I had somehow managed to be elected president of the Western Reserve student council, I quickly became the only president ever impeached for failing to attend a single meeting.

Given either the disregard or kindness of the university, my four-year scholarship was allowed to stretch to five and a half years. When I finally was graduated, President Dr. John Schoff Millis handed me the diploma, whispering, "About time, Perkins."

College can be a challenging time for faith. I think back to the parable of the seeds as the boy Lutheran had read it. The first seeds were spread across the path where they could not take root, then the second group of seeds fell where there was only a shallow sheath of soil over unyielding rock. So the seeds could, at first, take root. In college, one of my majors was religion, a lot of reading about people's multifarious ways of seeking and beseeching their deity. As a social study, taught by an engaging professor, it fascinated me. But it didn't take hold. It was a subject to study, a class to pass, not a way of life to consider adopting. I was shallow soil masking unyielding rock.

I was thinking too much. Can a person really think too much? Well, if the process of thinking suppresses or even supplants feeling, heeding, attending, or believing, then yes, that is thinking too much. You can think yourself out of believing.

College is the ideal way. You not only cut an umbilical, losing your accustomed support network; you go off unawares into a new world, a mostly secular world that worships knowledge. Its clergy are teachers, professors, PhDs. They are the ones who know; you are one who doesn't. They teach you not so much how to think as what to know. They test your thinking but reward your knowing. In college you *are* what you know. Your knowing is the measure of your being. Nobody cares what you may *believe* about anything, only what you know. Belief is theory; the only accepted currency in college is fact.

This son of a rational engineer, this lover of cloistered hours in library stacks fine-tuning arguments for debate or Extemp, this college student whose favorite course was Syllogistic Logic, this staunchly, tenaciously left-brained thinker, unknowingly but inexorably in college began thinking himself even farther away from believing. Small-town kid became big-city man. And professional journalist to boot! For a journalist, as for an academic, the only thing that counts is what you know. In journalism, speculation, conjecture, purveying the unproven are forbidden. (Or used to be.)

There was a church on the campus of Western Reserve University. I usually worked Sundays, my communion at the radio station being a bag of White Castle burgers and a quart of chocolate milk. I didn't miss God. I didn't have time. What with work and school and fraternity life and extracurricular activities, I hardly had time for a few hours in the bunkroom at night before I had to get up and go, either to class or to work. There was no space for God. That's how I thought. Nor did I feel deprived. I was not interested in anything like a Creator, which I couldn't rationally, logically substantiate.

I was doing fine. Life was good.

My decision in college to avoid a journalism or speech major was because I didn't want to learn *how* to communicate and not *what* to communicate. Better to study something a journalist needs to know about—history, economics, social studies, the cultures of the world—or anything that intrigues. I went through Reserve with a double major—poli sci and religion—joking that I wanted to know what both sides were up to. Actually, I made those choices because I was drawn to the engaging professors who presided over those disciplines. They were challenging professors who taught a great deal more than what was in their syllabuses.

Throughout my years as a reporter, I continued to be drawn to the engaging and strong figures I was privileged to meet. Some of my colleagues were attracted to controversy, crime, and corruption. They found fame from their ability to confront wrongdoers, exposing evil. I was never good at that. That puts it kindly. Fact is, when required to spring upon an unwary villain, at least once I got physically sick. The resulting story won me an Emmy, but to this day I won't look at it. My distaste for such ambush journalism was partly from a sense of common decency and partly from shyness. It seems a contradiction that one in the public eye as much as I came to be might be shy, but many are, and I was.

Rather than chase, accost, and accuse, I preferred to know what makes a person tick. Some thought of me as a "human interest" reporter, but I found that term vague, if not meaningless. Indeed, thinking of it now, I wonder if there should be anything other than "human interest" reporters. If a story isn't of interest to humans, why tell it? Of course, the risk there, and we see it too often, is journalistic pandering—telling stories that are superficially interesting but of little or no consequence. Which celebrity, famous for being famous, is in rehab or in jail? What politician makes a promise that he or she knows, as well as we, will never be kept? What drunk or druggie commits what offense against decency? These we really don't need to know. We don't *need*! But apparently, according to those who measure ratings, we *want*.

Today, if called upon to define my preferred kind of reporting when things seemed a bit more consequential, I would simply say I liked telling stories. (Echoes of Dick Morrison's barbershop.) Especially stories of people who, as Buckskin Bill said, made oompahs. He was no celebrity, no politician, and committed no indecencies, but he had something to say worth hearing and considering.

Since, throughout my TV career, I often was granted the liberty to choose my own subjects in what I came to think of as my journalism of self-indulgence, there were many stories of the people I wanted to meet and figured viewers would as well. Today I realize that as I met them to tell their stories, a veiled part of me also was parsing the state of their faith.

Côte d'Azur, France — One of the twentieth century's giants of modern art was Spanish-Catalan artist Joan Miro. He was the giant we flew to the south of France to meet. A grand *Vernisssage* or celebrative exhibition of his work was being mounted, and a lavish celebration it would be! There've always been many who didn't appreciate Miro's surrealism, but many others who were grateful that his art was intended never to be a mere depiction of the world (how dull that would be!) but a separate world tumbled about and spattered with bright illogic.

Spying him for the first time, across the atelier, I was struck. He was a miniature. (Why do we expect our giants to be tall?) Delicate, scarcely more than five foot, and at age eighty-six, hunched, slippered, leaning on a cane, tired and frail.

He was about to watch as the first proofs of his latest lithograph were pulled from the press. A printer operated the machinery, but Miro himself stood by to ensure that each reproduction was true to his vision. Charily, Miro edged closer. As the press rolled, it seemed that Miro, too, had been switched on. Dull eyes grew bright, sparking and sparkling. Tired face beamed with a broadening smile as he gazed, approvingly, on the first print. His art came to life; he came to life. He had created it; now it, in turn, re-created him.

I asked him a question. He had seemed so skeptical before the print run began. "Yes," he replied. "I am often skeptical. In studio, in life. But, you see, the more skeptical I become about the things around me, the closer I become to God. It is good."

That evening, he and his wife, Pilar, spent but a few minutes at the grand party for him; as she saw his energy flagging, she steered the master to a quiet departure, as if eager to return to the relative solitude of their island home on Majorca.

Island home. I think now that I must have tucked that pleasant phrase away in my unconscious, while also, as one who used skepticism as a tool of his profession, I stashed Miro's words that "the more skeptical I become about the things around me, the closer I become to God."

Skepticism fueling faith. Interesting idea.

As my memories of the TV years are often of people, so are my memories of college time. My first year, I pledged to a fraternity, Phi Gamma Delta, and moved into the Fiji House with a diverse bunch of guys. I sang in a quartet, The Fiji Four (lots of Four Freshmen tunes, a few Four Aces, although we never mastered the tight harmonies of the Hi-Lo's), and cowrote the annual student musical comedy with the rip-off title *Pal Josie*. Seems much of what I did in those years — what we all did — was derivative and naive. We were still so malleable, still taking form as adults.

Derivative, too, was my work on the air in those forming years. Let's say I was "suggestible." As I blow the dust off old recordings of early work, I can identify the year by the influences swaying my delivery at that time. For a while, I was Edward R. Murrow (solemn, stern). I tried Charles Collingwood (urbane, sophisticated). Robert Trout's wit infected me for a while. Later in my career, I fell too easily into the speech patterns of David Brinkley and, always, the induplicable meter of Paul Harvey.

In each of these cases (I slowly realized), it was not just the speaking style that defined the newscaster; it was also the writing — mostly, the writing. Read the scripts of Murrow's reports during the London Blitz and you'll understand. Or read a David Brinkley script from the *Huntley-Brinkley Report* era: supremely taut. That was the heart of it, I came to understand — the *writing*. Brinkley became my ideal and, a few years later, my mentor. Whatever success I had in the years to come I owed greatly to him.

A call from a man named Don Perris started my television career. He ran Cleveland TV station WEWS. It had been the first TV station in Cleveland, first anywhere between New York and Chicago, but had never gotten around to starting a news department. Now he wanted to. He had heard my work on radio during the Sheppard case and had decided I should be the one to do it.

What was it about my on-air work that impressed him? My

deep Murrow voice (bass in The Fiji Four), stylized Harvey delivery? Neither. Don Perris said he liked the way I never sounded like I was a newscaster *reading* the news but just a fellow talking to people, telling stories. Accepting his offer, I found myself just out of college, into TV, and at a perfectly propitious time.

Back east, NBC was launching a new broadcast, *The Huntley-Brinkley Report*, bringing together the resonant baritone of Chet Huntley and the engaging drawl and wit of David Brinkley. WEWS was an ABC affiliate, but the NBC station in Cleveland opted not to carry *Huntley-Brinkley*, so we jumped on the opportunity. In those days, instead of always flying its own correspondents around the nation to cover stories, NBC chose to draw on reporters from local affiliates. Soon the nation grew accustomed to the sign-off signatures of a new generation of journalists reporting from the home front — Floyd Kalber, WMAQ, Chicago; Dick John, WKY, Oklahoma City; Ray Moore, WSB, Atlanta. And before long, whenever NBC felt moved to catch up on doings around Ohio, national viewers started hearing the name Jack Perkins, WEWS, Cleveland.

One viewer in particular liked what he heard. Reuven Frank, the creator and executive producer of *The Huntley-Brinkley Report*, called one day to offer me a job. It would not be on the air — not to start, anyway — but it would be with the network, in New York, where Huntley anchored his half of the two-city program. What young television journalist would turn down New York?

Mary Jo and I — married by this time — were shiners. In life, there are shiners and whiners. Shiners you can take anywhere and they'll find something to like. Whiners will moan and harp on every discomfort or inconvenience. As shiners, we've always somehow discovered the simple pleasures of wherever I've been posted, even in places we mostly didn't like. New York we mostly didn't like. We considered ourselves fortunate to find a tiny basement apartment where our bed was wall-to-wall and the early-morning Gristede's grocery carts kicked city grit through open street-level windows onto our pillows. One day we were burgled, and *every* day we had to listen to the woman in the apartment next door pounding her head against the wall for some reason. In Ohio, one made an effort to find out why, but New Yorkers, we learned, knew better than to ask. Manhattan was never to our taste. For all the years thereafter, whenever I had to make a trip to New York City — and I made many — my comfort was the return ticket tucked in my coat pocket, my lifeline home to Mary Jo and the small-town satisfactions we never outgrew. Once, a son told us that he was the only one of his childhood friends in Los Angeles with parents who were still together. For us, that was a measure of small-town values, to be sure, but also of our abiding love and willingness to work through problems and disagreements rather than run away when difficult times came.

Dutchess County, New York — The Cagneys were still married. And still enjoying lives away from big cities.

The sign on the rail fence surrounding their 750-acre horse farm in upstate New York read simply "Verney." (The first syllable of his wife's maiden name combined with the last of his surname.) The farm rolled softly on the misty morning.

Driving up the gravel road, we saw, first, a small log-and-rock cabin we figured to be an outbuilding and kept driving to locate the main house of this wealthy retiree's estate. But, of course, we had just passed it. That simple cabin was James Cagney's home, squat and sturdy, appropriate for the man.

"'Mon in. How ya doin'?"

The unforgettable voice from the familiar square face, broader now but with the same sandy eyebrows, green eyes. Star aura and Saturday-night memories settled stoutly in an overstuffed chair by a bold rock fireplace blackened by years of use. He did not rise to greet his visitors, and that was fine. Eighty-one and in recent years victim of both stroke and acute diabetes that had jellied muscle and rusted joints, Jimmy Cagney was entitled to stay seated.

"Mr. Cagney," I started, and was immediately interrupted.

"Red."

"Excuse me?"

"Call me Red." He was one of the best Hollywood ever had, but he wasn't having any of Hollywood's pretensions. Never did. As soon as a film wrapped, he was always on the train headed home. He knew what, for him, was real, and it wasn't a set-strike party or Brown Derby cocktails with Hedda or Louella.

"So what was your question?" he said to get us back on track.

"Simply to ask why you quit. At the top of your game, why you chucked it twenty years ago." (Was a similar idea already forming so prematurely in my own unconscious?)

He launched into the story. He'd been shooting the Billy Wilder film *One, Two, Three*, a frantic farce with the pacing of a Bugs Bunny cartoon — exhausting work for an actor half his age — storming around in a pool of Klieg lighting amid the darkness everywhere else on the soundstage. When there came a break in the filming, he stepped outside for a breather. It was a beautiful day, sunshine and breezes. He took it in for a few minutes, then was called back to the set, from the sunlight and fresh air into the stuffy darkness. Which did he want for his life? he found himself wondering. He decided right then, between takes, that this film would be his last. The next train ride would take him home for good.

"After quite some career, Mr. Cagney."

"What did I tell you?"

"Red."

"Yep, some career."

And he launched into a gracious replay from his first taste of showbiz, impersonating a female to get a job on a women's chorus line, through the days of villainy as he broke into films, wielding tommy guns, smooshing a grapefruit into his leading lady's face (his own addition to the script), ultimately getting into comedies and musicals and becoming a favorite target of impressionists, hitching up their pants with their elbows, shrugging, and snarling, "You dirty rat."

"Never said it," Cagney told me. And the pants-hitching? "Did it in one picture, just once. Used to know a kid in the city who did that. I copied him. It caught on." A twinkling smile for a trademark understatement.

With difficulty he hoisted himself from his chair and led the way to see his stable full of Morgan horses, like him, compact, muscular, and all American. For years, riding them was his great joy, but it was now a joy denied.

He took us to his studio, where he used to paint. He'd been good until disease and dimming eyesight robbed him of that pleasure too.

Nowadays even getting around was hard. "Pick up your feet,

Jamesy," chided his caregiver as he walked slowly across the stubbled grass. He picked up his feet. And oh, one recalled, how the man used to pick up his feet! Well deserved was the Oscar won for the memorable song-and-dance film *Yankee Doodle Dandy*.

Now, all but immobile in his chair back at the house, he was being asked by his visitor one last and probably impertinent question. "Looking back, when you were making all that money years ago, were you smart about it? Did you do well?"

His answer was four words, that's all, but the timing and looks were a seminar in delivering a line. Head lowered, eyes peering up through overhanging fringes of brow: "Bought land." Pause, just long enough. Then the head lifted, brows springing in delight, a cocky Irish smirk dancing across the face: "Not bad."

Vintage Cagney. You knew in that instant this cunning old codger had been more than simply smart and was now more than merely solvent, and you knew one other thing. This was still, twenty years after his last performance, part crippled and blind, a transcendent master of his artistic tools — his face and body. So a screenwriter produces weak lines? No matter. Mannerisms, timing, the tiniest gesture can bring the character to life. It's the greatest skill in communicating — economy.

Bought land. Not bad.

No, buying land isn't bad, and Cagney's epigram, too, stayed with me — advice for the future, if not quite yet.

Our week with Stephen King and his family up in Maine was drawing to a close. We wandered with him one afternoon to Westways for the weekly dirt-field, good-buddy, pickup softball game, an affair happily fueled well into the darkling dusk by jovial camaraderie and a couple of pony kegs.

The next day, hiking the woods with the camera crew trailing us, I asked him why, able to afford a home anywhere, he remained in Maine. He spoke passionately of his feeling for this land, of enjoying woods and gentle people. Late afternoon, we headed down to the lake with a rod and a six-pack, the pond truly golden at that hour just before sunset, Stephen casting and not caring that there were no nibbles. That was not the purpose of the exercise. The purpose, as he explained it, was simply to sit there long enough and time it well enough that the sunset and the six-pack came out even. "What more could you ask of a day?"

Nothing more. Except to share it.

Stephen and his family, the Tripps' and theirs, the lubricated chums of the softball game, the lake and loons, the fishing without fish, the sunset without equal—I wanted my high school sweetheart to know all these. To see if they spoke to her as they were shouting at me.

And so, a week after completing the Stephen King interview, having made hasty arrangements for time off, I was back at Westways, this time with Mary Jo. At one level, it was a week for dispelling myths, such as the stereotype of laconic, aloof Mainers. Those we met were neither distant nor taciturn. They were people we enjoyed being around. Theirs was scenery you were privileged to gaze upon. Especially the birches and firs.

Birches and firs and blue water, the dappled shade along lakeside trails—at first Jo and I felt profound comfort in these but didn't associate them with anything else. Then we realized they were powerfully remindful, and it clicked: this was Canada, the Black River Club that Jo's dad and his cronies formed in the wilds of Quebec, those idyllic summer vacations in the rustic cabin on Green Lake, only Jo and me, our kids, and her mom and dad, no one else for miles around. Fishing and family love; nature and natural ease; simplicity and remove. Now, looking on this lakeside idyll in Maine, those were the images our unconscious minds reflected, the remembered love and communion of a cabin in Quebec.

We admired what the Kings had. We were fascinated by what the happily relocated Tripps had accomplished.

Could we?

Never mind, I told myself. *I'm not old enough yet to be thinking like that.*

No, I answered myself, *but I am young enough.*

3

SMALL
LIES

We came prepared. Before returning to Maine the next year, Jo and I decided that one day, to be sure, we would like to find a place of our own here, a place where we could build a small vacation house, a retreat to fly to a few times a year, and in the meantime dream of, the dreaming being as important as the being there.

Throughout my life, I thought myself a rigorously logical man. Impulse, when I allowed it to steer me at all, had to be buttressed by fact. This went back to the days in the library stacks, I guess, prepping for debates. Now, years later, I was reading cover-to-cover each issue of *Downeast*, buying copies of *Yankee*, studying *Country Journal* and *Mother Earth News*, and returning, with keener interest than ever, to the essays and letters of E. B. White.

From bookshelves, I took down Louise Dickinson Rich's classic account of moving to Maine, *We Took to the Woods*. In Kenneth Roberts's *Trending into Maine*, I was fascinated by his list of Maine authors and artists and his speculation as to why there are so many of them. It might be, he wrote, that iodine released from seaweed by the pounding of surf caused artistic stimulation. If so, he conjectured, "some day the mere intravenous injection of iodine into illiterates who have something to say may make them into authors." Or, the thought occurred to me, the removal of iodine from writers who haven't anything to say might stop them from trying. This pseudoscientific silliness made Roberts my kind of thinker and his state even more appealing.

I collected other tidbits equally specious, but where Maine was concerned, I was credulous. In a profession where skepticism is an essential tool, now and then credulity is therapeutic.

Maine is the easternmost state.

Maine is the foggiest state.

Maine's tides, the most assertive in America, rise and fall as much as fifty feet in the Bay of Fundy.

Maine's coastline, unfolded, would be 3,500 miles long.

Maine has more offshore islands than all the rest of America combined, one of the densest frecklings of islands in the world.

Maine is 90 percent woods, the most of any state.

Maine has no poisonous snakes.

Maine's Moosehead Lake is the largest lake contained in a single state.

And finally — my favorite — it was a Maine inventor who conceived of coffins fitted with shelves and rods, designed to be stood up in the living room and used as cupboards until otherwise needed.

As I considered each of these nuggets, what I was doing, of course, was rationalizing. It was the ever-logical, over-logical mind cataloging reasons to justify a feeling that in fact was not reasonable.

So I thought at the time. Now I figure that in fact it was all very reasonable. The reason was that we were in the process of being led where we needed to go. I don't mean Maine. That was not our ultimate destination. Never was. Our ultimate destination we didn't yet know, but there was one.

We started reading real estate ads. Those that most intrigued us were for islands. What *is* it about islands? What is it that, through centuries, has enthralled human imagination and yearning? "Islomania," author Lawrence Durrell has named the fascination, claiming that islomaniacs are direct descendants of Atlanteans, atavistically drawn toward the lost Atlantis, and that's why they find islands irresistible. There was a magazine devoted to nothing but islands.

From *Treasure Island* to *Robinson Crusoe*, childhood tales instill the magic. But if the child in us might seek adventure, is not the wish of the adult island-dreamer separation, apartness? Are not islomaniacs, put simply, trying to escape? Escape urban blight, crime, drugs, pollution, cacophony, anxiety, insecurity — all these might be left well behind when one crosses to an island. An island affords insulation, isolation.

Or does it work the other way? Does a person forge isolation within himself, and locate an island to serve as its setting? The world at large he can hardly influence and certainly not control, but an island can be his own miniature world with him at its center as protector and sovereign. A world that can be paced from end to end is measurable, comprehensible. How appealing: a comprehensible world.

Before our minds could conclude, our hearts decided: an island it would be. And of all the ads we saw for islands over all the months we looked and daydreamed, none was more enticing than this: "Bar Harbor, Maine. Truly unique island property located in Frenchman's Bay, 500 yards from the town and connected to the mainland by a traversable causeway for private access at low tide. A naturally terraced terrain rises to a 170-foot plateau, affording a 360-degree panoramic view of Frenchman's Bay with Cadillac Mountain to the south. Fields, woods, and gravel roads are contained within the 30+ acres, with 3,350 feet of deep-water shore frontage. The western half of this island is owned by Acadia National Park, thereby insuring its perpetual natural beauty."

The entire ad was an aerial photograph, the text laid in white over the patch of sea in the lower third of the image. In the middle was the island, part woods, part meadow, rising to a peak to the left; beyond it was a clean reach of water leading to the Atlantic; closer by, the shore of the mainland, with a small town nestled below modest mountains that loomed, beclouded, in the far distance. The ad was handsomely composed; there was dignity to this dream.

An island! But more than that: an island that was *not* an island when the tide went out. The best of both worlds.

A price was specified—barely affordable, but, for a dream, one should be required to stretch. In the lower righthand corner was the name of the realtor: Carl Small Associates, Route 1, Sullivan, Maine 04689.

In three decades as a reporter, I had honed the skills of prudent skepticism. Having done many interviews, covered many political campaigns, heard many self-serving justifications, I knew the tricks of misdirection, could decipher the codes of deception. It was second nature to me. So how did I let Carl Small humbug me? Why did I fall for Small lies? I had called him from California to inquire about the island. Encouraged by his responses (intentionally misguided), we flew east in high anticipation. Settling in at Westways with a son and daughter, we felt like old friends delighted to be back.

Sullivan, Maine, was four hours' drive, a chance to see more of our adoptive-state-designate, which was best known for its rock-bound coast and lighthouses on bleak promontories. This, though, was inland Maine, a rolling world of fields whose crops were rocks, and the crops were prodigious; of farmhouses grafted to barns so that in winter no outside steps need be taken between hearth and chores; of the rugged tumblestone fences. This was the Maine of small country stores at quiet crossroads, of white spires rising above trees up ahead announcing towns to come and faith abiding. Here were cows and horses and lifeless car carcasses, wealth of will amid poverty of cash. Sullivan was about two-thirds of the way along the coast, past Bar Harbor, the last of the resort towns, down where Route 1 was reduced to its essence — two lanes, plain blacktop.

Carl Small *was* small. Five-seven or so, he had a small man's way of compensating by being ebulliently outgoing. His voice had the lilt of the quintessential Mainer, the sharpened *a*'s, swallowed *r*'s. To our insistent questions about the island, he responded by locating it on a map and saying, "Bar Island. Like I said, it's a beauty. Show ya some other places first."

As he took us to those other places — bleak, raw, uninspiring barrens — he spoke geography. This part of Maine near Bar Harbor was where worlds met, botanically, ornithologically, and socially. For plants and trees, it was the transition zone between northern forests of spruce and fir and the birch, beech, poplar, oak, and maple groves that range to the south. For birds, it was the meeting place of species north and south. For people, it was where Maine, "Vacationland" as it declared on license plates, met the workaday Maine that saw few camera-toting tourists and was too busy scratching out sustenance to notice if it did; beyond this point, lobster boats didn't take tourists.

Carl drove us due south toward the rounded mountains of Mount Desert Island. "L'Ile des Monts-Deserts," Champlain had named it back in 1604, the Isle of Bare Mountains, for the peaks were treeless, scoured bald by the Ice Age ten thousand years earlier. The highest was Cadillac Mountain, only fifteen hundred feet, not a mountain, perhaps, as "you Californians know 'em, but, in fact, the highest point along the American Atlantic Coast anywhere north of Rio." That was his geography lesson.

And this is how he broke our hearts. Having avoided specifics about Bar Island, now, as we finally approached it, he dropped this: "A man named Rulison bought it, ya know. From New York. Has a company makes baseballs or something. Likes to walk his dog out there, through the woods. They have a great time."

Bought the island? Did he mean that years ago this man bought the island and now wants to sell? No, he meant *two months ago*. The same ad we saw, that man had seen, but he moved faster. A man who made baseballs or something, a miserable New Yorker, had bought our island out from under us, and I bet that beast he called a dog was a pit bull.

"Golden retriever," Carl was saying.

How could it be? Why was he telling us just now? If we had known the truth a week ago, we wouldn't have come. Moreover, we *could* have known the truth a week ago had I exercised my

normal, second-nature skills. I had let my unconscious mind
(or something!) blunt my critical abilities so that I heard what
it wanted me to hear. I had missed the clues, the verbal parries
that were not answers, as in: "Is that island in your ad still available?" "Oh, Bar Island? Beautiful place. Yep, it's still there. I'll be
happy to show it to you. But I've got other places you'll want to
see." I had asked *was it available*; he had answered *it's still there*. A
crafty Mainer can convey as much in what he does not say as in
what he does. That's the nut of New England taciturnity: the joy,
even perverse delight, in misleading by saying too little to people
accustomed to hearing too much.

The day had turned drizzly. Why should we even go look at
Bar Island? "Well, if you really like it," Carl was saying, "Rulison
might resell a section to you."

A section. Half a loaf.

In three hours, I was supposed to be driving halfway across
the state to Augusta to catch a flight heading back to California for a business meeting the next morning, only to return and
rejoin the family back in Maine that evening. Not brilliant planning, bicoastal breakfasting, but the president of NBC News, Bill
Small, didn't understand the concept of vacations. We had three
hours, but the Mr. Small of this coast said that the way tides ran,
the bar over to the island wouldn't open up in that time. Without
a boat and unable to drive or walk to the island, we would be able
to see it only from afar.

We peered at the island through a smudge of drizzle the color
of loose lies. In so many ways, at that moment, the island was
beyond our reach, but perverse as human nature is, that made
it all the more appealing, the damsel in the castle tower, wearing
the allure of the unapproachable. All we could see through the

mists was a monochrome hump lying dark on the water. It was not, by itself, a sight to thrill, but superimposed over the image in the magazine and our daydreams about magical islands and, especially, its uniquely accessible isolation — with all that swirling in our minds — we stood and stared and pondered.

We could not dismiss the facts. Someone had already bought the place, it looked like a dingy hump, and in a few hours I had to be hundreds of miles away.

Carl drove us through the heart of Bar Harbor, past handsome shops, galleries, restaurants, an art-deco movie theater, the classic white-steepled church, an old graveyard; it was a fetching place, host to happy tourists we could not join. Regaining our rental car back at his office, we bade Carl Small an ambivalent farewell and drove off. Had our dream just dissolved? I was not accustomed to dreams dissolving. For me, they always seemed to come true.

Washington, D.C. — After less than a year in Manhattan working for Chet Huntley, I was moved to the *Huntley-Brinkley Report* unit in Washington to work for David Brinkley. I would be formally listed on the union records of the Writers Guild of America as David's writer, which was absurd. David — only David — was David's writer. What I would do is take camera crews to congressional hearings or other public happenings where Brinkley's presence would have been distorting of the event, report the essentials back to him, then oversee the cutting of the film as he wanted it for his story that night.

Jo and I purchased our first house, a new three-story place on Lake Barcroft over in suburban Virginia, and we loved it immediately. Rolling green lawns out back, terraced down to the lake at the end of the dam that contained the two-mile-long lake. What a splendid place to begin our new family. Neighbors in the area included many who made the daily drive down Columbia Pike to the Capitol, White House, or Supreme Court to tend to the work of governing the nation in an era when that profession was still considered admirable. Just four doors from our house lived the bushy-browed, cigar-smoking, debonair, and driven Pierre Salinger, President Kennedy's White House press secretary. He was a fascinating man to talk with — erudite, elegant, and with stories to tell: stories from a career in newspapering; the story of being discovered by Bobby Kennedy to be an investigator for his justice department; another of the president, a fellow cigar-smoker, directing Pierre to acquire at least a thousand fine Cuban cigars. Delivering *two* thousand to the Oval Office, he watched the president reach into his desk drawer, pull out and sign a document that put into immediate effect a trade embargo against Cuba, cigars and all.

One evening, Jo and I were invited to the Salingers' to play bridge. Pierre had been traveling with the president on a campaign swing out west, but the trip had been canceled in Chicago because the president was said to have come down with a cold.

Repeatedly, our card game was interrupted by phone calls that Pierre took privately in the bedroom. He'd return, we'd play a few more tricks, and then the phone again. That's how it went for two or three hours until, finally, Pierre and Nancy, as gracefully as they could, said we should call it an evening, and Jo and I walked home not yet realizing what had just happened.

Next day, the president revealed to the nation the frightening news that became known as the Cuban Missile Crisis. Pierre had known about the looming threat for several days, how Russia was installing offensive nuclear missiles on the island of Cuba. That — not a cold — was why he and the campaign had returned prematurely to Washington, everyone urged to appear to have a normal weekend so as not to arouse public or press suspicions. But three major newspapers had gotten wind of the story, and it was Salinger's job to persuade them to sit on it for now without publishing. That's what he was doing on the phone while presumably having just an ordinary Saturday evening at home with friends playing bridge.

What I have not mentioned is that Mary Jo, at this time, was in her ninth month of pregnancy with our first child. What a terrible time for that. Today it may be hard for a reader to remember, or for some readers even to know, how frightening that time was in our nation, in our world, fraught with shivering fears of a very likely nuclear Armageddon. It's no exaggeration to say that a mother-to-be had to fret whether she dared bring a new life into the world at such a bleak time.

The world teetered and trembled for two fear-freighted weeks as I sought some kind of balm. I had once hosted a banquet for Dr. Robert Schuller of the Crystal Cathedral in California, at which time he presented me with a leather-bound copy of his Possibility Thinkers edition of the Bible. I opened it for the first time. In the back was a list of Positive Verses for various occasions. The first I turned to was in the book of James, first chapter, verse two. It was headed "Profiting from Trials," and it began, "My brethren, count it all joy when you fall into various trials."

Joy? The paralyzing fear and burning uncertainty tearing us apart should make us joyful? Read on.

"Knowing that the testing of your faith produces patience."

The testing of *my* faith? I had none. I felt none. Way things were going, I didn't even have faith in myself. What else was there? No, I had neither faith nor patience. Bible away!

On Sunday the 28th, the damning world crisis still unresolved, Jo said it was time to make an early-morning dash from Virginia over into the city, to Columbia Women's Hospital.

From the day it was founded just after the Civil War until it was turned into condos in 2002, Columbia gave birth to a quarter million babies. Only one matters. That boy baby was born after several hours of labor for his mom and several hours of anxious waiting by his dad — more anxiety than most fathers experience, no doubt, because the world that day remained a nervous place.

But then something extraordinary happened, something that even a not-always-keen young reporter and an exceptionally distracted father-to-be could not miss.

As Jo was in labor inside (in that dark day when fathers were not allowed into birthing rooms), I was waiting outside on the hospital's balcony. It was a balmy autumn shirtsleeves kind of day, and I was trying to say a prayer for my wife and our soon-to-be-born. I was trying to pray because I was scared and understood that praying is what some people do when facing anxious unknowns. Even if I felt no faith and the trials of the time had not produced in me any joy, I tried to pray. But how?

God is great, God is good; let us thank him —
Irrelevant.

The Lord is my shepherd, I shall not want; he makes me ... something or other. Twenty-Third Psalm, wasn't it? (As I've said, my religious life till this time was limited, enough to emboss "Lutheran" on my dog tag but nothing on my heart.) Wasn't there something else in that psalm too about "though I walk through the valley of the shadow of death, I will fear no evil, for you are with me"?

The world this very day was walking through the valley of the shadow of death. There was evil aplenty to fear. But was he really with us? Indeed, was there a *he*?

I closed my eyes, lowered my head, didn't really pray, didn't know how, but figured that if there were a *he*, perhaps I could just talk to him.

God, I don't know if you know me; I don't know if I know you; but I need help. I guess a lot of people do. But I really do. This world needs help. The baby son or daughter you're about to place in our care will need help, and most important, my dear, dear wife needs help. We don't know where else to get it. Whom else to ask. So — I'm not on my knees; I hope that's all right — I am asking you. Begging you. Praying to you. I guess that's what I'm doing, praying. I'm praying to you, God. Thank you. Amen.

If my prayer lacked religious grounding, it was a gesture. Maybe that was all God wanted. I didn't know. Slowly I raised my head and opened my eyes. Bright, balmy autumnal shirtsleeve day — but something more! Something was happening below me, down there across the street, something that ignited the dormant reporter in me. There was a black limo, and I could make out several of my colleagues hanging around it, cameramen along with secret service agents gathered outside St. Stephen's Catholic Church. The president must be there. I watched for fifteen or twenty minutes until church let out and I saw John F. Kennedy, a man who had been bearing inconceivable stress for more than a week, emerge from that church — smiling! A broad, carefree smile lit his handsome face, and seeing it, I felt anxieties within me begin to dissolve.

Why the president's smile? In the memorable explanation spoken later by Secretary of State Dean Rusk, "We were eyeball to eyeball, and the other fellow just blinked." The Russians had agreed to back off from the "quarantine" line of US Navy ships, turn their own ships around, and pull out their missiles. The nightmare, it appeared, was over. The president had just learned the good news that morning and presumably had gone to church to thank God, then walked out beaming like the sun itself beamed on that bright October day.

And at that moment — almost that exact second — Master Mark Christopher Perkins decided it was safe to come out into a world that apparently was going to survive after all. And the prayer — my awkward prayer that wasn't a prayer — could that have had anything . . . ? Never mind!

What mattered was that this was to be a time not of ending but of glorious beginning. Once more things were working out for us, even if we didn't yet really understand.

Actually, Mary Jo probably understood better than I. Her family had been godly believers. Mine had gone to church sometimes, our occasional churchgoing more a social than a spiritual commitment.

I wasn't atypical. Considering the matter today, I note that religion is little contemplated in our time. Not little discussed, to be sure, not little pretended, but little contemplated. More Americans argue about prayer in school than pray; more mouth the commandments than obey them. What is the problem? For one thing, some have been too busy fighting for their success at the expense of everyone else's. They've been too busy preying to pray. Some of us are too absorbed in ourselves. Surrounded by and enamored of our own human accomplishments, we fall victim to that most evil form of idol worship wherein we ourselves are the idols. Others among us succumb not to idol worship but to idle worship, whiling away the hours once devoted to church, prayer, and thoughts of religion.

For myself, I long had thoughts about religion, but my primary intellectual commitment was to logic, to thinking things through, and thinking through religion inevitably brought me face-to-face with the wars and horrors waged in its name, to the grotesqueries and contradictions of some biblical literature. It's not popular to talk about those. People who like to cite Scripture usually isolate the passages that comfort rather than those that puzzle or repel. Rarely noted are the murders, massacres, rapes, disfigurements, and plagues that a biblical God putatively caused or condoned. Never offered as godly advice is Deuteronomy's command that "if a man has a stubborn and rebellious son," he shall turn him over to the elders of his city, who shall "stone him with stones, that he die." Which of us today doesn't find that prescription abhorrent? Christians and Jews alike were appalled when a leader of Islam pronounced a death sentence upon an author for writing a book the Ayatollah considered blasphemous, but were those same Christians and Jews familiar with Leviticus 24:16 in their own Book, in which God is represented as directing that "whoever blasphemes the name of the LORD shall surely be put to death"?

Pastors, priests, and rabbis, facing such quibbles, reply that, in the end, faith in God is not a fact to be proved but a decision to be made.

Even before I made that decision, however, good things kept happening to me, wonderfully unbidden graces that I happily accepted even if I didn't know whom to thank. It is the miracle of God's grace that it can work for us even without our knowing.

My flight would be leaving Augusta, Maine, for Boston, then LA, in two hours — barely enough driving time to there from Bar Harbor, although the point became moot when the right front tire on the rental car went flat. It was a sign. Now, a skeptic might not be willing to accept a flat tire as a sign, but here's the wonder of it: if something that happens causes you to change your course, and that course-change brings you unwonted benefactions, then I argue that anything, even a flat tire, can be a sign.

The nearest rental office was at the Bar Harbor airport.

"Any flights out of here down to Boston? I've got to connect to LA at 5:30." Nothing. So, two choices: take off driving now, fast. We might make it across to Augusta in time, maybe. Or the other choice, which seemed far more appealing.

Only a close friend should you ask to lie for you. Bob Eaton, a producer with whom I had worked for twenty years, was a close friend.

"Having a great time, Bob, and in case you can't guess why I'm calling, let me give you multiple choices: (a) I have developed an acute ear infection and am advised by a doctor not to fly; (b) it is pea-soup foggy, no flights getting out of Maine this afternoon; (c) death in the family, anyone you want to make it; or (d) use your judgment."

"Where are you?"

"Bar Harbor."

"Fog. I'll tell Small how hard you tried and how grievous is your regret." As he said Bill Small's name, the irony hit me. From Carl to Bill — what balance to the day. Small lies received, Small lies given.

"Bob, I owe you."

"Enjoy. And how are things going really?"

"I'm not sure yet. I think maybe terrific."

We called Carl, told him we had changed our minds. As we awaited his return, we wandered town a bit. It was in a grocery store that I saw a woman coming down the aisle toward me with what seemed a look of recognition.

"Oh, my gracious!" she exclaimed. "Don't I know you? Didn't you used to be Jack Perkins?"

"Yes ma'am," I said, practicing a Mainer's restraint.

"I thought so," she said, proud of her powers of perception. "So tell me, whatever happened to you?"

I don't think I answered, just smiled and shrugged. While thinking, *A lot, madam — and still is.*

Carl had changed into white sneakers, a white print short-sleeved shirt, dark sunglasses; he looked California. We, in sweaters and jeans, classic L. L. Bean, looked Maine. Carl carried a long roll of surveyor's plans and used it as a pointer.

"Island's a half mile long, west to east, and about a quarter mile wide," he lectured. "Park Service owns the western half: part of Acadia National Park. Second busiest park in the country. Three and a half million visitors this year."

The fog had lifted, yielding a sunny afternoon. We walked across the bottom of what just hours ago had been the sea. Now it was a causeway for us and a buffet table for gulls, picking up periwinkle or mussel shells, flying into the air twenty feet to drop their prizes on rocks below, where the shells cracked, exposing the meat. Ingenious critters. After ten minutes' walk, the bar ascended, then leveled, and we were on the island.

Walking around the Park Service gate, we wound up the slope through apple and oak, reaching a clearing, a meadow eighty feet above sea level, where waving grasses were speckled with tiny blossoms and then regal stands of lupine.

"Park's land goes up to that big oak." Carl pointed. A grand-father oak, six feet across, fifty feet tall, a majestic creature rising at the far end of the meadow surveying his kingdom. We approached with admiration and respect. He had preceded us; he would outlive us. And he lived where we fancied. A footpath split off to his left, but we stayed with the dirt road, such as it was, bearing to the right.

"This is the land you could buy if you wanted," Carl said. "Twelve acres. Starting at the oak, it goes from the south shore to our right all the way over to the north shore. About three hundred fifty feet of coastline on each side." He had unrolled the maps and began tracing for us the perimeter of the twelve acres. The path, choked by brambles and brush, headed south toward the slope at island's edge. Amid eager young moosewood trees with their slender green-striped trunks and broad maple leaves, there, rising importantly, was an old rock chimney, massive, the date inscribed on one of the rocks, 1906. We smiled at the view that must have thrilled the people who lived here: the harbor, bobbing with lobster boats at moorings; the little town, nestled against its waterfront, its streets a-bustle; and beyond, the rounded mountains of the park. We surveyed the vista and exclaimed to ourselves, *How blessed were these people.*

As we might one day be?

For two happy hours, we tramped Bar Island. We walked soft paths beneath arches of birch, watching light-sprinkles dance on mosses and duff. We skittered down slippery rocks to cobbly beaches to take census of tidepools, to inventory driftwood. We wrestled through groping darknesses of spruce to exult when a clearing opened and once more we could breathe. Occasionally, Carl found a surveyor's flag, unrolled his map, and—his pitch getting more certain in response to our patent delight—declared, "Here's where the northwest corner of your land would be."

Our land.

As we left the island, walking back across the bar with many glances over shoulders, I thought of Robert Frost and his poem "The Gift Outright," in which he had written of fledgling Americans as colonists come to this continent while still bound by ties of culture and tradition to their old countries.

The land was ours before we were the land's.

Why did I think of that then? Those twelve acres whose boundaries we had so carefully paced, among whose waving lavender lupine I felt that never had I seen a place more beautiful, that sweet green quilt of grasses and woods where once people had lived in what contentment we could only imagine—now, as we walked away from it after only two hours, before we could rationally consider whether one day we should own it, it already owned us. Frost in reverse.

We were the land's before the land could be ours.

Washington, D.C.—Today, I see how pieces fit together. Frost had written that poem for the Inaugural of President Kennedy in 1961. Two and a half years later, the Cuban Missile Crisis well behind us, Mark Christopher Perkins smooshed his face into his second birthday cake, happy, hungry, and healthy. Thanksgiving was coming up, and Jo and I had much to be thankful for. Until ...

One thirty in the afternoon, November 22. David Brinkley and I were at lunch when UPI's legendary White House correspondent Merriman Smith, out in Dallas, commandeered a phone to feed the first word to his agency, which immediately sent it out as a flash to newsrooms everywhere. Shots had been fired during President Kennedy's motorcade through Dallas.

Abandoning lunch, we dashed back to NBC, where, after a frantic few minutes, David was on the air and I was setting up a clearing desk just off-camera. For the next harrowing hours, I received the incoming wire copy as well as dispatches from our own correspondents and producers in Dallas, filtered them, and funneled the most germane to David as he told the story on the air. He managed at first with very little information but with a great need to keep telling whatever we did know to those just tuning in and to those who had been listening but needed to hear it over and over before they could even begin to absorb the horrible news. At first, the incoming reports came sporadically, with maddening gaps. The president's motorcade had been passing through Dealey Plaza in Dallas, headed to the site of a presidential speech. There had been shots. They may have come from a building. Witnesses saw blood on Mrs. Kennedy's pink suit. The president had been rushed to Parkland Hospital. Hospital not commenting. People gathering outside.

And then, within the hour, the announcement from the hospital: the president is dead.

Through the long, dark afternoon, the story deepened, broadened. NBC remained on the air nonstop, but about a half hour before six, Brinkley left the anchor stool to pull together the facts and write his lead for the evening's regular *Huntley-Brinkley Report*.

My time working for him had been a master class in television-news writing given by the man who pretty much invented the craft. There had been many lessons. Now again I saw him apply them on the air, live.

Another anchor in another time might have started the newscast differently: "Good evening. Our nation today suffered a grievous loss, an historic crime in which the President of the United States was cruelly cut down by an assassin's bullets." Or, "Splashing blood across the pages of history, a brutal assassin today wantonly took the life of President John F. Kennedy."

It *could* have been written like that. But as Brinkley had taught, that wasn't how it *should* be done.

At six thirty, as the nightly news broadcast began, David said simply this:

"Good evening.

"The essential facts are these:

"President Kennedy was murdered in Dallas, Texas.

"He was shot by a sniper, hiding in a building beside his route. He was dead within an hour.

"Lyndon Johnson is President of the United States. He took the oath of office in a jet airplane as he was returning from Dallas back to Washington."

Simple, declarative sentences, no ornamentation. *The more important the story*, he had taught in master class, *the less importantly you need tell it.*

His delivery was calm, balanced. *You don't have to act dramatic or write dramatic to convey drama that's already there.*

There was another important lesson he had taught in master class, not so much about writing as about making decisions in life. I still remember his words: *Jack, when it's time to do it, and you know it's time to do it — do it.*

The day after we walked the island, we bought. We called Carl Small from Westways, asked the price for our "half a loaf," and agreed. Not the prudent way to do business, but something in us — or above us — had overwhelmed our prudence. I still wouldn't credit it. That would come only later. For now, our conscious minds, reflecting on our impetuosity, could only conclude we had recklessly undertaken a burdensome commitment with little thought.

In the months that lay ahead, there were many more critical decisions to be made, some most daunting. At any of those junctures, it would have been easy to resign the game. Staying with status quo is comfortable; changing takes effort. But anytime I was tempted to turn tail, I felt myself inexplicably prodded, encouraged, and lifted by words heard years earlier: "A man's gotta make his own oompahs." Those words may have been Buckskin Bill's, but the way they kept intruding on my mind was surely — I acknowledge it now — the work of the Holy Spirit, of God, gently changing our lives.

4

CIVICS
LESSONS

Jack, like to invite you to breakfast." Les Brewer was not only the owner of Bar Harbor's Golden Anchor Motel, where I was staying, but also a significant property owner around town and a founder of the renowned College of the Atlantic. He thought maybe he could introduce me to some people who might help us build over on the island.

Next morning at seven, I was at Jordan's, the locals' breakfast hangout, being introduced to big, overalled Doug Gott, who commanded a battalion of earth-moving equipment and could do our site-clearing work if we wished; retired stonemason Jimmy Murray, happy to check out the integrity of that old chimney; and builder Vic Mercer, who asked if we intended to use an architect. When we asked what he advised, he said he thought architects mostly design monuments to themselves. If we wished, he'd be glad to design a simple place for us. Just let him know what we'd like. "Maybe sketch some ideas for me," he said, "and I'll take it from there."

The "blues" were terrific: a stack of blueberry pancakes drenched with Maine maple syrup. The conversation with this group of new friends, colleagues, was encouraging. Except ... these were people we barely knew. Still, it felt right. And feelings had been good to us so far.

On another day, I had flown to Bar Harbor, trying to reassure myself that it was truly the thing to do, building over on that island. If there was a God and if he wanted us to find this beautiful new life, I might have expected him to welcome me to a radiant, sunny day, but no, if I wanted bright and balmy, I'd have to imagine. (Of course, now it's understood that the power to imagine is his gift as well.)

Walking the town in a light rain, I tried to picture having a vacation getaway here, far away from the hectic city we called home. What would our dream house be like over on the island? Ah, but to imagine a dream house, I first had to remember how to dream. I practiced on that drizzly day.

Down at the Village Green, I dreamed a dozen bandsmen in crimson uniforms with gold braid sitting with gleaming brass instruments on the bandstand. Blankets were spread across sun-dappled grass as cicadas and Sousa sounded vespers. Back at the harbor, I pictured a Fourth of July evening, dark sky, dark water, both exploding with color. Then Christmas. Downy snow on the sidewalks of Main Street and, over there in the distance, on that island where the Perkinses had their vacation place, a few distant twinkles of celebration and the rising white smoke of a warming hearth.

It was three o'clock, and as the water ran ever shallower over the gravel bar at the end of Bridge Street, bare rocks began to peek through lapping waves, until those waves receded farther and patches of rock and shell were dryly exposed, then those dry patches connected in a chain, and that chain stretched unbroken the half mile from town to island.

As I climbed the path to the meadow, how bleak it appeared in this nameless season between fall and winter, summer's green grasses gone brown, its maples and popples dark traceries in the dusk. It was only three thirty, but already the day's meager light was fading. Sunset (at 3:57, according to the local newspaper) wouldn't be noticeable. I followed the road to the big king oak and beyond it to the land that owned us. No lavender lupines waved welcome. No birds trilled hello. I slogged through yesterday's raspberry canes imagining tomorrow's, swam through spruce boughs and branches of moosewood, and considered that we needed some name to call this place other than "the place on the island."

Moosewood. I had relished the word the first time I'd heard it. I admired this species of small tree, modest and unpretentious, an understory tree with oversized leaves to glean enough sunlight to flourish. It didn't need to be a top-story tree; it was content not to rule the meadow. It had nothing to prove.

The species had other names — prosaic *striped maple*, pedantic *acer Pennsylvanicum* — but *moosewood* was poetry, distilling into one word a wilderness of animal and plant, scenery and soul. (To be sure, there was a well-known cookbook titled *Moosewood* after a restaurant in Ithaca, New York, but what did they know? The leaves on their cover were oak.)

I stood in squishy shoes and sodden pants, doubts insisting:

Should we really build here? Bleak, lonely. If there was beauty, it was meant for subtle discerning. Wasn't it nonsense to plan a vacation place so far removed from our real home? I brushed my way back through trees to the meadow, walked the length of the island, and retraced the bar, by now a hundred yards wide. I walked without thinking. But not without feeling. I did a great deal of listening. By the time I got back to the motel, there were still many *reasons* for doubt, but oddly, in my mind, there was no longer doubt.

"How is it?" Jo asked eagerly on the phone.

"Well, you know the old saying, 'This isn't the end of the earth, but you can see it from here'? Well, from here you *can't* see it because of the fog."

"Sounds depressing. But you don't sound depressed." She knew.

In the gloaming now, I could barely see the island's shaggy silhouette. It was four thirty. My visit on this grim day had caught both town and island at their dreariest time. And still . . .

"Joey, how 'bout we call the place Moosewood?"

Back in LA, we shared ideas. An open structure with few walls, we wanted. Internal walls were the invention of wealthy homeowners centuries before to shield them from having to watch servants laboring around the house. Today, for folks with no servants, walls separated families during much of what could be their time together, and set kitchen work apart as something undignified, unseemly. Jo and I had already spent too much time apart; it would be good to be able to look up from wherever we were in the house and see each other.

We agreed I'd try to sketch something for Vic. Consequently, on airplanes careening the country for stories, or commuting each week between Los Angeles home and New York studio, on wobbly airline tray tables, playing architect, I ran smack into another wall — the wall of my own ignorance. Simple things. Wondering if a closet would fit in that awkward accident of geometry I had drawn between bathroom and stairway, I realized I didn't know what size a closet should be. Or a bedroom. Was twelve by sixteen good? I paced out the cramped dimensions of interchangeable hotel rooms from one city to another, imagining other rooms. Envisioning kitchen counters, rehearsing the reach from stovetop to sink. Deciding how wide the living room should be. Twenty-four feet? I paced off eight strides in a motel lobby from registration counter to Coke machine; if this were the living room, would a couch fit there by the map rack?

How long *was* a couch? How much space did a dining table and chairs require? In a bathroom, how big was a tub? In the kitchen, how deep the counters, how wide the refrigerator? I envied architects. Equipped with standard specs for the basics, free to let minds soar, they could be dreamer, plotter, and creator at the same time. I didn't know the size of a toilet.

I didn't know. I hated admitting that. Coming from others, it always sounded like a feeble excuse. Coming from me, it was an embarrassment. But I was the boss of this project, so I bulldozed ahead, not admitting out loud how little I knew.

As Builder Vic finished his plans based on the sketches we had worked out, as he filed for permits and readied for construction, suddenly, surprisingly, our dream house came under attack.

The first forays — and for me, the most stinging — were from the local weekly newspaper. In an editorial that broke our hearts, the *Bar Harbor Times* urged the locals to "take strong, immediate action to discourage" our building on the island. It printed letters from environmentalist groups like the Maine Coast Heritage Trust, whose Gary Friedmann complained that our home would substantially change the character of the island and the harbor, forgetting or not realizing that other families had lived on the island decades earlier. How dismaying when someone you don't know accuses you of destroying the sanctity of your own sanctum. How unnerving to be condemned for exploiting, when your intentions are to cherish and preserve. And yes — and wasn't this the heart of it? — how damnable to see a bright-eyed liberal, as once you thought of yourself, accusing you of thinking and acting as you promised yourself you never would. Had I changed since my days as a crusading newsman? Had "I" become "they"? Was despoiling nature justifiable when the pronoun was first person, or was what we planned despoliation at all?

Repeatedly, the newspaper's editor, Earl Brechlin, preached to his readers that the Perkinses should not be allowed to build on Bar Island. Then one week he changed tactics and preached directly to *us*. The nasty puddle of vitriol smearing his editorial page was titled "Fantasy Island" and warned us that whatever our delusions, should we try to live on our island, our lives there would be a nightmare. He drew quite a bill of particulars. Our car would get stuck in the mire of the bar. We'd be stranded in town one dark night in January. Needing to depend on a boat, how could we use it with town docks pulled and ice clogging the harbor? In summer, swarms of tourists would inundate the island, "trampling your flower beds and peeking in your windows." Island life would be noisy, since sound carries over water, and we would get tired of being serenaded nightly by squealing tires on the town pier and drunks in town yelling obscenities. Island air would stink of town "french fries, diesel fuel, and exhaust fumes." Given all this, Editor Brechlin felt a duty to warn us that "living on Bar Island would be far from a dream. It would be a nightmare."

We studied his tirade and felt sick. Sick because no one wants to feel shunned by the community he's chosen, sick because a fellow journalist with more zeal than objectivity was trying to intimidate us, and sick because, to be honest, we didn't know how much of what he warned us about would prove to be true.

My initial instinct was to lash back, to out-write the man. I could do it. I sat at the keyboard and vented four pages of vituperation. I showed it proudly to Mary Jo and then, as she suggested, tore it up.

Our battles were not over.

First, our local government determined that its zoning map had been mistakenly colored so that our homesite would not permit a home. Unless they changed colors, Moosewood couldn't be. That was local government.

Then came the feds, joining the war, bugles sounding. I wrote in my journal of "a self-important document arriving in our California mailbox today from a certain Ronald N. Wrye, Superintendent, Acadia National Park."

We don't know this man but from the letter, we sure know the type. "It has come to my attention," he writes prissily, in the sclerotic stuffiness which to the bureaucrat denotes gravity, that surveyors have gone to the island on our behalf and "We can only presume they came across the bar and through our gate." He cautions that his government lawyers aren't sure we have any right to cross park land, so, to prevent us, he has changed the locks on the island's gate. We're locked out!

Now, in our deed we have a clear written guarantee of easement across the park's half of the island. The language is specific, irrefutable. Ronald N. Wrye, Superintendent, denying us access, is an outlaw. He wants our land to add to his empire. He ordered a minion to go change the gate lock, then sat down to dictate his missive to us. He is a dictator, dispatching an arrogant fiat he believes will make us cringe.

It makes us furious. Not so much for what it threatens, since we know the threat is hollow. More for how it confirms Balzac's sour assessment that "bureaucracy is a giant mechanism operated by pygmies," and reminds us that increasingly we are all becoming people of the government, for the government, and by the government.

This was the United States government hulking its full weight to intimidate where legally it had no right to regulate. For many reasons — our dream of building on the island only one of them — we would *fight*.

The Bar Harbor lawyer we located by phone endeared himself with his first advice. Fred Burrill advised us not to sue the feds. He was sure we could win, but he wanted to try something else. With the enemy demanding our surrender, Lawyer Fred, like General McAullife in the Battle of the Bulge, cracked, "Nuts."

As for the town, he said, let it be: Those folks, in the best of possible outcomes, will be your neighbors. They're fair and sensible people. Trust them.

Isn't it liberating to be able to trust? First, to trust yourself, of course. But also to learn to trust others. Oh, now and then, your trust may prove to have been misplaced. But isn't it better to suffer a loss now and then than to live your entire life distrustful and paranoid? At Moosewood, we intended to build a place that had no locks. If we were away and people got lost on the island, stranded by the tide, they could find refuge at our place. We would trust. I had already lived through our nation's time of mortal mistrust. I knew what that was like.

As I thought about what we faced, the battles that impended, my mind raced. How can simple citizens contend against abusive or misled government? How do you stand against all the pressures for what you believe is right?

I recalled a woman I had met once. Thinking about her now, I feel that even to put ourselves on the same page is blasphemy. The problems she faced were of such a different magnitude as to render our concerns insignificant. We were quibbling over zoning maps and building permits. Her struggle was life or death. For herself and many, many others.

Ruleville, Mississippi — "I didn't know," she told me, shaking her head. "I was old enough, I should have known, but you've got to remember what it was like here in Mississippi those days." A heavyset woman, Fannie Lou Hamer had a round face splashed with moonlight in the middle of the day as we sat at the kitchen table of her small house. She wore a simple frock, what my mother would have called a housedress. Her eyes instantly engaged me. She was the youngest of twenty children, had worked in share-croppers' fields since she was six, and never knew until she was well into her forties that a black woman like her had a constitu-tional right to vote. No one had ever told her. Mississippi whites didn't want Mississippi blacks to know.

On August 23, 1962, though, she attended a program at a black church in Ruleville and heard an organizer for SNCC, the Students' Nonviolent Coordinating Committee, deliver a sermon and then urge blacks to register to vote. Who was willing to be the first to register? Fannie Lou Hamer's was the first hand raised, and a week later she was on a rented bus keeping her nerve up by singing hymns on the way to Indianola, where she signed up to become an American voter.

That simple act cost her. Almost immediately, as word got around, she lost her job on the plantation (the term still applied), and daunting death threats began.

"I guess if I'd had any sense," she told me at her kitchen table a year later, "I'd have been scared. But what was the point of being scared? The only thing they could do was kill me, and they'd been trying to do that a little at a time since I could remember." That was a statement she made more than once, as if reminding her-self. She also often repeated as her mantra, "Nobody's free till everybody's free."

They did try to kill her. Arresting her one day in Winona, Mississippi, on a trumped-up charge, cops put her in a cell and let men with blackjacks come after her. "They just kept beating me and telling me, 'You nigger bitch, we're gonna make you wish you was dead.'" Left very close to death, she suffered injuries that kept her in pain for the rest of her too-short life. Yet she was always resolute and always joyful. By instinct, she did what her favorite hymn instructed: "This little light of mine, I'm gonna let it shine."

"Find that hymn-singing woman," an SNCC representative directed a colleague. And before long, Fannie Lou Hamer was hired to become a cofounder of a planned Mississippi Freedom Summer.

The infant Civil Rights Movement was the story of the century, and though I was still officially David Brinkley's writer back in Washington, he wanted me on the story, so I was dispatched with a film crew to report those sickening times of attack dogs and fire hoses; NAACP leader murdered in Mississippi; Sunday schoolers killed in a church bombing in Birmingham; black demonstrators gassed and beaten on a bridge to Selma, Alabama; three young civil rights workers from up north murdered by thugs of the Mississippi Ku Klux Klan.

I had met those three — Michael Schwerner, James Chaney, and Andrew Goodman — at a training session organized by SNCC in Oxford, Ohio, just before they went to Mississippi. This was 1964, and Lyndon Johnson, a wily, masterful legislator suddenly given the power of the presidency, had seized the brief window of opportunity following John Kennedy's assassination to break through generations of resistance and push the historic Civil Rights Act of 1964 through Congress, guaranteeing rights regardless of race.

At the training session in Ohio, the earnest young volunteers were instructed in nonviolent reaction to violence. They were cautioned that they would certainly meet resistance and that their lives could be in danger. They were told that over and over.

"And I know that," Goodman said to me during a break in

their classes. "But I also know I have to do this. I can't stand by while a whole population of citizens continue to be denied their rights."

With steely resolve, he and the other young activists headed into the miasma of Mississippi, from which he and two others never returned. Arrested on their very first day, supposedly for speeding, they were hauled off to jail for a few hours and then released into the waiting hands of the KKK. Their bodies weren't found until years later, buried in an earthen dam.

The young Freedom Summer volunteers who had the privilege to meet her considered Fannie Lou Hamer their away-from-home mom. Oh, but she could be tough. When black Democrats in Mississippi fielded their own slate of candidates, including her, for their party's national convention, they discovered in her a born politician with no hesitation about speaking out. The whole nation could hear as she addressed the convention's credentials committee, decrying how just the attempt to vote in the South got people like herself arrested, beaten, or worse. Fannie Lou Hamer quickly became a national figure. President Lyndon Johnson, campaigning to be elected to the office that had fallen to him, told aides "that illiterate woman" had to be dealt with. He dispatched his running mate, Hubert Humphrey, to see to it. Humphrey, a supposed champion of civil rights, pleaded with Hamer, telling her his own position on the ticket was at risk if she didn't accept compromise. To which she replied with a soft but stern rebuke, "Do you mean to tell me, Mr. Senator, that your position is more important than four hundred thousand black people's lives? Senator Humphrey, I know lots of people in Mississippi who have lost their jobs trying to register to vote. Now, if you lose your job of vice president because you do what is right, God will take care of you." And then with a maternal smile on her moonlit face, "Senator Humphrey, I'm going to pray to Jesus for you."

Was the power of this woman evident to someone chatting with her at her kitchen table? It was to this someone. There was stubborn determination in her, mellowed by humility and the glow of a passionate faith that was not a matter of choice or ambition. Her greatness did not advertise itself, as one is accustomed to find with political figures. There was nothing calculated or orchestrated or self-serving about it. It was, simply, her nature. Isn't greatness all the greater for seeming not to recognize itself?

I said to her once, "Ma'am, a lot of people think you're a great woman for what you're doing."

Her response was, "What I do is what God asks me to do. It's God that's great."

She became a powerful force in the civil rights struggle, but as Margaret Thatcher would say in a different day and in a different context, "Being powerful is like being a lady. If you have to tell people you are, you aren't."

Fannie Lou Hamer didn't have to tell people she was powerful. Fannie Lou Hamer didn't have to tell people she was a lady. Nor could she make any clearer the source of her strength. She was a woman of faith, guided by God.

I know now that I might never achieve the power of that woman's faith, but I will never forget it.

While waiting for our lawyer in Maine to work something out with various government agencies, since the Bar Harbor weekly newspaper was already a combatant against us in the war, we turned to the daily paper out of Bangor fifty miles away, whose reporter had requested an interview. I sat down with him on what felt like the wrong side of the interview table. I assumed that, at the outset at least, he would accord me some credibility if I just explained the facts in a dispassionate tone. (Which probably meant I secretly wanted to manipulate him. Should a reporter use a reporter?)

We talked for an hour. What were our plans now, he asked. Was it true that, as some were saying, we intended to bar visitors from our land? Would the house cost what rumors said it would cost? What did we think of the Park Service officials and others who were opposed to our plans? (How candid should I be on that one?) Since the Park Service expected Congress to soon pass legislation absorbing all of Bar Island within the boundaries of Acadia National Park, were we just trying to enhance our bargaining position before the time came to either sell the parcel or have it seized?

He was a good reporter. He asked tough questions.

The story ran the next day, June 3, and, to our happy surprise, it was fair.

"NBC Newsman Willing to Let Public on Island"

GOULDSBORO — Jack Perkins has no intention of buying "No Trespassing" signs for his nearly 12 acres of land on Bar Island.

In fact, the NBC News correspondent, who plans to build a home on the island, appears to be stopping just short of laying welcome mats at the boundary to his property.

"We love that land and know that people love to go on it," Perkins said Thursday. "We would do nothing to deter them from that. We would invite them and encourage them to, because it is a beautiful place. We certainly aren't going to be ordering 500 yards of chain link fence and concertina wire" to surround the property, he said.

Perkins disputed some suggestions that he is building a home on the island in order to jack the price of the property when, or if, it comes time to turn it over to the park.

"We are not buying a piece of real estate. We're not making an investment. We're not buying for a profit. We are buying our future."

Let people read the truth. Work for change by changing attitudes, defusing prejudices, fears, and anger as well as the lies and misperceptions driving them. It worked in Selma and Birmingham. Would it work in Gouldsboro?

Given that article and Lawyer Fred's truculent demands, once the US government understood that we insisted on our rights, and by the time the town council and good citizens of Gouldsboro read the newspaper account of two outsider folks who loved the island, would welcome visitors, and were willing to defer to the town's verdict — once it was clear we were not ogres but stubborn Americans like them, unlikely to give up, astonishing reversals began.

The first white flag was hoisted by the Park Service. Anytime we wished (we were informed by the regional Boston office of the National Park Service, Superintendent Ronald N. Wrye's superiors), a key to the new gate lock would be ours, and Wrye was specifically instructed no longer to interfere. Further — even more astonishing — if we still wanted to build at our original site, down at the old chimney overlooking the water, the United States Interior Department would formally plead our case before appropriate local authorities. The feds were not just surrendering; they were joining us.

As for the town, it would have to amend its entire zoning code, an extreme measure, but — next surprise — the county planning commissioner agreed to do exactly that, fashioning seven amendments to create an entirely new category of shorefront zoning applying to virtually no one but us. Now there was only one remaining hurdle: the citizens of the town would have to vote to ratify the zoning-code changes in a special town meeting — that quintessentially New England institution, the purest expression of democracy remaining in our land, where the townspeople assemble to discuss, argue, and resolve the countless trivial issues affecting their society. As a rule, town meeting was held only once a year, in late winter. This year, there would be a second meeting to consider just one issue — whether Mary Jo and Jack Perkins would be allowed to build their dream house. The county planner, town councilmen, and federal Park Service supported us, or at least declined to oppose us, and believed we would win. But now it was up to Maine voters, a notoriously independent-minded and contrarian group.

Journal entry from a nervous night back in California:

Town Meeting Night — What is being said? How are the voters of Gouldsboro thinking?

I'm glad we never tried to bully the town. We didn't launch frontal attacks when denied, nor try to intimidate. Our neighbor-to-be, the New Yorker Fred Rulison, has been vainly trying to subdivide his eastern end of the island and sell lots for profit. Lots of profit. When rebuffed, he threatened. Swore to fight in court if need be, an obstinacy which only stiffened town backs. That much remains true of the New England stereotype. They don't take kindly to folks "from away" bullying. As they go to vote on us now, we're glad they needn't think of us as adversaries. How will they vote?

We raise a simple, pleading toast to people we don't know, three thousand miles away.

And the day after:

It must be over by now. I feel a twinge of anxiety as I get the number from information and dial.

"Town Hall," a woman answers.

"Good morning, I'm calling to inquire ..." As she goes to check the vote count, I wonder. There are twelve hundred registered voters in the town of Gouldsboro to which Bar Island belongs. Many would not have come out for a special, one-issue meeting, but precisely how many did? All the publicity, dispute, rancor ... it often seemed to us as though the whole arca were fixated on us and Moosewood. So when the roll was finally called, how many of those twelve hundred good citizens and true were present? And did they give us a yea or nay?

"Okay, here it is. There really wasn't much contest. According to the minutes of the meeting, the zoning changes were approved ..."

Hallelujah! Hosanna! We did it!

"... eighteen to one."

That's it? That's all? All the time, all the fretting, all the anguish and—only nineteen people cared enough either way to even show up, of whom eighteen shrugged their okay, and one guy was against us? My sour inclination was to fret over the one. Mary Jo's was to say a thankful prayer for the eighteen.

5

A FAINT
VISION
OF GOD'S FACE

Builder Vic joined us at the homesite, said he was ready to start digging, but only—he said ominously—only "if this is really what you want."

"Of course it is," we answered, too immediately to satisfy him. After all that we had gone through to win approvals, after all the uncertainty and worry that had finally been resolved, how could we bear to put off the groundbreaking another moment?

It was not in Vic's gentle nature to lecture, most of all lecture clients, but clearly, something troubled him. "I guess what I mean ..." he began haltingly, leaning against his pickup truck, trying to pry the words out of his reluctance. "I guess ... this house we're talking about, I wonder, is it really what you want? Before you answer, let me say what I think, okay? I may be out of line, but I want to make sure you've thought about this.

"When we first talked," he recalled, "you used the word 'simplicity.' Wanted a simple life, simple place, you said. So look what we have," he said, spreading out the blueprints.

He had designed, and we enthusiastically approved, an over-sized, cathedral-ceilinged great room, the wings to either side — three thousand square feet in all, and that didn't count the basement. Far too big, Vic felt. Plus which, plans called for woodstove heating with an oil furnace backup, propane for water heating, cooking, and refrigeration. Counting gasoline for vehicles, we were depen-dent on four different fuels, which was decidedly unsimple.

He shifted his feet, looked us in the eyes. "Don't you think you should reconsider? If you want a house that's easy to heat, it should be smaller. You want simplicity? Eliminate some of the fuels. Rethink the size. Rethink the whole thing."

We stood stunned, saying nothing, looking from him to each other, then back at him.

"Can I make a suggestion?" Vic said, breaking the silence.

"Sure," I responded, eager not to have to come up with an idea myself.

"How about a camp?"

The word threw me, he could tell.

"That's what we call a smaller place, a cabin, simple, rustic. Very livable but very different from what you have here on these pages. And, by the way, though I haven't costed it out precisely, if you want an estimate of what all of this is going to cost ..."

The figure for "Moosewood Mansion" was far more than he believed we should spend, far more than we knew we could spend. He drove us back across the bar, saying, "I'm willing to build whatever you want, if you still want to build at all," and deposited us at Bridge Street. We walked toward the inn, walked in a silence that was tacit confirmation of all he had said. The house through whose imaginary rooms just yesterday we had strolled, on whose porch we had lounged with fancied friends, could never be. Should never be.

Ironic. The National Park Service, the *Bar Harbor Times*, the Maine Coast Heritage Trust, the League of Women Voters, the Hancock County Planning Commission, the Gouldsboro Planning Board and Board of Appeals—all of those we could beat, accommodate, or ignore. But the truths Builder Vic had just forced upon us were irrefutable.

"What do we do?" I asked as we slumped into chairs in our room at the inn.

"What do you think?" she prompted.

"What do you think?"

Silence, prolonged.

Then finally, Mary Jo's face lit with a childlike smile and she said, "I think it's time for The Barn."

"It's raining out there."

"Only water," she said, and off we went, walking the two blocks to our afternoon haunt, our faces tilted to catch the gentle rain on our faces, a calming therapy we needed. Ordering cones (I, blackberry; she, ginger), we took seats on bent-wire chairs of the little ice cream parlor and quietly gazed through the windows at the rain, coming a bit harder now, people scurrying into doorways, under awnings.

"We can't do it, can we?" she said.

"Not like that," I agreed.

"It would be awfully big."

"Not simple."

"Not inexpensive, either."

"I've loved the name Moosewood because it's such a small, unpretentious tree, willing to live in the understory, not needing all the attention. That's how I figured our time here to be. But that name sure wouldn't fit the place we thought we wanted," I said.

"So should we do it at all?"

In an instant, the thought and the day were lost to the now raging storm. Only barely, through windows almost opaque with the drumming rain, could we discern blurred bodies rushing for cover. For some reason, moved by some impulse, we chose to move against that flow and stepped outside. Our dream had exploded. The weather, most would say, was miserable. To us, warm rain pounding on our heads and shoulders was a knot-easing massage.

(As I look back on it now, I think of those rains as baptismal, our christening into a new life and a promise of a new faith.)

The sky brightened a bit in the west, sun poking through. We wondered if there might be a rainbow. Scanning the high sky to the east, we saw only the dark wall of continuing rain, then there were people running down the street. Clutching quickly grabbed cameras, dozens of people dashing east toward the town pier. We raced after. The street widened, Agamont Park to the right, pier to the left, harbor and *our* island ahead of us — and there it was. There *they* were. Not just a rainbow but *two* glorious rainbows tracing parallel arcs, perfect in form but barely rising above the horizon. We had been looking too high to see them.

We had been looking too high. Our dream house over on that island hadn't exploded; it had imploded, collapsed under its own pretentious weight. Moosewood Mansion would be a spectacle — and wrong. Wrong for the island, wrong for us, wrong for the community. Vic could have profited more by building the palace; he was willing to earn less to do right.

I thought of a line of Thoreau: "The most interesting dwellings in this country ... are the most unpretending; it is the life of the inhabitants whose shells they are ... which makes them picturesque." I told Jo. She agreed. Simple was right. Small would fit.

Dripping, clothes soaked through, but not caring, we stood on the pier, heartened by the rainbows that Thoreau had called "a faint vision of God's face." I remembered that and wished I believed it. Wished, too, that I accepted the notion that we were blessed by that, as by the godly insight that flashed in the lightning before our eyes and spattered our faces. Those rainbows weren't just a "faint vision" but biblically, I knew from college religion classes, a sign of God's covenant with Noah. Might they prove to be his promise as well to us?

A stocky, flannelled man approached. He too had hastily grabbed his camera when aware of the scene and walked the short block from his office on Main Street. I recognized him from his picture in every issue of his paper.

"Mr. Perkins, my name's Earl Brechlin. You might not want to meet me." Rain dripped down the bearded face of the young editor, and he was right; recalling what he'd put us through, he and his newspaper, my first reaction was that indeed I didn't want to meet him. But almost instantly a deeper reflex took priority.

In a town so small, in a life so short, there's not time enough for grudges. We are all neighbors. Or soon will be.

"Hello, Earl." I shook his extended hand. "This is my wife, Mary Jo."*

---

* In coming years, Earl and I grew a friendship, he never mentioning his campaign against Moosewood, nor we our disgust with him. He would be supportive in reviewing a book I would publish; I would credit to him the inspiration for an essay I broadcast on the *MacNeil-Lehrer Report*.

6

BUILDING
MOOSEWOOD

For a builder, it was the ideal commission —
to work without hot client breath down your neck, no prima-
donna vacillations, no last-minute changes. It was ideal for us too:
Not having to make the tiny decisions. Which direction to swing a
door? What cupboard knobs? Not being tortured by subcontrac-
tors' delays, by work done needing undone and redone. Spared the
misery of yearning for progress when weather decided whether.
"Most agonizing time of your life," it is said of building a house, but
from most of the agony, we were protected by a three-thousand-
mile cushion and a week's delay in mail.

The first picture to arrive was from the *Bar Harbor Times*: a
shot made by a wide-angle lens to exaggerate the awful hulk of the
backhoe in the foreground, making it appear like a frightful strip-
mining operation. More innocent were shots from Builder Vic's
Polaroid showing two concrete trucks poised among autumn-
leafed trees, their chutes readied over plywood foundation forms.

In the same packet, the foundation magically in place, and here, in one corner, a window! Our first! What a difference! Walls, by themselves, were *construction*. Windows were *house*. House that might one day be home?

We analyzed each new packet of pictures like CIA photo interpreters working over film from a recon satellite with magnifiers and rulers. We read closets and rooms that were still two-by-four skeletons; watched trusses, unmoving, being raised; heard silent saws ripping CDX plywood; saw workers frozen in midstride who, from photo to photo, somehow accomplished amazing feats.

December was about framing and roofing. January was an envelope of shots from inside looking out at snow through the still-labeled glass of the living room window. Spectacular view! Inside, as Vic swung his Polaroid around, we had our first look at how he was handling the walls — uncompromisingly rustic, bare studs facing into the room, the glimpse of unfinished walls that thrills homeowners before the finishers throw up wallboard and paint everything moonbeam white. There would be no delicate inner skin on our walls. Vic intended to leave those electrical switches and outlets hanging there, exposed, the wires feeding them running nakedly beside the studs. No pink rolls of fiberglass insulation; this house would not be stuffed with cotton candy.

"Don't know about that," we said to each other, studying these anomalies that would never pass inspection in Los Angeles, and our words expressed our state of mind precisely. *We didn't know about that.* But in our exhilaration, we didn't *need* to know; we savored the liberating feeling of once more unburdening ourselves to pure trust. Learning to trust here and now was the essential first step toward nurturing a faith that would be the ultimate trusting.

February's photos told of a battle with weather. Heavy equipment and trucks with materials timed their crossings of the bar with the tides, but laborers came and went by twelve-foot boat whenever they could. Vic called the team Mercer's Marines, and in February there were days of nor'easters so fierce the Marines' two-horse outboard could not land them at the beachhead.

Once back on the job, the workers would face their own challenge of trust.

Before we bought the twelve acres, we'd been assured by realtor Small that there should be no problem getting electricity run to the island, no problem at all. We and neighbor-to-be Rulison could share the minimal cost.

After we'd bought, and our plans were being drawn, Mr. Small dropped this on us: "Bangor Hydro says it could lay a submarine cable from town around to the far side of the island, the other side from where you want to build. They can't come straight across from town because that's navigable water, and they'd need the Corps of Engineers' permission on top of the town's, the county's, and the state's. So they'd go around the long way and come up on the north side of the island. They'd do it … for a price."

"How much?"

"Something like a hundred and sixty-five."

"A hundred sixty-five?"

"Thousand."

"A hundred sixty-five *thousand dollars*?"

"Yup."

"To get power to the *wrong* side of the island? A *quarter mile* from where we want it?"

When Bangor Hydro says $165,000, you can't go to a competitor; there's no Volts R Us factory outlet offering a bargain. So?

First option, of course, would be to do without, to live without electricity and get by with kerosene lanterns. No pump, no microwave, no radio or CD player. No television.

No thanks.

A diesel generator would work, but at the cost of frightful noise and the constant need to truck in a fuel supply.

Power by wind generation was feasible in some places, but Maine, especially on the coast, was not such a place. Winds were erratic and could be too strong. We heard of turbines being ripped apart by nor'easters, owners repairing and replacing exotic equipment over and over, an impossible expense. The investment in turbines and towers worked out to be affordable only when the installation could be tied to the power grid so the excess produced in high winds could be sold to the power company and some of the profit used to draw power from the grid when the winds were calm. That was the whole problem for us: we couldn't tie into the grid.

Solar? Photovoltaic cells had come down in price and up in efficiency, but enough? It would be years, experts said, before solar electricity could compete in cost with utility-generated power. There was promising research, but for the foreseeable future, solar was not economically feasible, the publications I researched agreed — unless, perhaps, a fellow were foolish enough to contemplate living on a remote island where the power company wanted no part of him. Then it might make sense if there were enough sun. Daylight gets short, come winter in Maine. Fogs hang thick for days. There were charts in library books that were not encouraging, but, on the other hand, there was a headline in the latest *Downeast* magazine about a man named David Sleeper. Apparently, this guy had it worked out.

The people of Maine's Monhegan Island had found him first. The handful of year-round residents there had long relied on diesel-powered generators for power but were sick of the relentless thrum that at times became insufferable clatter. A former engineer for Scott Paper, Dave Sleeper had studied alternative energy sources with some success, so the good folk of Monhegan invited him out to lecture. They thought he would talk about wind power like the other experts, but they were surprised at what he told them.

The more David Sleeper had researched wind power, the more his engineer's mind had turned toward the quiet sun. The citizens of Monhegan listened, and David Sleeper's limitless, youthful confidence, plus something else — a familiar version of Yankee ingenuity — persuaded them that he could track down the requisite technology and begin covering their roofs with photovoltaic panels, eventually freeing Monhegan from diesel drone.

By the time we connected with him, he had done more than a hundred residential photovoltaic installations, probably more than anyone in the nation. His was a cheerful, melodic phone voice.

"What you've gotta do," he said, "is decide how much power you need. Make a budget. That's the first step. Then we can talk about what size installation."

"What's an average?"

"What's an average?" he repeated. "Irrelevant," he said. "You have to know how *you* want to live."

"It'll be just a vacation house," (we still thought), "so there won't be huge demands."

"But what will there be? You've got to know. What lights, what appliances, for how long each day?"

Whereupon we lurched, once more, into a precinct of ignorance. How much power did we intend to use? How much did we use now? Our monthly bill in Los Angeles gave a figure in kilowatt hours, but what did it mean? How did it relate? The house on the island would be smaller, fewer lights, but how much savings would that mean? What were our hungriest power gobblers? TV? Cooking? Lighting?

Over coming weeks, analyzing, we learned that our heaviest power user by far in Los Angeles was the pump on the pool. No worry about that at Moosewood. Next biggest: electric range and oven. We could use propane, refills delivered across the bar at low tide. How about refrigeration? Propane for that too? The largest propane refrigerators to be found in the fascinating Lehman's catalog out of Amish country in Ohio, a book full of items for people wishing to live off the grid, was no larger than nine cubic feet — only a third or half of what most homes had. Would that do us? A big color TV burned five times as much juice as a small black-and-white. Would black-and-white television keep us happy? Electric heat and water heating we would avoid. The small appliances most wasteful were those that heated by resistance — iron, toaster, electric skillet. That last one, we would jettison, the first two use sparingly. When it came to lighting, fluorescents were twice as efficient as incandescent. We would minimize incandescent.

A solar-powered system would produce primarily 24 volt DC current. We would need special fixtures and bulbs. It would incorporate an inverter to change that DC into standard 110 volt AC to run appliances as needed, but sparingly.

How would it add up? How much electricity would we need? List each light, each appliance, its amperage and hours per day of use. Hard to do. How many hours will reading lights burn? In summer when the sun sets at nine? In winter when it's dark by four? Use a microwave oven? In total, on average, how long? How to figure an iron? Its heating coil cycles on and off. How much on, how much off?

So much to figure, so much to stop taking for granted. One ought to be aware how many lights were on around him and when, but wasn't. Awareness. That's what we were being forced to develop — awareness of some of the simplest realities of our daily lives. It was a valuable exercise, not because it taught us the amperage of every appliance we owned but because it made us cultivate cognizance.

All during the construction of the house, the workers had been told that the house would be powered by the sun. Sure, sure, they seemed to say, hearing but not gullible enough to believe.

In March, Dave Sleeper rolled up onto the island in a truck groaning under thirty-two model RA 30 Mobil P/V modules, thirty-two Delco 2000 maintenance-free photovoltaic batteries, a 5.0 KW Best power inverter, a 7.5 KW redundant propane generator, along with assorted racks, control circuits, cables — requisite paraphernalia to erect the largest residential solar electric system in Maine at that time. (Though much smaller than would soon start appearing on extravagant houses up and down the islands offshore.) Till then, the workers had been powering their saws and drills by portable generator.

"Give me a couple of days," Dave told them, "and you can hook up to this."

Sure, sure.

In a couple of days, he had the solar panels firmly anchored to pipe racks on the south-sloping roof, cables run from there to the basement (where the energy would be stored in battery banks), and the inverter installed, and he announced that it was time for workmen to cut their umbilicals to their construction generator and plug in, for a change, to the sun. This is a change mankind worldwide may one day make — and, no doubt, as skeptically and reluctantly as Mercer's Marines at Moosewood.

The first carpenter to proffer his trust plugged his Skilsaw into Sunny Dave's contraption and was amazed that it whirred with the same speed and, applied to lumber, ripped with the same ferocity. Others plugged in. Tools spun. Doubters became believers. Whether or not they understood the technology — cells of crystalline silicon photovoltaically transforming solar energy to electricity to be stored in wet-cell batteries tied in parallel to yield 24 volt DC, which, run through the modified sine-wave power inverter, emerged as 110 volt AC — they had to acknowledge: it worked. Energy was converted; so were they. Their tools really were being powered by the sun. The energy of nature. The warming, illuminating gift of God.

What is the quirk of human nature that having worked, worried, and waited so long for a precious moment, when finally it impends, we stall? Is it the wish to treasure not only that ultimate moment but also the penultimate? To prolong not just the penultimate but also the antepenultimate? And … what's the one called before *that*?

Vic said the house was ready. We should come.

But we didn't rush. Having flown to Boston, we lingered, remembering E. B. White, for whom nothing, it seemed, was indescribable but who confessed he could not describe his exhilaration on crossing the bridge over the Piscataqua River and into Maine. It was, he wrote, "like having received a gift from a true love," a sense of belonging that "grants exemption from all evil, all shabbiness." We knew another Mainer who said it happens immediately. Cross that bridge and the air smells different, is instantly more invigorating, and the sky — whatever the weather — causes palpitations of the heart. He said that every time he crossed into Maine, he rolled down his window and blew his horn in celebration.

We blew the horn, rolled down the windows, inhaled deeply, sighed profoundly, and from that moment on, what had seemed blight along stretches of Route 1 — "Factory Seconds," "Your Home Away from Home" cabins, pure kitsch — no longer disturbed us. Exemption from shabbiness. Our antepenultimate moment.

The penultimate was stopping in Freeport, Maine, home of L. L. Bean and the other outlet stores up and down its main street (sleepy Freeport having become the outlet capitol of the Northeast) to get a start on furnishing our little house. Usually, homes are filled by haphazard accretion over years. To start from scratch was a challenge and a tremendous privilege. After five hours, we were on the road again in a rented station wagon chockablock with snowshoe chairs and three small tables, pots and pans, tableware and glasses, towels, sheets, pillows, pillowcases, quilt, candles, kerosene lamps. We had already mail-ordered to Vic a mattress and box springs and a kit for a colonial-reproduction, four-poster canopy bed I would assemble and lovingly polish. Spare furnishings, but sufficient for our little cabin. The penultimate moment lingered nicely.

And finally, the ultimate. Vic was waiting for us at the foot of Bridge Street. Whatever words we exchanged would not be remembered. The vivid memory would be of piloting the overloaded station wagon down onto the bar and stopping to look across and see our house for the first time, through trees and at a distance. A tantalizing appetizer.

But this was not the time to linger. No longer. Now we jounced across the rocky spit, scrambled up the slope onto the island, through the gate, and kept going. Through the meadow, past the noble oak, past the raspberry brambles, through the pin-cherry and apple trees until ...

Stunning! A house with tidy lines, low-lying, stained a weathered gray among popples and birch, spruce, fir, and moosewood. Jo and I stood with our arms around each other.

"Beautiful! Victor, it's beautiful!"

Uncomfortable with our gushing, he turned away to open the door for us.

It was ... *woody*. No white-painted gyp-board on walls. Our hands ran inquisitively over timbers and boards, softly sanded, lightly stained. Feeling their fiber, we sensed their soul. The *structure* of the house was its decor. Electrical wires, snaking up studs in full view, which we'd thought might be jarring, were strangely appropriate. This house was honest, forthright.

And the view: a panorama of sea and far-off mountains that filled the broad south windows of the little "great" room, the bedroom, and the guest room. Looking down the short hall, we could see that on the east wall of the bedroom a tall, slender window framed a perfect cluster of white birch. To the north, from the kitchen bay window, a stand of brooding spruce, a good place for feeders.

"Vic, we've studied every inch of the pictures, but seeing the place, it's so much more than we expected! It's everything we wanted, which is amazing because we didn't *know* what we wanted. Glad *you* did!"

There is a quality some houses exude when you enter them the first time, something ineffable except that the house feels homey. There are degrees. A house can feel homey in a qualified way: your homey, their homey, but not *our* homey. Moosewood's feeling was unqualified. Instantly, without the first stick of furniture in place, this house was our home.

Did I say home? Did I mean that? Or did I mean simply our vacation house?

Mary Jo, our resident artist, soon in those earliest days found time to illustrate a small plaque to adorn the new place with a meaningful verse composed decades earlier by a woman who lived just a few islands away along this same coast:

You don't know why and you can't say how
Such a change upon you came,
But once you have slept on an island
You'll never be quite the same.

— Rachel Field

7

ONCE
YOU HAVE SLEPT
ON AN ISLAND

Birdsong. A churble of finches, the secret
Sam-Peabody-Peabody-Peabody of a white-throated sparrow,
soft music punctuated by the squawking of bluejays, the cooing
of doves, and the cawing of crows. Such a diverse avian passaca-
glia was the way of waking on a Moosewood vacation morning.
Morning was the soul of the day.

Whether the day was sun-spangled or befogged, though woodstove fire be yet unlaid, teeth unbrushed, day's garments unchosen,
we found ourselves irresistibly drawn to the living room window,
where other chores were more compelling. First, the mergansers
and buffleheads that rafted offshore must be found in binoculars
and admired, for they liked that. Late-starting lobstermen should
be cheered on their way. In the sky above, there were clouds to be
examined for weather omens; in the waters below, the state of the
tide to be determined, the moment's shoreline mentally mapped.
Familiar birdcalls needed acknowledgment, and unfamiliar ones

needed attention. On a foggy day, the threnody of the horn on Egg Rock wanted harmony; if sunny, with flittering sparkles on the bay, each ephemeral light-flake dared to be counted. Branches, depending on the season, offered snow, ice sheaths, melt-drops, buds, unfurling leaves, catkins, blossoms, cones, acorns, autumnal color tinges, or leaf-fall. All of this deserved to be seen and respected.

Our Moosewood vacations, which we took as frequently as we could manage, weren't shiftless, slothful weeks. There was work to be done. Hours of screwing things into walls, assembling what should have come assembled, peeling unpeelable stickers from plastic utensils, filling shopping carts and emptying wallets, reading books of instructions that mostly were cautions and warnings so fearsome that the safest course seemed to be leaving the gadget in its box. Measuring, plotting, cutting, fitting, then waiting for tide-turn to cross over to town for yet one more handful of screws. Much mundane work, but much satisfaction: To see homemade gingham curtains hanging at the kitchen window. To sleep in a canopied bed I had fitted and joined, sanded, stained, and rubbed to warm luster. To discover that the antique cupboard we had shipped to Builder Vic, but had arrived too late to be installed in the kitchen, fit just right in the bedroom. To see tools organized on new basement shelves, wastebaskets and a couple of flower holders handfashioned of birch bark by the creative Moosewood craftswoman, wall studs supporting boards to serve as bookshelves bearing bird guides and Thoreau.

Still, whatever chores there were to do, each day we made time for exploring, for poking about the island to discover and name Pillow Rock, the thickly moss-covered boulder ideal for laying cheeks upon and inhaling its earth-musk; for hacking through underbrush to discover an ancient lumberjack peavey where it had been impaled years before in a stubborn stump; for treading gently through leaf-fall and duff to spy the rare bloom of a pink lady's slipper; for shinnying down to the rocks of the shore to study tidepools, gather driftwood, fling seaweed, or just wander along wondering if the old saying that, like snowflakes, no two beach rocks are the same is a myth and, in fact, there *are* two rocks alike on each beach — only two — and a life of contentment might be spent in their quest.

Often, though, a warming summer day was an invitation to plop down on grasses — faceup if one decided to take the Rorschach test of the clouds; facedown if he shared the belief that heaven is under our feet as well as over our heads. Peering down, he could discover minuscule wonders: the nodding frailty of blue-eyed grass; the soft dark-green carpets that, closely inspected, resolved into myriad tufts of hair-cap moss, their spore-capsules borne atop miniature pedicels, stately, small, and usually overlooked.

There were few large mammals on the island. Deer, capable swimmers, came and went. We found scat of red fox, and a few times spotted those secretive animals. There might be skunk and porcupine, and we knew there were raccoons.

One afternoon, threading through a dense stand of shadowy spruce on the island's north side, Jo stepped over a fallen log, but I, paces behind her, stopped in my tracks. In the shade of that log, two feet from my two feet, lay a full-grown coon. So well did it blend into the shadows that Jo, usually keenly observant, had missed it. It stared at me with a wide-eyed look of — fright? Supplication? Awe? For a moment, we locked eyes as though trying to climb into the other's mind, the other's world. Which of us would break the moment? The coon did, suddenly heaving itself from under the log and scamper-waddling away as I heard myself whisper, "Thank you."

Respecting nature is the first step. But only the first. Time comes to move beyond that.

At this point in my telling of the story, I have a problem. Today I know that something very important was happening to me on that day, but of course it was not just that day. It wove through many days, the process of spiritual awakening. There was no blinding flash of lightning on a road to Damascus, no burning bush, only — when it finally resolved — a book, a dinner, and a walk on the bottom of the sea.

Start with the book. One afternoon, as we waited for the tide to uncover the bar so we could walk to town for a special dinner, I was reading from the writings of Lincoln and discovered the catalyzing words. With the Civil War at its raging peak, Lincoln, in March of 1863, proclaimed a National Day of Prayer and Fasting with this universal reprimand:

> We have been the recipients of the choicest bounties of Heaven. We have been preserved, these many years, in peace and prosperity. We have grown in numbers, wealth and power ... But we have forgotten God. We have forgotten the gracious hand which preserved us in peace and multiplied and enriched and strengthened us; and we have vainly imagined, in the deceitfulness of our hearts, that all these blessings were produced by some superior wisdom

and virtue of our own. Intoxicated with unbroken success, we have become too self-sufficient to feel the necessity of redeeming and preserving grace, too proud to pray to the God that made us.

"Jo, look at this. I believe Lincoln knew me. What he wrote here could be my personal confession." As she read the passage in silence, the unheard phrases echoed in my aborning awareness:

Recipient of the choicest bounties of heaven. My "accidental" career, my high school sweetheart become wife.

Preserved in peace and prosperity. All of both I ever needed.

Intoxicated with unbroken success. Never been fired; never out of work; never had to look for a job.

Have vainly imagined. Plenty of vanity.

That all these blessings were produced by some superior wisdom and virtue of our own. Just as college had taught and a TV ego had gladly accepted?

Have become too self-sufficient, too proud to pray. Too proud? But why? Proud of what I had done thus far in my life? But what I had done I was able to do only because of what I had been given — some talent and many serendipitous opportunities. Of neither could I be proud. Of all I should be thankful. Thankful to whom?

To the God that made us. Amen.

"Powerful words," said Jo as she handed back the book.

"And you know," I replied, "it strikes me: maybe this is why we're here. Why we're allowed to have Moosewood and enjoy it. To learn that it's not about us. We haven't earned this; we don't deserve it. Like the skies and the trees, the coon and the voles and the eagle and the eider, God made us and makes us anew each day."

"We are blessed," she said. "Truly blessed."

The tide had begun to clear the bar. By the time we walked to the end of the island, we could get across. Leaving the cabin, we barely spoke, too busy taking in the waving popples, the hawk-weed-speckled meadow, then the bar where gulls were already feasting at their twice-a-day banquet as the sun slid softly down the orange and crimson skirt of the sky. We did not need to speak. It was a passage of peace we shared, and in those quiet moments, I knew — knew with more conviction than I had ever known anything — that they were not gifts of nature we witnessed. Walking toward the old town pier, I remembered the double rainbow we had spied there back when we had to decide whether to build Moosewood, the bow that was a sign to Noah and — I knew it now — to us as well.

Whenever Jo and I had a special occasion — and tides permitted — we enjoyed going over to town to dine at George's Restaurant. George Demas had taught drama in high school. Then, when his time came to change his life, he turned to his other passion, opening this small restaurant to offer exquisite cuisine. After enjoying one of his magnificent meals, I always ducked back to the kitchen to congratulate and thank him once again.

It never occurred to me while there to thank the stove. But isn't that what many people do? For the bounties that God has provided, they thank nature (and even capitalize the word). They ignore the chef and thank the stove.

As we headed home, back across the bar, which soon, again, would be the bottom of the sea, we understood that every day of our lives at Moosewood we were surrounded with irrefutable evidence of a Creator. He laid before us as he did before the gulls a daily banquet. It was clear: there *is* a chef in the kitchen.

That Sunday morning, we attended the local Congregational church and were taken by the responsive text we were called upon to read with a hundred still-strangers around us: "Dear Lord, you were ready for us ages before we looked for you. You believed in us long before we started to believe in you."

We were starting, Mary Jo and I. Especially I. In those too-fleeting vacation days at Moosewood, there was a settling calm, a promising peace.

Ah, but remember Jesus' parable of the seeds? How some seed fell on the hard-pack path where it had no chance to sink roots; so I, though briefly involved in a church youth group, found, in my own home, no hospitable soil in which the seed might take root? Then in college, like the seed spread on soil over rock, though I studied religion, was intrigued by it, its roots were shallow and soon withered. The third part of the parable, then, referred to the seed that fell among weeds and thorns and was soon choked out. For me, that was the frantic pace of TV news to which I must soon return. That life always worked to strangle fragile new roots of faith.

Los Angeles — *Kennedy's been shot!*
What?
Bobby. At the Ambassador. Assassin.

No! Could the toxic year of 1968 become even more murderous? It was just two months before — to the day — that Dr.

Martin Luther King Jr. had been shot down in Memphis. Bobby Kennedy had interrupted his presidential campaign speech in Indianapolis to deliver an extemporaneous eulogy for him, urging Americans to "tame the savageness of man and make gentle the life of this world." And now the savageness of man had shot down Bobby in a kitchen passageway at the Ambassador Hotel in Los Angeles.

He was rushed to Good Samaritan Hospital, where I arrived hurriedly and climbed atop an NBC mobile unit to begin reporting the story the nation didn't want to hear but had to. I told it, and told it again and again. There was little news to add as the vigil went deep into night: the senator's family and staff were gathered inside; the doctors were doing whatever they could to save Bobby's life. Night became day, and day wore on, the reporters still talking, the audience still listening, people speculating, conjecturing, philosophizing, recalling, analyzing — but no one *knowing*.

Many people around the hospital, inside and out, were praying. I was reporting.

For a reporter, it was a near-impossible challenge. I thought of Brinkley and the JFK assassination. How to convey the distressing urgency of the story, the horrible drama of it all, while reporting it with neither distress nor drama. Just the facts, which were maddeningly hard to come by: The senator was undergoing surgery. Three and a half hours. Still alive. Cause for hope. Wife, Ethel, near his side. His vital signs weak but steady. There'd been three gunshots. The surgery went as well as could be expected. Doctors would have nothing more to report for a few hours as they monitored the results of surgery.

The crowd outside, respectful, silent, grew vast. Flowers

appeared. Prayers continued. "A few hours" became several, and several dragged into many. Day passed once more into a dismal night that seemed to erase whatever hope there might have been that morning. Night closed on all, on sympathizers clustered around the front of Good Sam, on medical people being careful to say only what they knew for certain, on reporters, exhausted and word-worn. And inside, night closed too on the young senator's life.

Twenty-six hours after celebrating the most dramatic electoral victory of that dramatic year, Robert Kennedy was dead. One of his closest friends said, "I'm sure that one day we will smile again. But we'll never be young again."

Chicago—Then came the brutally, violently, and mortifyingly dramatic Democratic nominating convention. Mayor Richard Daley had sworn, "No thousands will come to our city and take over our streets, our city, our convention." But they did. Ten thousand driven young people poured into the city to stage ever more strident protests against the Vietnam War and the old-line pols "stealing" the nomination from antiwar Senator George McGovern in favor of Vice President Hubert Humphrey. Day after day, Chicago police tried to break up their assemblies with tear gas and arrests. Then, on August 28, the convention's culminating night, thousands of protesters moved *en masse* to the convention organizers' headquarters at the Hilton Hotel at Michigan and Balbo in the heart of downtown Chicago. This was the epicenter of the horror that, months later, a federal commission labeled a "police riot."

I stood atop another NBC mobile unit smack in the center of that intersection — which is to say, smack in the middle of the riot, the clubbing by police, the rock-throwing by demonstrators, their shouting and cursing met with yet more exploding canisters of tear gas. I was coughing, choking as I described the scene to the nation.

"You can hear the throngs here shouting, chanting. Let me hold out the mike to pick up what they're saying." Extending the mike, through my earpiece I could suddenly make out what they *were* saying: "One, two, three, four. We don't want your ..." Oooops. I snatched back the mike, but not before the rest of the chanted obscenity had gotten through.

Another wave of police tear gas blew our way, and atop the mobile unit, I was having a terrible time breathing, let alone talking. One of the young people on the street reached up to me a piece of cloth. "Use this!" he yelled. I followed his gesture and, holding the wet cloth over my nose, inhaled a few times. My lungs quickly cleared, and I could start talking again, reporting again. He knew his history, that young man. Knew that in the First World War, soldiers faced with German mustard gas learned to urinate in a handkerchief and use it as a gas mask. I didn't describe on the air what had just happened, how I was able to talk thanks to an unknown benefactor's kindness, but I did call attention to what the crowd now was shouting, the phrase that would prove to be the most memorable slogan of the entire night, the entire event, a line from a Bob Dylan song, and never more appropriate: "The whole world is watching! The whole world is watching! The whole world ..."

Out at the convention hall, Senator Abe Ribicoff of Connecticut went off-script during his speech nominating Senator McGovern to inform delegates of the rioting going on at that moment on Michigan Avenue: "With George McGovern, we wouldn't be having gestapo tactics on the streets of Chicago."

Whereupon Mayor Daley leaped to his feet, shaking his fist and yelling obscenities, profanities, and vulgar racial slurs. Those, interspersed with our tapes from the ugly riots downtown, made for a regrettable but never-forgettable drama.

By the time that painful and poisonous year of 1968 was gone, I, like most Americans, didn't even want to see it in the rearview mirror. There were memories we would never lose, but none we wanted to keep.

For me, the antidote was to seek out stories that were neither argumentative nor controversial. Stories meant not to tear people down but to build us all up.

Off I went.

Off to Baja, Mexico, for the annual migration of gray whales, petting the head of one of those great creatures as a cameraman and I bobbed in a Zodiac inflatable to record my standupper, petting it five times when the bouncing camera didn't catch the first four.

Off to Budapest to meet the brilliant Erno Rubik and slowly learn the technique of mastering his fiendish creation, the Rubik's Cube.

Off to follow a man who not only knew how to have fun but had ample means to do it. When Malcolm Forbes did something, he did it all the way. His goal this time was to fly all the way across America — West Coast to East — by hot-air balloon. No one had ever done it, and when you have Forbes's kind of money and his delightful amalgam of seriously mature business sense and playfully childlike panache, you seek pastimes like this.

A crew and I covered his oft-delayed departure from Coos Bay, Oregon, and then picked up the story days later in the middle of Nebraska, where fickle winds had deposited him and his chase team in an unwary farmer's millet field outside the little town of Gurley. As always, the farmer and first arrivers were presented traditional bottles of champagne as Forbes and his team headed to a small motel. By the next morning, though, local schools had been let out, and it was not just a few but hundreds of people and dozens of cars and trucks trampling down the millet field, awaiting the famous flier's grand ascent. Which did not go exactly as he had hoped, especially with our TV camera once again recording the historic journey. With the burner firing and heating the air in the balloon, inflating it, Malcolm gallantly climbed aboard and, to the cheers of the crowd, slowly ascended — oh so slowly — oh, *too* slowly! Clearing the ground, but just barely, the basket began moving, sweeping sideways directly toward the parked cars strewn across the millet crop. Malcolm was waving, as though unaware that the heavy basket was about to collide with a car. The balloon still wasn't heated enough to lift away from the danger, so the basket swung and slammed into the windshield of the car, shattering it and causing the basket to swing even harder, pendulum-like as it came up to a second car, smashing the side of that one and swinging once more to take out another windshield. Forbes, all this while frozen in his buoyant smile and waving arms, ignored the havoc he was wreaking on the ground.

The closing line of my TV report that day was this: "Imagine those car owners explaining to their insurance agents that they'd been sideswiped by a hit-and-run balloon."

Another story I thought would be fun ended up more prickly than expected. I realized going in that the man was a grandiose boor, and his latest grab for attention a thing of pitiful prospect, but why not check it out?

So this time, off to Twin Falls, Idaho, to prepare for Evel Knievel's Great (at least greatly hyped) Snake River Canyon Jump on a rocket-powered craft named *SkyCycle 2*. (*SkyCycle 1* having already crashed.)

We showed up a week before the jump to do a few feature stories and arrange for the event itself. At the jump site, Knievel had headquartered himself in a grand trailer painted (as was everything associated with him) red, white, and blue with gold-spangled lettering. A wooden deck had been built as a porch outside its door so he would have a platform on which to stand above the crowd when the press gathered to hear his daily wisdom.

Our cameraman was Jim Watt, one of my all-time favorites, though a colleague who created a problem whenever we shot a standupper — me on camera setting or wrapping a piece. Problem was that I was six-three, Jim five-six, so unless I wanted the camera shooting up my nostrils, an unflattering angle, either he had to get higher or I had to get lower. Many a standupper we did with me spreading my legs as far apart as I could manage and Jim shooting me only from the waist up so it wouldn't show. With affection, we called him the Camera Dwarf.

One afternoon, after Knievel and his team had spent the day

checking and testing, jiggering and jabbering, clearly anxious about the odds of success in the hazardous venture, Evel came out onto his royal platform (late as usual) and launched into his barrage of braggadocio for the assembled press. There were probably thirty reporters and cameramen clustered below, taking it in, when suddenly Knievel's eyes fixed on the Dwarf and his camera in the front row. Jim had a grim look on his face. (He considered Knievel a thug and a lout and didn't hide his feelings while doing his job.) Why Knievel even noticed, I don't know; perhaps there was something in him that expected universal adulation and, not getting it, erupted.

"Hey you, down there."

Jim replied meekly. "Me? You mean me?"

"You," Knievel barked. "I don't see a smile on your face. When you're facing me, you'd better smile. Understand?"

Jim's reply was terse and unyielding, not discourteous but explanatory. "I only smile when I want to."

Knievel's answer came not in words but in action, leaping down from his platform and launching into the Camera Dwarf, wildly flailing his gold-headed walking stick at Jim's head and camera, smashing the lens and doing no favors to the head. Jim was pounded to the ground before some of us surrounding the melee managed to pull Knievel away, ending the absurd assault.

Two things followed: First, another network let us use their footage of the beating, which we aired across the nation in our story that evening. And second, a person not given to any act that even suggested rebellion, rebelled.

I used to kid Mary Jo that she was such a stickler for rules and propriety that she wouldn't get in the "ten-and-under express lane" if all she had in her cart were two six-packs. But the next day, still incensed at Knievel's inexcusable attack on Jim, she went out to a local store to purchase some supplies—three dozen white T-shirts in various sizes, some paints, stencils, and brushes. Returning to our room at the Twin Falls Holiday Inn, she set up her production line and started to work.

At the same time, Joe Esterhasz began writing. Years later, Joe gained notoriety, and a lot of money, for penning such lurid movies as *Basic Instinct* and bragging of bedding its star, Sharon Stone, but at the moment he was still a newspaperman covering the canyon jump for *Rolling Stone*, telling his audience of Knievel's whacked-out bludgeoning of the fellow Joe called the Dwarf Cameraman. "Whacked out" was a phrase used by *Rolling Stone* readers to refer to someone who was drug crazed, and Joe's allusion may have been valid. It's hard to understand how a simple remark like Jim's could cause a sober person to erupt so violently as Knievel had, even a man under stress as Knievel certainly was.

The great daredevil's official pre-jump press conference was scheduled for the next afternoon at the hotel. By that time, there were more like sixty press gathered. And Mary Jo's makeshift production line had been productive indeed. By the time of the press conference, most of the T-shirts she had carefully inscribed in— what else?—red, white, and blue were spoken for by our own crew and the other TV crews present, as well as Esterhasz and many other reporters and even Knievel's principal press handler, Shelly Saltman.

The press conference began late after two o'clock, Knievel being introduced and stepping to the podium to begin fielding questions as cameras rolled. Halfway through his first answer, however, he looked down at the front row to see all of us looking up at him grimly while wearing the same shirts, white T's defiantly stenciled, "I Only Smile When I Want To!"

He saw us in the front row, looked around and spotted all the others in the room wearing the same message of overt insubordination. He didn't see the one his man Saltman wore because Shelly, cowardly but wisely for his own safety, had it covered with a leather jacket.

"If that's how you want to play," snapped Knievel to the assembled media, "that's the end of the press conference." Off he stormed, leaving the newest arrivals among the press wondering what had just happened and why, while the rest of us, in our uniforms, reveled in conspiratorial triumph. And Esterhasz added that to his story too.

None too soon came September 8, 1974, the day of the Great Jump. *SkyCycle 2* prepared to fire Knievel up and, possibly, across the canyon to the other side. Just possibly. But he and his team had never had a successful practice run; they had failed twice with their rocket-powered bobsled gadget launched from a metal incline. Two failures, no successes. Why should anyone expect it would work this time?

But Knievel was committed, significantly, by contract. He was being paid $6 million to make the jump live on *ABC's Wide World of Sports* and to a pay-per-view audience. Neither his ego nor his bank account would let him back out. So, as he wrote in retrospect, "I climbed up and got strapped in, and when I punched that power button, I thought, 'God, here I come.'"

He didn't make it to God. Not yet. He didn't even make it across the canyon. Seconds after *SkyCycle 2* cleared the launch ramp, its parachute deployed prematurely. Horrified, his team and friends and ABC's millions of live viewers saw the vehicle plunge into the canyon, dropping, it seemed, directly toward the river, which would have meant his certain death.

Ah, but how many times before had he cheated the Reaper? And once more he did. At the last second, a gust of wind dragged the vehicle down onto the rocks on the far side of the raging river, and before long, Knievel was able to extricate himself, shaken, scared (though he would not admit it), bumped and bruised, but alive.

We had not been permitted on the grounds for the shoot, since ABC's purchased rights were exclusive, so how could we of NBC cover it for that evening's newscast? With a few still shots his people deigned to provide, and with perspective.

That weekend, we noted, relishing the irony, most of the sensible folk around Twin Falls were going to the county fair. We showed folks visiting livestock in 4-H barns, checking out the blue ribbon pie winners, smearing faces with cotton candy, kids climbing onto tractors, and handsome young farm boys trying to impress girlfriends by winning a stuffed animal throwing balls at wooden milk bottles. We showed, in other words, what the good and godly people in that part of Idaho really cared about that day, not some idiot outside of town trying to kill himself on a foolish homemade rocket. Reality versus fantasy, and most folks chose the former.

There's a follow-up: One day, years later, I got a letter. There was no question whom it was from. The envelope was boldly emblazoned in red, white, and blue with the single name in gold: Evel. The letter inside was shakily written; he was not a well man. Though we had not seen each other since those ugly hours in Idaho, the letter was graced with a familiarity as though we had been buddies all along.

Dear Jack,

I have wanted to write this letter for some time concerning our meeting in Twin Falls, Idaho, on Sept/8/74.

I guess the reason is because of my watching you throughout the years on T.V. since 1974 + trying my best to watch + listen to you on certain subjects that for the most part make good sense + pertain to things that are very important to our society + free world. You seem to have only positive sensible statements to make about things (events etc) that are not derogatory + that make me feel good to hear especially now since I have a 17 year old daughter + seven grandchildren by my other children + a grandmother (103) who raised me since I was six months old—she has lived with us for many years.

Jack, as time goes on I wonder why I was so tough on myself, + at times so difficult? As a young man now that I think back I know for the most part I acted as a young stallion with not much horse sense.

Today, because of my wild whiskey drinking ways driving myself to the extreme, in every way, I have liver disease, hepatitis + diabetes, it may be a blessing in disguise, I don't drink anymore and watch my diet very carefully. I am on a lot of medication but think I'm much easier to get along with—my thinking seems to be much more conservative + caring for others is a big part of my life (not that it has not always been in some ways).

Someday I hope that I get to see you again. Maybe I just might have one more beer to "make you smile," I still remember the T-shirt + press conference.

I wish you the best + good health, regardless of our

thinking and disagreement at the time I want you to
know that this letter has been written with respect and
friendship.

Sincerely

Evel Knievel

We never got to have that beer, and I'm sorry. Friday, November 30, 2007, Knievel had trouble breathing, and before the ambulance could arrive at his Florida condo, he was dead, that crippled and burned-out old man who wasn't old.

In his life, he had been a wild man, savage and brutish, but also, as attested by many, a profligately generous man, picking up tabs for strangers in restaurants, tossing off hundred-dollar tips. He had been a reckless (not wreckless) daredevil and a consummate showman. If he used and abused other people, even more did he use and abuse himself. Toward the end of his life, he underwent what friends reported was a heartfelt conversion to God, his newfound faith encouraged by his reading the book *The Case for Christ* by Lee Strobel, to whom he reached out in a series of inquiring and inspiring phone conversations, calls sometimes an hour long, discussing faith as the former reprobate locked in his new beliefs.

Looking back, I figure his letter to me at about that time was just one more step on his way to the Way.

Today, as I write these words, I smile.

Because I want to.

8

SIGNS, VOICES, AND THE FRYEBURG FAIR

Maybe we already knew. Maybe something inside us had known from the beginning that our plan to build "a little vacation place" was subtle self-deception, that it was always intended to become a place to rebuild our lives from the ground up. Even before we acknowledged the role God and the Holy Spirit played in orchestrating the "coincidences" that brought us here, maybe we knew. Maybe, at least in our subconscious minds, the seeds had been planted way back with the Kings and Tripps at Westways, had germinated under Carl Small's glib fertilizing, and burst into flower with the lupines of the meadow. Maybe Mary Jo and I long had intuited what was about to happen.

We felt good at Moosewood. As we thought about it and talked about it, it was not just that we liked this place better than we liked LA; we liked *ourselves* better when we were here.

We had lived in Los Angeles nineteen years. My reasons for staying were money and recognition, but mostly because it was what I did. Radio and TV were all I had ever done. But now, at Moosewood, I realized that to the question, "Is this what you want to do with your life?" the answer, "It's what I do," is a sign of spiritual atrophy. Whatever I had done and however well I had done it, did I want to end up saying, "That's all I tried"?

We were sitting on the deck, idly gazing across the waters of Frenchman's Bay glittering in the sunshine this sweet, bright afternoon, when I asked, "Could you see us living here full-time, Joey?"

A lobster boat was chugging in with its day's harvest. Looked like Robin Young. Jo spoke. "Remember that day Vic proposed we build just a simple place like this; he said he didn't figure this was going to be our permanent home anyway. He couldn't see that. It'd be too small, he said, for 'the Perkinses of Los Angeles, California.'"

"I remember. But maybe ... Whaddya think? Maybe for a change, the Perkinses of Moosewood, Maine, would like to live small."

"Maybe, with God's help."

There would be signs. That summer, while we were gone from Moosewood, we talked about how we might landscape when we went back. (*Landscape* — shibboleth of the suburbanized American.) We thought about bush roses to climb and cover the rock walls, delphiniums or larkspur, perhaps, to stand tall along the side of the house, and asters, phlox, coleus as cover.

Returning to Moosewood, though, we were reminded how superfluous are people's anthropocentric intentions. Without us,

God had employed nature to do his own landscaping. Where bare earth had glared three months before, rolling green mounds of horsetail fern were the cover, bush dogwood the form, and lupine, daisies, clover, and hawkweed the color accents of a garden more lush than any catalog could offer. When last we had seen it, the deck outside the bedroom stood three feet above bare brown soil. Now that nakedness was clothed in a green, white, and yellow robe of such lushness it rose level with the deck: thousands of oxeye daisies gently undulating in the breeze, so thick it looked as though one could step off the deck and walk right across them. Best of all, there were no weeds! Everything was what and where it was meant to be. The surprise profusion of wildflowers seemed to have been put there to give us an urgent message: *You'd better hurry and get here for good, folks, because it doesn't get better.*

One day, far afield from Moosewood, another sign. We visited the ruins of Tulum in Mexico, seeing images of the Descending God carved in stone centuries ago by the ancient Mayans. A guide was explaining how the Mayans, like later Toltecs and Aztecs, worked with two calendars: lunar, 365.25 days (yes, even then, they knew the need for leap years), and a religious cycle of 260 days. As the math of it worked, those two calendars, wheeling simultaneously, came into congruence once every fifty-two years. Observing that holy conjunction, Mayans chose that cycle to renew and rebuild their great temples and monuments and rededicate their lives. They erected new walls to surround old buildings, their temples growing like tree rings marking these times of rebirth. Renewal, rebuilding, growth — every fifty-two years. Next year, I would be fifty-two.

One evening at Moosewood, we listened to a man on the radio reading a book, *Evening Stars*, Barbara Matusow's account of the growth of network television news, and, at one point, we heard my name mentioned. How ironic, I thought, to be sitting by kerosene lamplight in a cabin on an island off the coast of Maine hearing my name float by among those of great broadcasters I had always venerated. But also, I thought, looking out at the popples that waved and waters that glinted, how irrelevant, not worth even mentioning over a stack of blues at Jordan's. A sign.

Another evening, I was rereading Anne Morrow Lindbergh's *Gift from the Sea*. About to end her own island vacation thirty years earlier, she fretted that back in the city, she would be "submerged again not only by distractions but by opportunities, not only by dull people but by interesting ones." She feared the world crowding in on her again "with its false sense of values, values weighed in quantity, not quality; in speed, not stillness; in noise, not silence; in words, not in thoughts; in acquisitiveness, not beauty. How shall I resist the onslaught?" A voice.

Another day, Jo was curled in her chair, legs tucked under, reading Edna St. Vincent Millay, a Mainer, born in Rockland. We realized that when she wrote

All I could see from where I stood
Was three long mountains and a wood;
I turned and looked another way,
And saw three islands in a bay.
So with my eyes I traced the line
Of the horizon, thin and fine,
Straight around till I was come
Back to where I'd started from;
And all I saw from where I stood
Was three long mountains and a wood.

she was describing the scene around her beloved Camden, Maine, but also, almost exactly, our view from Moosewood. The poem was meant for us, especially its title: "Renascence."

I wish I could recount one single moment, the dramatic flash when our decision was finally sealed, but there was not one. Maybe there usually is not. Maybe it is like the way people fall in love: by the time they get around to putting it in words, they have already communicated it a hundred times with eyes, touches, and it is understood. The unconscious has already decided, and it remains only for the conscious to hear of it and agree. How does that happen? For us, it meant the Fryeburg Fair.

Fifty years earlier, E. B. White, making his migration from New York City to the Maine coast, while sorting through a lifetime of accumulated possessions, "right in the middle of the dispersal, while the mournful rooms were still loaded with loot, I had a wonderful idea: we would shut the apartment, leave everything to soak for a while, and go to the Fryeburg Fair, in Maine, where we could sit under a tent at a cattle auction and watch somebody else trying to dispose of something."

There were many summer fairs in New England, but Fryeburg's, over in western Maine, was the last of the season and the biggest. What wonders it offered! Should we dash first to the pig scramble or the ox pull? The fiddlers' contest or the firemen's muster? Soap-makers' demonstrations or the pie competition? We certainly would save time to tour the sheep barns and poultry displays; we'd miss neither the 4-H nor the canning exhibits. Whatever we could imagine, and many things we couldn't, we would find at the Fryeburg Fair.

Except we wouldn't find Lerch's donuts. Wayne County Fair, Wooster, Ohio, late thirties and forties. Walk in the gate, the first thing you see are the tractors to climb on, where you can sit up there on that wide-saucer seat and go *hroom, hroom* with your hands on the wheel. They let you: the grownups in charge let a kid sit there and *hroom-hroom*. Fairs are for that. And for the booth just down the way toward the grandstand, the one you smell before you see it. Mom says the odor is rancid oil, but a kid knows it's Lerch's donuts, lifted hot and dripping from the oil, some dipped in powdered sugar but the best ones left plain, a bit of crunch to the crust and still steaming. Only at fair time do the Lerches make donuts. Lerch's donuts make fair time.

At Fryeburg, though, instead of donuts we found stalls hawking fried dough fished from evil-smelling oil and rolled in powdered sugar. I did not try it. You should not mess with memory.

The midway was five-decade *deja vu.* Tilt-a-whirls and Ferris wheels? *Still*? Throwing baseballs at fur-fringed cats and white wooden milk bottles? Were the cons all the same?

One thing had changed: at the booth where kids aimed air guns with crooked sights at conveyor-belt rabbits, a winner, when there was one, got his choice (or the young lady's choice) of either a Day-Glo stuffed animal or a three-by-four poster of AC/DC.

There were tractors and kids climbing up, and if the tractors were Kubota and Mitsubishi instead of John Deere and International Harvester and that seemed strange to some, it did not seem strange to the kids. To them, things foreign weren't foreign. It was older kids like us who thought it inappropriate that across the cattle barn, as eager 4-Hers groomed potential ribbon winners, the cornhusk voice of Casey Kasem on the radio counted down the American Top Forty above the milking shorthorns of the Fryeburg Fair. Not right, I moaned. But I realized I was caught in the nostalgia seeker's paradox, the self-centered notion that it was more important for me to re-create my past than for today's kids to create theirs. One day, their memories would include the tent at the far end of the midway, ominously dark inside, anxious feet shifting this way and that in the sawdust, bodies above writhing in exquisite concentration, the darkness blasted with rat-a-tats, unearthly shrieks, withering musical chords: the Fryeburg Fair had a tent full of video games.

Over by the racetrack we found a parade of vintage automobiles. Those old cars had been *new* cars last time I'd been to a fair. The attraction that seemed most lightly attended was the Freak Tent. "Nature's Mistakes," screamed the sign and the barker below it. "See them all live! Not stuffed or padded! A four-winged duck! The elephant-skin dog! The part-bull, part-heifer, five-legged cow! Straight from Ripley's Believe It or Not!" the barker shouted at no one. It wasn't a matter of kids not believing; they didn't care. Had freaks gone out of fashion? In a world of Pee Wee Herman, female mud wrestling, kidney transplants, UFOs, and the *National Enquirer*, were freaks mundane?

So much about fairs had changed, because, I suppose, so much about people had changed. On the other hand, down deep in us were immutable memories, and there was much to be found here that brought them back to the surface. A glass jar packed with watermelon pickles. A cozy quilt hand-pieced and hand-stitched. If products like these, quality like that, had gone missing from our lives, it was simply because we had stopped looking for them. They were still to be found, right here at the Fryeburg Fair, and no doubt at hundreds of other country fairs just like it. These were not faded memories of a lost time and place, objects in a museum. They were *here*, all around us. But for how much longer? If the simple enjoyment of straddling a rail fence to watch sheep-dog trials was an endangered pleasure, it was time to rescue it.

I had worked in broadcasting thirty-three years. It had been a rich and fulfilling career. Yet even as I admitted that, I realized the sentence was cast in the past-perfect tense. Past-perfect denotes action completed.

The timing was awkward. I had just signed a three-year contract with NBC. Younger son, Eric, still lived at home between college terms; his senior year was a year away. We could wait that long, but no longer. The Lord, who appeared to us daily through nature at Moosewood, had plans for us, we believed, plans that we needed to discern and fulfill.

We had ridden life's Ferris wheel up and around, around and down. From the top, it was a dazzling view, but now, not unwillingly, we would ride it back down, alight softly, and while the calliope still played, saunter contentedly down the midway. Where *were* those 4-H exhibits?

9

SHEDDERS

The moment two people commit to marry, the marriage, in a sense, has begun. The working through of problems together, the sharing of joys and the learning of the delicate dance steps of assertion and yielding, insistence and compromise — those are the true marriage. The wedding ceremony, when it comes, is merely ratification.

Once Jo and I had committed to living full-time at Moosewood, each minute spent thinking about what we were going to do was in fact *doing*. Since we didn't wish to waddle as lame ducks through work and life for a year, we chose, for the moment, to keep our plans secret. That was good. For one thing, if we should change our minds, the opinions of others would play no part in the change. A purpose of such a move, we figured, is to free ourselves of others' expectations.

Maine itself offered the ideal metaphor for our transition: wc were shedders, the term for lobsters that are just beginning to wriggle out of old shells, as lobsters do when old shells start to bind, and fixing to construct new ones for themselves to allow room for growth. Lobsters, in such matters, aren't stupid. Instinctively, they know they mustn't begin shell-shedding until they're equipped for shell-building. We needed that kind of prudence, to ensure that before casting off old lives, we were prepared to construct new.

What would mine be like? How did I want it to be?

Over years, I had spent many hours in editing rooms admiring the creative eyes of many great cameramen. I didn't want to shoot video, but I did want to test my own creative abilities with photography — large-format photography such as Ansel Adams, Minor White, Edward Weston, Alfred Stieglitz made famous. Landscape photography. That I would enjoy. In TV, I had done what I had done and done it well, but that didn't mean I might not do other things well. God, I was confident, had given me more than one talent, and it was time to start using others. I needed to put myself in a place where I was inexperienced and open to failure. That would signify my shedding.

For her part, Mary Jo had set aside her artistic skills during most of our marriage, channeling her creativity into the challenge of raising children while I was off on assignments. She maintained a sane home environment as we were transferred around the world. Even so, she managed to advance the art studies she had begun in college. She studied oriental art during our years living in Hong Kong. She learned basket-making and bought herself a pottery wheel and fired ceramics. What she didn't have, of course, was enough time to do those things to her satisfaction. She had undertaken one gigantic project (or two, depending on how you count), measuring one thousand strings to a length of a hundred feet each, balling each up and bundling them carefully together, and then slowly—very slowly—knotting them into macramé drapes for the twenty-foot picture window of our Los Angeles living room. It took her most of a year. Whereupon, with a patience I could barely fathom, she started all over to make them for the *other* window.

After our move, she'd have time for so much! She would be free to become herself rather than selflessly expending so much of her energy and creativity on husband and children. She used our "engagement" year to plan how she would use that freedom, signing up for more classes in crafts she had not yet tried—weaving, stained glass. Her Christmas present from me that year was a loom. Her gift to me, a framed collage of Maine autumn leaves we had collected together that she had assembled and framed, inventing her own techniques.

It was a bittersweet year, a litany of lasts. Our last season of Friday nights at the Hollywood Bowl, last season of Raiders' games, last Thanksgiving dinner shared with the Eatons. Eric's twentieth and Mark's twenty-third birthdays, the last celebrated in the home in which they had grown up. The last time my parents and their cat would fly in from Ohio for their holiday visit, the last Christmas tree in the living room, stockings at the mantel. Would we miss these? We chose to think this way: we were not losing these joys but imprinting them indelibly on our minds, storing them as memories in a more attentive, loving way than if we took them for granted, never expecting them to be the last times, as any of them might prove to be anyway. And we thought: If lasts are so precious, how much more so are firsts?

We could not put it off forever: it was time to ready our California house for market. Jo repainted, repapered rooms. I waded into the workshop and inventoried the toxic-waste dump of decaying chemicals that once, to us or predecessors, seemed essential for tinting a wall, killing a plant, reviving a plant, burnishing, burning, buffing, or bonding. I counted 176 cans, bottles, boxes, pails, spray cans, cartons, and squeeze tubes of white enamel, sulphur spray, liquid iron, water putty, white enamel, snail and slug pellets, fruitwood penetrating stain, antique glazing compound, white enamel, grafting and pruning compound, vinyl adhesive, slate dressing, fish-based fertilizer, white enamel, lawn pest control formulas, screen printing ink, tree-trunk white, antifreeze, green blackboard paint, conditioning enamel, acrylic violet base, acrylic sculpture coat, repellent and sealer, white enamel, linseed oil, multipurpose dust, liquid olive control, paint and varnish remover, and one more can of white enamel. I heaped half a rented dumpster with these expensive testaments to the modern faith that there's a chemical solution for every problem. At last, the shelves were bare, save for six fresh cans I had just purchased for Jo's room-freshening campaign: six gallons of white enamel.

I found myself wondering how many people, fixing to sell a house, felt overrun by an avalanche of possessions that had accreted over years? Here was one more reason for getting out while we were still relatively young: it was a rare opportunity to excavate ourselves free of so many clinging possessions we had forgotten we possessed. And, for that matter, to shake ourselves loose from the clutter of styles, habits, and priorities that had outlived their usefulness. Reminded us of the great George Carlin speaking of a house as simply a place where people store their stuff while they're out getting more.

In our small place in Maine, we would not have that luxury. So, staging a garage sale, we managed to turn much of our stuff into *their* stuff and move on to the house itself. The imbalance in that transaction stems from the fact that a buyer buys only a house; the seller sells a home. It is beyond most humans to remain coolly businesslike when giving up a home on which years of love and caring have been lavished. We feared the house might not sell for a year, planned on a sale in six months, hoped it might go in three. It sold in ten days!

It was time to go public. We felt the need for ceremony. Celebrating the close of the old life would help clear the way for the new, fortify us against any doubts that might arise.

Our next-door neighbor, disc jockey Rick Dees, that morning on the air reporting the weather had said, "First day of spring, going to be a beauty, high of eighty-five Dees-grees. Hey, be glad you're not living in Maine. Can you believe they're reporting a windchill of twenty below zero?" The crack was coincidence. He didn't know. None of our friends did — yet.

The announcement deserved production. For dinner, we invited old friend Bob Eaton, whose fibs to management allowed us the extra day when we first saw Moosewood; his wife, Betsy; and newer friends, Nick Clooney, with whom I worked on two shows a day, and his wife, Nina (parents, as the world soon learned, of George). Just four friends at first — the announcement deserved production, not overproduction.

Warm spring evening. It wasn't easy, as guests arrived, to pitty-pat around for an hour and a half without blurting out the one thing we were bursting to say. For dinner, pastas with choice of monkfish or yellow tomato sauce. Jo pruned her herb pots to season a salad. We poured champagne, and Jo delivered a dessert of lemon cake drizzled with blueberry sauce for symbolism.

"I'd like to propose a toast." At the head of the table, I rose impatiently. I could feel the glass in my hand tremble and stifled a laugh at myself. "Forgive if I'm nervous." I looked around at each curious, expectant face. "This is a moment Jo and I have been waiting for and looking forward to for a long time."

Bob knew me best — how I thought, how I wrote, usually where I was going before I got there. This time? I tried to read the look on his face — puzzlement? He was such a political animal his face was unreadable. Surprise him, and he could convince you he'd known all the time. This time, did he know? Had he guessed?

"The choice of blueberries with dessert is intentional," I picked up. "Sort of setting the mood." I raised my glass. "A toast to Maine, to that little place in Maine we call Moosewood, a place that Jo and I love so much" — pause for effect — "that we're going to move there for good ... this summer!"

Nick sprang to his feet, beaming. "Wonderful! Tell us. Really?" Nina smiled. Betsy — and I had never seen this of her — had tears in her eyes. Bob? Still that enigmatic half-smile, that faint nodding of the head. All were standing, glasses raised.

I pressed on. "We wanted you to be the first to know, because you people are the measure of how dearly we seek to make this change, to enjoy the peace God offers us on that island, that we are willing to leave such fond friends to do it." I raised my glass to join theirs. "To you. To Maine."

"To you," all responded. Flutes were tipped, the bubbles infectious, soon everyone talking, excitedly, simultaneously — questioning, answering, marveling, laughing, shaking hands, patting backs, exclaiming, exulting, Betsy, gently wiping her eyes, asking with tender concern, "But have you been there in winter?" We laughed. And Bob? His head was shaking in astonishment. He had had no inkling.

The next ritual took me into news director Tom Capra's office. "Tom, I've got a big one to lay on you." I was nervous, mindful that I had only recently signed the new contract. I took the chair in front of his desk and could feel my heart pounding, the pulse throbbing in my neck. Here was a moment I had thought about for years.

When I broke it to him, there was not an instant's hesitation. He threw up his arms and exclaimed, "Beautiful! That's just beautiful!" Not sarcasm, not the reaction of a boss losing an employee, but a friend delighted for the good fortune of a friend. We talked about Maine, about the timing of the move, and about the wording of the press release the station would send out. He wondered if there was some way they could keep me on the air once we'd moved. I said I wasn't sure I'd want to; new life would bring new interests.

"Well, Jack, when you look back, never underestimate what you've done here. NBC will miss you — that goes without saying — but beyond that, this city will miss you. Don't overlook that. What you have done here through your reports and commentaries is encourage people to *think*. That's a great thing to do."

Which reminded him of a story about CBS's Eric Sevareid. How, when Sevareid was doing commentaries on the old Cronkite show, someone hoping to hire his services for CBS radio as well approached Don Hewitt, Cronkite's producer, to see if he would object. He most certainly would. "Mr. Sevareid," Hewitt supposedly replied, "only thinks once a day, and when he does, it's for the *CBS Evening News.*"

From now on, we joked, I wouldn't have to think at all.

" 'Of all the people on our staff, Jack Perkins is the least replaceable,' said Tom Capra in announcing Perkins' departure" (NBC News press release).

The *Los Angeles Times* sent writer Lee Margulies for an interview, and his piece was especially touching because it mentioned our sons. Our impending move was not going to be easy on them. Younger son, Eric, had come home from college one weekend to find his room, formerly slathered with sports posters, redone in pale pink with flowered curtains. Older son, Mark, living in his own apartment, when he visited stayed in the yard, preferring not to enter the house he had grown up in because our redecorating was already making it someone else's. The kids all understood what we were doing and why and, I think, approved. Still, even before we could leave town, moving away from it and him, Mark resigned a good job he had had for five years and headed to Canada. That's how the *LA Times* piece began:

> Perkins' 23-year-old son recently quit his job to move to a cabin he owns in British Columbia. Perkins, who makes his living sounding off for NBC, Channel 4, started to lecture the young man about responsibility.
>
> It turned out to be one of his shortest commentaries.
>
> "But, Dad," son Mark shot back, "that's what you're doing!"
>
> "He was absolutely right," Perkins recalled with a chuckle. "So we moved on to another subject."

The piece described Moosewood, sketched my career.

"I try to avoid the word 'retirement,'" Perkins said of his decision to leave, "mainly because if people think I'm retiring, they'll think I'm old enough to!"

In truth, silver hair and beard notwithstanding, Perkins is 52. And he's not retiring. He's just not sure what he'll be doing next in the way of earning an income.

Seeing the stories, friends began a barrage for which we weren't prepared. We were girded for curiosity, for attaboys, maybe envy, but not for an onslaught of kindly incredulity.

Fred and Suz Rheinstein hosted a splendid dinner but could not accept that we and Maine were really meant for each other. There were pizza and pasta with Joan and John Marshall, one of the few other couples we knew in our ego-pumping, time-devouring business whose marriage had survived. They, too, were not persuaded we were going for good. "You'll be back!" Joan merrily insisted.

Why wouldn't people believe? Why wouldn't they stop asking why?

Our official going-away party was at the Eatons', in their gardens on a balmy Saturday eve. One expects to be humbled by praise at such a do, then humiliated by the gag "roast" videotape later. But what nearly brought me to tears were the special moments when two of the guests, longtime colleagues, took me aside. One, an editor and technician with whom I'd worked many times, traveled with, played tennis with, and depended on, earnestly confided that, whether I had known it or not, for years he had been professionally inspired by my work. In the hundreds of times we had talked, he had never said that.

The other surprise was from a young woman who had become a superior television news producer, one of the best. She pressed into my hand a note to read later.

Jack,

When I came to NBC 7 1/2 years ago, there was this master storyteller. He made me cry. He made me think about happenings in the world & about individuality and style. For a kid with a penchant for perfection, he was an idol to dream of working with someday. In this rapid-fire business you rarely get a chance to take the time to thank those who knowingly or unknowingly play a big role in shaping your life. But every once in a while you have to stop & do just that. This may be the most difficult note I've ever written . . .

To the master of "less is best," I guess the bottom line of what I'm trying to say is THANK YOU. For inspiration, guidance & for making it all look so good.

All my best

Why do we wait until someone dies, retires, or moves to an island to say things like that?

When a lobster wriggles free from its outgrown shell, for a while a flexible, translucent sheath is its only defense. What must the lobster do? It pumps itself up with water as big as it can so that this new shell, when it soon hardens, will be roomy enough to allow it to grow. Retirement parties are like that: a brief window of vulnerability when tough guys go all mushy, a bit of the inner self shows through, and the guest of honor is encouraged to puff himself up outrageously.

A deluge of incoming mail helped.

"Philo T. Farnsworth said, 'Television is a gift from God and God will hold those who utilize his divine instrument accountable.' You have nothing to fear."

"Our three-year-old daughter came running in to say, 'Your friend is on TV.'"

"My first impulse after the stunned feeling of your leaving was pure anger: 'He can't do this to me!'"

"We wish you and your wife a beautiful time of renaissance in the pure air of your island."

"While you enjoy your new life, please remember that you leave behind a sad but admiring audience."

"Don't disappear altogether into the Maine woods, for we will be much diminished if you do."

Each day, faced with a deskful of letters and cards, I closed the door, shut off the phone, and wallowed. But, of course, not all the mail was positive:

"The airwaves is ridding itself of much pollution when you leave. You are full of hostility, rancor and misinterpretation."

"Choke on a Maine lobster."

"So you are leaving! We no longer have to look at that bald head, bulbous nose, bleary eyes, shaggy beard, plaid shirts and listen to that vitriolic mouth."

These and others, obscene and profane, helped ensure that this lobster didn't get himself *too* pumped up.

Bob Schuller — the Reverend Dr. Robert Schuller — invited me to come on his weekly *Hour of Power* national broadcast before we left. There on the chancel of his Crystal Cathedral, he asked why I was leaving, what I intended, asked about my work in the past, and finally asked what, through all, was the source of my strength. It was clearly an opening for me to witness to a religious faith, but I didn't. I still couldn't. I thought of myself as a believer now, but I wasn't ready to make a public declaration. So my answer was evasive, if loving: "The source of my strength? Right there in the fourth row," and a camera picked out Mary Jo. People thought it was chivalry. I knew it was a cop-out. Dr. Schuller knew too.

Suckers for symbolism, never reluctant to belabor the obvious, Jo and I scheduled our departure for the Fourth of July, Independence Day. The Friday before would be my last day at work. End of a thirty-five-year career?

A crew from another station, Channel 13, came to our house that morning for a goodbye interview and shots of my getting into the car for the last drive to work. Outside the NBC studios, people queued for that day's *Tonight Show* taping called out, "Jack, we're going to miss you!" A woman blurted, "Don't go!" A man left the line to come over. "For years," he said, "I have enjoyed your work. Now I hope you enjoy your retirement."

Back at the office, newsroom friends had a cake frosted with island and pine trees, and a framed picture one of the artists had drawn and colleagues signed. In caricature, I was a baseball player, bat in hand. Caption: "Jack, Thanks for the trip to the Big Leagues." Tears.

Phone calls. All afternoon, coworkers and friends the country over phoned to reminisce, wish well. And viewers. "You don't know me, Mr. Perkins, but before you leave, I just had to thank you." By the end of the day, I was floating on cheer and love.

Then it was time. So few such moments are given in one's life, snapshots of time that you know, before they develop, will be treasured for the rest of your days. You try, as they happen, to absorb every nuance.

Our daughter, Julie, was in the control room as technical director for the broadcast as I was introduced for the evening's commentary.

"I've been thinking a lot lately about ..."

I paused. I paused and did something I had always wanted to do on TV. For five, ten, fully fifteen seconds I sat there, staring at the camera, saying nothing at all. Nothing. Until finally, "Silence. How in the clangorous life of the city it has become such a rare and precious commodity. Silence. Space. Solitude."

At the end of a commentary, there was usually music as the broadcast broke for commercials. This time instead of music, soft applause. While I had been talking for two minutes, struggling to hold composure, outside the ring of lights that flooded the set, the darkened studio had filled with people. At first nothing was said, just the applause. Then I was up, co-anchor Kelly and I hugging, people surging around, Kirstie bestowing a kiss, Christina hugging, David shaking hands, Liz smiling, a bouquet of red roses thrust into my hands, and in the control room, the technical director, our Julie, calling, "Reveal Chyron," as on television screens over the wide shot of the celebration unrolled the words, "Good Luck, Jack."

The walk from the studio, as I think back on it now, blurs. The flow of goodwill transported me numbly out the door, and before I could mark for personal history the moment of departure, it was past, and I was on the Ventura Freeway sailing west for the last time. How dare there be a jam at the Hollywood! I floated over it. As I drove, from some mean corner of my mind, intruding unbidden, came a petty thought: *They didn't give me a gift. All the times over all the years I've ponied up for someone's going-away gift, and when it's finally my turn ...* Then I remembered that studio, the gentle applause, the dignity of that everlasting moment. Oh, they gave me a gift!

I planned what to say arriving home. Few words were needed. The essence of all that I felt, of the adventure before us, fit comfortably into two meaty words.

Jo was out the door as I pulled in, running to meet me. I grabbed her and hugged her; I sobbed and she sobbed, and I said only, "I'm home."

To which she replied, simply, wisely, "Not yet."

10

TALK ABOUT BEING TAKEN OUT OF CONTEXT

After the lobster has cast off its old shell and pumped itself up to ensure that its newly forming shell will be capacious enough for the next phase of life, it crawls under a rock to hide while the new shell hardens.

We needed a rock, a way to provide ourselves an inviolable time of transition. The best way, we decided, was to put ourselves in a situation of no demands, where the stimuli acting upon us were fresh and unfamiliar, where inspirations from the Spirit could float on the air like yeast spores to leaven. Leavening was needed (if I may jump metaphors from lobsters to bread). The dough had been kneaded, stretched, and punched down. Now, in warmth and under cover, we needed to let it rise.

No hurry. We would go leisurely, that leisure being the first big change of our new God-granted lives. We would let things happen, keep ourselves open to the little epiphanies that God might provide to guide us forward. And to make sure I didn't overlook any moments of potentially life-altering significance, I decided I'd put everything down on paper, the trivial as well as the momentous, since everything from now on would be out of our ordinary. Journaling had helped in our times of testing, providing a place to vent and reflect. Now a journal would help fix those wisps of thought which otherwise might escape. What we express, we remember.

July 4 — Ives plays us off as we depart LA. Appropriate. Charles Ives wove music so complex — polymetric and polytonal, wisps of summer cloud rent by stabbing white spires, prayers whispered across picnic grounds, marching bands oompahing through celestial choirs — that for decades, defying performance, his works went unheard. Today, to listen to these recondite collages is to marvel at how a human mind could conceive such complexity. But of course, that is the nature of a mind — a tangle of thought-threads, ever snagging and interweaving. Especially this morning. Especially the open, intentionally unfocused minds of two people whose lives today change.

Today! Today the last LA breakfast, the family goodbyes. Today the drive east on the freeway, NBC studios receding behind us. No regret. Today the burn of the rising sun in our eyes and a sepulchral radio voice introducing Ives's *Fourth of July*. Today the contentment in knowing that our wanderings across the land, while ultimately purposeful, can be as random as we wish them to be, no schedule, no committed itinerary. All these thought-threads, flashing, disappearing, flashing again, like sun-slants on the whizzing pavement. Like themes of Ives.

Sights trigger thoughts. We climb the high desert — red rock, sand, aridity. I think it forlorn. Characteristically, Jo finds the beauty.

Sprouting like cactus across the desert, trailer parks — northerners' paradises. Not for us such gritty bleakness.

Lunchtime in Las Vegas, a place we loathe for its gaudy excess, money lust, trivializing of marriage, worship of neon, but, as though driven by a perverse impulse to suffer the worst of the worst, then put it behind, here we are, at Circus Circus, which is Vegas cubed. Here are the tables and wheels, slots and cards, dice and keno, like every casino, but here, too, suffocating those, are both the huckstering games of a carnival midway and a full-scale circus, aerialists trapezing over craps tables, wild animals roaring into the din of carny barkers — garish grotesqueries.

For a claustrophobe like Jo, to whom crowds are punishment, Circus Circus is excruciating. After five minutes among sweaty tourists swarming like black flies in the Allagash in June, she bolts in panic toward the only exit in sight, marked "Employees Only," slams through to another door, this one wired for alarm, which she also ignores, bursting outside, where the desert air is oppressive, but to her, released, cools like lemonade.

"Scary thing," she says, looking back, trembling, "that so many people seem to like that."

She's right. The press of the crowds, the clangorous blur of energy invigorate some people. For them, it's tonic. For us, toxin. That doesn't mean that they are wrong and we are right, but it sure means we are different. That is what life is for, isn't it? To find our way to the place and the pace fitting for us.

This first day of driving is long. Intentionally. Hereafter, we'll go slowly, feel the pulse of people and towns, stop early and absorb.

But today, as though needing thrust to achieve escape velocity, we grind out four hundred miles, reaching St. George, Utah, with just enough time to find the road that switches to the top of a mesa where we and a hundred carloads of townspeople settle back, take a breath, and watch fireworks.

To us, I'm sure, this celebration today means more than it possibly can to any of those around us: Happy Independence!

July 5 — There are layers to cast. The new life we seek is not meant to be an alien branch grafted onto the stalks of our stale selves; it is a seed that has long been carried within us, waiting to germinate. It needs light and air. To admit those, the husks of old habits must fall away. The peeling begins today.

Ahead, reports Jo, navigating ("nag-ivating," she calls it), we'll come to the fork of Routes 15 and 9: fifteen the fast freeway route to Salt Lake City; nine the scenic detour down country roads through Zion National Park. Which way do I want?

The extra distance going nine would add more than an hour to the day's drive, the narrowness of the road, another hour. Old habit insists on speed and directness: I figure fifteen. Jo does not object. (Another old habit.) But I do. Maybe for the first time ever, I question the preemptive way I have once again made the decision as though decision-making is the masculine prerogative. With us, with me, it has always seemed so. That has to change.

"What would you like?" I ask, enjoying the strange sound of the words. We take nine.

Nature is sly. For hundreds of miles it parches a traveler's senses with beiges and browns, then suddenly conjures lush little

Edens of green with names like Springdale, and while the appreciative mind relishes those verdancies, suddenly, there looming ahead — Zion! Not the holy site of ancient Jerusalem but the holy site in Utah, offering the grandeur of contrasts. Rich, soft vegetation set against starkly weather-beaten rock. Green against red beneath blinding blue. To wind through Zion is a backroad traveler's reward. A gift almost neglected.

July 6 — Straight through Salt Lake City, no stopping. No time for big cities this trip, this new life.

July 7-8 — White-water rafting, horseback riding along mountain trails among moose, mountain wildflowers, mountain sunsets, mountain moonlight — the Tetons never stop overwhelming. Nature never stops. God never stops.

July 10 — For forty years, Jo had a dream I never knew about. A few weeks ago, when I laid out the map with our tentative route, her eyes came alight as she saw the pink felt marker line bisect Wyoming. "Can we go to Horse Creek?" she bubbled with childlike excitement.

"Where?"

"Ever since I was a kid," she said, "I've wanted to go to Horse Creek, Wyoming. I used to want to live there."

I'd known her thirty-six years. She'd never mentioned Horse Creek. All these years, she'd been hoarding this childhood dream patiently, silently.

"When I was a kid, I loved anything horsey," she explained. "So one day, looking at a map, I saw the name Horse Creek in Wyoming and decided right then that one day that's where I'd live. I drove Mom and Dad crazy talking about it."

"But you never saw it?"

"No. Could we go there?"

So on a brilliant, high-sky morning, here we are, cruising up a road from Cheyenne through country I remember from Saturday matinees, Roy and Dale and the Sons of the Pioneers. This is the range where the pronghorn antelope play.

A sign promises "Horse Creek, One Mile," but we can see for miles in every direction, and there's no town. Better stop here, take pictures of the sign — that may be all there is — then drive on.

We pass a white Conoco station, two houses, cross a stone bridge, and then for two miles nothing but more antelope. Not even horses. Better turn around and ask back at that Conoco station.

Which, of course, *is* Horse Creek, Wyoming. This single, simple, white wooden building is post office, gas station, general store, sandwich shop, lending library, snack bar, souvenir concession, and, come evenings, taproom. As Jo takes pictures outside, I enter. No one here. To the right, a glass display counter in which the sparse merchandise is carefully arrayed so that seven candy bars, four bags of potato chips, and three cans of deviled meat appear at a quick glance to fill it. To the left, shelves hold collectible glass insulators (a hobby I've never understood), well-worn paperback books, and a decoupaged copy of *Desiderata*. At the rear of the room, an arthritic old postmaster's cage, floor to ceiling, khaki metal, postal boxes built into it, a counter with bars above it and on the wall behind, a sign reading "Buy Stamps: Support Horse Creek."

"Hello," I call out. "Anybody?"

"Yeah." The voice comes from a side room and is followed by a wiry young man in jeans and a Coors T-shirt, a tousled fellow looking rockier than the road into town and muttering about a hard night last night but if I want stamps, he'll open the cage early.

"You the postmaster?" I ask.

"And the mayor." He smiles wanly. Name is Keith Wisepka; midtwenties.

"My wife's outside taking pictures we want to mail to her folks from here." Which, I feel, requires explanation, so I tell him of her lifelong infatuation with the idea of Horse Creek, expecting to see amazement or puzzlement on his face, but I don't. Her fixation does not surprise him.

"'Bout once a month," he explains, "a letter arrives addressed to the Horse Creek Chamber of Commerce — I'm that, too. And it's some schoolkid somewhere saying they saw the name Horse Creek on a map in geography class and thought it sounded so neat they want to know everything about it. So I answer. I tell them I think it's great that they have a dream and we're it."

"And what about your sign up there? 'Buy Stamps, Support Horse Creek'?"

He laughs. "Well, ya see, when I took over a few years ago, this was only a two-hour-a-day post office. The Postal Service measures post offices by how many stamps they sell. If ya sell only so many, ya can only stay open two hours. So I've built it up now to where we're a four-hour post office."

155

"And the more hours it's open, I bet, the more the postmaster is paid."

"You got it."

"So 'Support Horse Creek' means support the postmaster."

He flings out his arms. "Who else do ya see?"

Jo joins us. We buy some stamps, and Keith includes a postage-free envelope so we can mail in — to him — to buy more. "I've already got one couple from California who buy all their stamps from me," he says with satisfaction. "Now maybe I'll have another."

"Not really," I say.

"Not because we won't buy stamps from you," Jo hastens to add, "but not from California. We're moving to Maine."

As I hear her say it, I think how nice it sounds. We talk with Keith about our move. No, that's not where we're from. No, we don't have relatives or friends there. So why? Following an impulse.

"That's how I got *here*," he says, remembering. Five years ago, his last year of college in Salt Lake City, he wandered up to Cheyenne for the Roundup and saw a map and the name Horse Creek. "That I gotta see, I told myself. So I drove out here, saw this building, and it had a "For Sale" sign on it. So, to make a short story even shorter, I came in, bought it, and I've been here since."

"Just like that?"

"Said to myself, if I don't do it now, never will. So I did it."

If I don't do it now ... In the words of this self-proclaimed mayor of the nontown Mary Jo used to dream of, we hear ourselves. How good to know that schoolkids across the land, seeing the name Horse Creek, still dream wandering dreams, and that grownups, sometimes, follow them. May we never lose that.

156

July 11 — Today is a day for considering time. What is a long time? As in, "I worked in broadcasting a long time." What is permanence? As in, "We're moving to Maine permanently." Usually *forever* is shrunk to human scale. If something will outlast me, or me and my issue, it's "forever."

The archeological dig outside Hot Springs this morning suggests another scale. We watch workers on hands and knees brushing dirt from fragments of bone embedded in rock. These were once bones of mammoths, creatures who rumbled these plains twelve thousand years ago. Long time.

Then, this afternoon, we reach Rushmore. Neither Jo nor I has seen this mountain and its massive sculpture. Nor is "seeing" what one really does here. One feels, one absorbs, one submits. There is majesty not only in the granite products of a dedicated artisan's years of blasting and chipping but, too, in the meaning that Mount Rushmore affords the word *permanence*.

Gutzon Borglum's team started mountain sculpting with a model he rendered in 1936. That was the year Jo was born. She and Rushmore are contemporaries. But the years yet allotted to her, if she and I are lucky, may be an additional fifty. Rushmore's?

The heads of four presidents are sixty feet high. The Harney granite from which they are carved erodes, we are told, at a rate of one inch every fifteen hundred years. We do the math. Recall how long ago it was back in prehistory that mammoths walked this earth; project an equal span of time into the future and, man's nuclear folly permitting, you arrive at a date twelve thousand years from now. By which time Mount Rushmore will have eroded less than one foot! All other monuments of today's mankind will be long gone — perhaps mankind itself will be long gone — but the granite visages of creatures who bore the strange names Washington, Jefferson, Lincoln, and Teddy Roosevelt will still gaze down unseeing from the Black Hills in the year of 13,986 AD.

Closing in on forever.

July 13 — Early on the road today, determined to reach Fairmont, Minnesota, by noon.

A new book, *Roadfood and Goodfood*, provides our destination for Sunday dinner in the heartland, where people still call the noon meal *dinner*, the evening meal *supper*. Edie's restaurant is described as "nothing fancy, with its green plaster walls, stamped tin ceiling, plastic and Formica booths, and paper placemats." And yet, according to the guidebook, "There is a touch of class about it: an individual sconce to illuminate each booth; pastoral pictures along the wall."

This is unpretentious country, and if Formica booths and paper placemats sound inelegant, so what? How's the food?

"The meals we eat are Mom's cooking, Midwestern-style. Roast turkey, sliced from a plump tender bird, was served on top of sage-scented giblet dressing, beneath a blanket of sunny gravy … accompanied by an item called 'pistachio salad,' which, for devotees of heartland cookery, is a quivering taste of heaven."

Famished, we reach Fairmont by one. Churchgoers on their way home fill most booths, good companions to dine with. The meal proves to be as advertised — plus. Tomato juice, salad, roast turkey, sage dressing, cranberry sauce, beets, mashed potatoes, gravy, rolls, butter, milk, strawberry shortcake, and real whipped cream. Tab for two: $9.96.

First job: Newsroom at WGAR Radio, Cleveland, Ohio. It was here on a Sunday afternoon that I got first word of what would become perhaps the greatest murder trial of the twentieth century.

October 18, 1959:
The greatest blessing
God has given me.
(See, dear, I do remember.)

Recording on a helicopter in Vietnam.

Refused to have tailored the traditional correspondent suit. Never did work to fit in.

Aerial photo of Bar Island, our home for thirteen years. Underwater is the bar that was uncovered at low tide, providing access to the town of Bar Harbor.

The start of another news magazine show for NBC. Chris Wallace, Tom Snyder, and I being introduced to a press conference.

While I was hosting A&E's Biography *series, they dressed me so well I hardly recognized myself.*

Moosewood from the water side, solar panels on the roof.

Bringing in our first harvest of potatoes.

Canoeing on a colorful fall day.

For our first Christmas at Moosewood, we sent this photograph mocking our holiday feast.

Our limited power system, running 12 volts, could handle only this small TV set, which we found we didn't mind at all.

*My beloved artist-in-residence
concocted this playful logo
for Moosewood.*

*When we were snowed in for
two months, this was our only
way of getting around. Here it
was strictly for fun.*

*From the
island, the
bar leading
to town.*

When Batian, William Holden's household cheetah in Africa, leaped into the room, Mary Jo got up from her seat next to Holden and immediately became enamored with the cat. Holden seemed amused at being upstaged.

Inspired by the time I spent with Ansel Adams, and schooled at the prestigious Maine Photographic Workshops, I began a rewarding hobby as a large-format photographer. No better subjects could I have than the beauties around us each day.

Symphony Hall, Boston, and a hundred piece orchestra. Were they really following me? I did a test and, indeed, they were!

Signing books when my first photography book was released.

The shore of our island, a great place for reflection.

At La Serre in Los Angeles, where friends hosted our bon voyage meal, my appetizer alone was twelve dollars. Meals for two, a hundred. Did we enjoy those meals ten times more? No. So why do people pay so much for meals that are different but no better than this? At least partly, do they enjoy doing it because others cannot? Most anyone could afford Sunday dinner at Edie's; dining here does not distinguish the diner. But it pleases, nourishes, and satisfies. From now on, for us, that is enough.

July 14, Oshkosh — An inn is on the shore of Lake Winnebago, a lake more comely than the roaming aluminum boxes that are its namesakes. It's our first stop on water this trip, and it feels good. Why? What is it that impels people to shorelines? This magnet that draws us toward Moosewood?

In the local paper we read that United Way is raising money by raffle. And what is it raffling? *An island.* The winner will receive title to sixty-by-ninety-foot Picnic Island in Bass Lake — not big, to be sure, but "a picturesque island ... dotted with oak trees, brushy ferns, and patches of wild blueberries." Hundreds of people are purchasing tickets in response to the romantic lure of owning their own island.

Bless the winner; bless us all.

July 15, Marinette, Wisconsin — A decade ago, a story brought me to this small town, a report on people fleeing big cities for new lives in rural America. A decade ago! We visited a middle-aged couple who had abandoned the busyness of Chicago for the quiet of small Marinette; another moved from Los Angeles to Eagle, Colorado; another from New York to the Ozarks. These were three surprise growth areas of America. It was the first time this century, demographers reported, that the population shift had reversed—more people moving *to* the country than *from* it.

The thought never left me. The values those people told us they had sought and found struck chords within me.

Now, demographers say, the aberration is correcting, population shifting back once more toward cities. Pity. We feel lucky and a bit smug to be exceptions.

July 16—The distinction of Mackinac Island—its pride—is that it brooks no automobiles. A two-by-three-mile outcropping of limestone in the straits separating upper from lower Michigan, Mackinac Island contentedly echoes the sedate clip-clop of horse hoof. Gay carriages rather than smoking buses transport tourists from ferry to hotel while bellhops glide bags on trailers behind bikes. Horse wagons deliver a new refrigerator, pick up laundry. Police walk. With all motorized vehicles forbidden save for a public works truck, a fire truck, and an ambulance, Michigan Route 185, ringing the island, may be the only state highway in the nation on which there's never been an auto accident.

Mackinac Island has an old fort, a few old houses, an historic trading post, several small hotels, and one hostelry so unarguably grand that for once the name Grand Hotel means it. Just one statistic: the porch extending the breadth of its gracious facade is a sixth of a mile long—the longest porch in the world. With a white wicker rocking chair every ten feet. So magnificent are the Grand's gardens and grounds, so spectacular its architecture and quaint the sight of liveried doormen greeting guests in fringed carriages, that even those who choose not to afford the nightly tariff of three or four hundred dollars, plus tax, plus service, willingly pay three dollars a head for the privilege of entering hotel property, walking its paths, padding its crimson carpets, and ogling its public rooms. Sampling the grand life, people seem to feel, is better than never knowing it at all.

We have to remember. I tell this to Jo, but I'm talking as much to myself. We have to remember this isn't the island life to which we are bound. Oh, no. There are islands and islands. There is Grand Hotel; there is Moosewood.

July 18—From grand to simple. From commercial to godly.

As we flow through central Ohio, we find that hayrolls are no longer mechanically compressed and deposited in fields like tidy droppings, the oversized scat of rumbling machine-beasts. Here, as it was a century ago, hay is gathered by hand into shocks, timeless sentinels, the providence of the plain people.

As children growing up in small-town Ohio amid the largest Amish population in America, Jo and I saw the black buggies jiggling along dirt roads and wondered about those strange folk named Hershberger and Troyer, Eli and Noah, the men with their beards, if married, clean-shaven if not, all wearing broad hats, and the women in black bonnets. They did not have buttons, we children were told, or pockets in shirts, or automobiles or electricity.

Why? What did those material matters have to do with religion? Most curious, we thought.

That was the difference between children and adults, and still is. What children don't understand, they find curious; what adults can't comprehend, they fear or scorn — or both.

Today we are adults. But today we are adults trying to be children.

At an Amish market, we buy the latest copy of the *Sugar Creek Budget*, the weekly paper reporting the folksy doings of Amish worldwide: There was a frolic at Levi Beachy's last Friday to build him a new hog building. Katie Zook is still poorly from her fall from the buggy when their horse bolted two weeks ago. We buy an Amish cookbook and, reading its prefatory description, are reminded of these gentle people and the precepts by which they try to live. Avoid violence, in war or self-defense; suffer injury rather than protect oneself by force. Depend not on the laws of men; accept injury instead of the protection of law. Keep simple ways so as to maintain purity of thought and commitment to God. If the world does not share these simple ways, be not part of that world; keep separate. Teach Amish children in Amish schools — attendance mandatory, misconduct impermissible. Hold church services in homes, choosing church leaders by lot. When one member of an Amish community has need, all assist: hence, barn-raisings.

That's how these "curious" people believe: that war is wrong, killing people is wrong, suing people is wrong, and that the world that doesn't agree with those itself is wrong and better avoided. They believe that public schools often teach wrong values, that friends are meant to help friends, and that rather than choosing leaders by election, you can do just as well by the luck of the draw. Across America, we're told, mental depression is ten times more prevalent than fifty years ago. But among Old Order Amish, there's hardly any. So we consider their values. Consider their lives. What's to scorn; what's to fear? The adult answer is: they dress funny; they're different. That's enough. For adults.

Here are Mary Jo and I, journeying from previous home to next home through the land of our original homes, drifting warmly through childhood reminiscences while yearning once more for childlike innocence. To be sure, we are moving to Maine as small-town kids returning to small-town ways. But part of it, too, is the wish to recapture some of the trusting credulity of youth. We don't want to be Amish, no, but living our lives as gas-guzzling, power-burning, war-making, litigating, self-centered, twentieth-century hedonists, cheering Rambo, wearing designer jeans, drinking bottled fizzy water, and gabbing on cellular phones in Porsches on the way to tanning booths is not the only alternative.

July 19 — It's been many years since we last saw our hometowns. According to the new sign up on Route 3, my hometown, Wooster, Ohio, is now a nuclear-free zone. Wasn't it always? WWST, where, in high school, I did my first radio broadcast, "Hi-Jinx Harmonies," is now Christian radio. It, too, converted. The old house at 1526 Overlook has shrunk. On the back road to Orrville, Melrose Orchards is still in business, and I tell the clerk it still smells the same — deliciously appley — after thirty-five years. She can only shrug. She's probably twenty. In Orrville, we stop by the high school to see if we can find Jo's name on the plaque she

won for citizenship, but it's Saturday, school's locked. Security is tighter in Orrville these days; perhaps it isn't nuclear free.

July 20— The Clooneys are back in Kentucky. Shortly after our little dinner party four months ago to announce our Moosewood intentions, Nick himself left KNBC News. Returning to anchor in Cincinnati, he and Nina moved back to their old house in tiny Augusta, Kentucky, near where he and his sisters, Rosemary and Betty, had grown up.

We float on the small ferry across the broad Ohio, and Nick meets us on the other shore. As he drives us through narrow streets, he is continually greeting and being greeted — the comforting familiarity of the small town. Appealing.

In the evening he takes me up to the outskirts of the city for a party, a nostalgic reunion of old broadcasters who, among them, have done about everything there is to do, known every triumph, suffered every setback possible in the business and come through it — some still working, some retired — with a sense of having been well rewarded, yes, but also of having served to entertain, to enlighten, to inform; these, they feel, are not insignificant contributions to the commonweal.

"That was back before there *was* an NBC. When it was still the Blue Network," someone is reminiscing. "Had only two seconds to air, and that rascal sets my copy on fire," laughs another. "Tell 'em how smart you were when you were doing that game show in New York," insists one old friend to another, who launches into a story that, clearly, he has told many times, a joke on himself.

"Well, I was announcing this quiz show called *Who Do You*

Trust? But I got an offer to emcee a quiz show across the street. I figured I ought to do it; it's a promotion, more money, and, after all, what future do I have playing second banana all my life to this guy Johnny Carson? So I suggested he hire a friend of mine from Philadelphia named McMahon."

All laugh. With the wisdom of years, they realize what I hope we, too, have finally learned: some decisions are wrong, but that doesn't mean they shouldn't have been made.

Wonderful yarns. Just retired, I already feel like a welcome and proud alumnus.

July 23 — Interstate 90 across New York State. Tire-thwapping, spring-banging, kidney-quivering, corrugated. In California, we were spoiled, neither roads nor people having to suffer the ravages of eastern winters, which we must now relearn.

"Niagara Falls! Slowly we turn, step by step, inch by inch." Three Stooges vaudeville routine.

But today, Niagara Falls isn't funny. It has become the epitome of nature arrogantly managed for the convenience of people. In a tourist brochure, the facts are proudly recited, how the flow of the river that creates these falls has been constrained, the awesome spectacle housebroken for one reason and one only: because people, confronting a natural spectacle, expect tourist accommodations adjacent; there must be a snack bar, a mailbox, a place to buy T-shirts, postcards, Snickers bars, and painted wood plaques reading, "Too soon oldt und too late schmart." Well, all these are conveniently, profitably in place today at the Niagara precipice, but the very force of nature which creates the falls erodes the rock beneath them. At the rate the river used to flow, it was eroding rock so fast that, by now, the untamed falls would have been a quarter mile upriver while the concessions were still down here. You can't sell plaques that way. The river had to be checked and taught manners: step by step, inch by inch, but don't stray too far from the cash.

The priorities are obvious. In the dining room directly overlooking the falls, we marvel at how many people sit here at windowside tables with one of the most breathtaking works of nature before them and don't look! Noses buried in menus, eyes cruising bodies, a man reading a guidebook, a woman reading soup. Apparently, these people came for lunch, not for awe.

Of awe, there is plenty. In tunnels below the river, behind the falls, one stands within fifteen feet of the falling water. That phrase doesn't capture it, *falling water* nowhere near strong enough. *Cascading, rampaging, torrential* — inadequate. The water of these falls, so close, is a booming, blinding blur, thunder vibrating the organs within us. Never, nowhere, can a person safely stand so close to such ferocious natural power. If one is not humbled leaving here, salvation is just the name of an army.

As it used to be, Niagara Falls was America's premier honeymoon destination. Not a bad way to start a marriage, being humbled by nature and moved to ponder its Creator. Niagara Falls was where people honeymooned, and marriages in those days lasted.

Today people honeymoon at Disney World.

July 24 — A pickup truck flashes past, impatient driver flipping us off. On his back bumper, a sign: "World Peace." Fella, ya can't get there from here.

During our eagerness for this move a few months ago, the lesson to be remembered was that living shouldn't be done in future tense. The lesson for today is this: past tense doesn't work either. Fine to recall fondly some tangerine moments of youth, but never expect to recapture them. Remember Paul Simon singing "Kodachrome": "Everything looks worse in black and white."

A summer town of my youth was Ganonoque, Ontario, and the inn was named Blinkbonnie-on-the-Saint-Lawrence. Speak it. Let it bubble from the tongue and lips. How a child years ago would delight in that sound, just as he did in the towering presence of the grand dame of the place, the white-haired old Scotswoman who tended her rainbow gardens, telling tall tales in a thick Scottish burr and making sure you understood that she did not accept just any tourists happening by, but chose at her whim; you were guests of her inn at her pleasure. We were honored. Many a summer did the old Ford or Lincoln Zephyr make the trek from Wooster to Ganonoque to afford us warm weeks of her quaint hospitality.

Blinkbonnie-on-the-Saint-Lawrence.

"Just Blinkbonnie, these days," said the distinctly non-Scottish voice on the phone when I called to book for tonight. That should have been a wave-off, but too strong was the draw to wallow in the past. Especially now. Because perhaps — I realize this as I tell Jo about my childhood memories — Ganonoque was the start of my lifelong infatuation with islands. Off its shore, in the river, are the seventeen hundred dots of land shortchanged by the name Thousand Islands. Was it glimpses of these years ago that first planted the seed? Was it while cruising among them, gazing upon them, that longings began which only now culminate?

Ganonoque is still trippingly euphonious, but what more can be said of the small town we find on this day? It still sports a village green, a bandstand, a summer repertory theater, admirable accoutrements. Small shops still advertise fine woolens. And here, round the bend in the street, is ... the Blinkbonnie Motor Lodge!

They shouldn't have.

Where the dear lady's gardens had waved fragrantly, a chlorine blue pool is surrounded by orange plastic colander chairs. Where her lawns rolled smoothly sprawl "fifty modern motel units." Her wonderful old inn has been *renovated*. And the lady herself, her distant successors barely remember. "Oh, I heard there was an elderly woman used to own the place. Years ago. Never knew her."

Our room, rankly disinfected, smells like the Continental Trailways station in Newark, New Jersey. Pillows are Kleenex packs. Mattresses, institutional hard. Decor, catalog cheap. In the dining room, with no view of the water whatsoever, even the thousand island dressing is tasteless.

They shouldn't have. We shouldn't have. We should have been willing to let the past remain memories, beautiful, Grand Dame, Simonesque Kodachrome memories. There's the sermon for the day.

July 26 — Saturday morning. From a pleasant auberge in Ste. Georges de Beauce, Quebec, to the border and across into Maine.

Moose River and Jackman, West Forks and Caratunk. This is the Maine of deep north woods, so remote that a seek-and-find car radio can't find. Woods around, woods ahead. Pine, fir, and needly perfume. In a world of confused cause and effect, might one be forgiven for savoring this air and thinking, for an instant, how much it smells like those cute little pillows they sell at L. L. Bean?

Moscow and Bingham. Skowhegan. Route 201 is designated a scenic highway. In all of Maine, we don't know one that isn't.

Canaan, Palmyra, Damascus. It was on another road to Damascus that Saul of Tarsus, persecutor of Christians, was struck blind, and then in his blindness given new sight, to continue his life as the apostle Paul. Lord, we quietly pray, give us new sight.

Bangor and Brewer. Final leg. Time for music. Good times, we believe, are best with Beethoven. A quiet evening cuddled by a fire with the *Pastoral* playing. A drive through colorful country to the *Kreutzer*. Walking woods humming "Für Elise." Or best of the best — our marriage twenty-seven years ago, celebrated with the Joy theme from the Ninth Symphony as wedding recessional. Not only is the Ninth the greatest creative achievement of mankind, there's something else. I am not willing to dismiss as mere coincidence the phonic kinship between the words *Jo* and *Joy*. For me, the two usually coincide. Further, in the Schiller "Ode to Joy" that Beethoven set for his Ninth, that blessed creature Joy is described as the "Daughter of Elysium." Isn't that how we idealize Moosewood, as our Elysium, our "place or state of perfect happiness"? Won't Jo soon be the daughter of our Elysium-on-Frenchman's-Bay?

We need the Ninth. I have it figured. If I start the tape in the car player leaving Brewer, the last movement should begin as we drive into Ellsworth. The bass will interrupt and the choral finale rise as we cross the causeway from Trenton to Mount Desert Island. The Joy theme will accompany our drive into Bar Harbor and across the bar (I'll slow down or speed up as required to fit), and the symphony will climax precisely as we drive onto Bar Island. I've imagined the moment in detail.

Also — foolishly — I've imagined that by popping into any

music store along the road we'll find the tape. But this is Maine. Restaurants serve red wine chilled, and in record stores the classical section is where they put Mantovani. In Brewer and Ellsworth, there's only one cassette of Beethoven's Ninth, and it has a glitch and won't play.

So we drive in silence. But though record stores failed, the mind does not. The majestic Ninth cues precisely as planned in my head. Aren't one's own resources — the resources accorded us by the Holy Spirit — ultimately sufficient?

We skirt Frenchman's Bay, slip through Bar Harbor, bump across the bar to the island, ceremoniously unlock the gate, climb the road through the meadow, and arrive at the house.

Somehow arriving does not feel like arriving. It is returning. As awhile later, hiking the island — scrambling down to the water at Pineo Point, circling around to Mussel Beach, climbing duff trails to find Pillow Rock and brush cheeks against moss — we are not exploring but renewing acquaintances, saying not "hello" but "hello again."

Come evening, I am moved by a keen sense that this first night of our new lives should be observed in some special way so that it might feel more portentous, but I don't know how. Champagne? Moosewood isn't a brut kind of place. Candlelight? Here, that's normal. Evening by the fire? Routine. The fact is, Moosewood already fits us so well that nothing about being here seems extraordinary. New shoes, if they're not stiff, don't seem new. Moosewood is not stiff.

Well, at least, on this christening night, can't we conjure some profound expression of philosophical contentment? The Bible must have something to say. But rather than search the Psalms or wherever, we quietly sit in the ungloomy gloom of flickering kerosene lamps as, outside, a full moon unrolls a gleaming carpet across the bay. Town lights sparkle. Lobster boat shadows dance on the water, and we reflect on the wisdom of Arthur. Remember toward the end of the film *Arthur* when Liza Minelli asks Dudley Moore, the millionaire scamp, what it's like to have so much money, a big yacht, and go cruising around all the time? And Moore/Arthur's only reply is a quizzical, "It doesn't suck!"

This first night of our new lives is celebrated by one of us softly murmuring, "What do you think?" and the other replying simply, in profound contentment, "It doesn't suck."

TO KEEP IT
NEW

Awaking that first morning as full-time residents of Moosewood, we exhaled great, gusty sighs and thought happily, "We've done it."

We hadn't. Not yet.

We went for a walk. Up the lane, across the meadow, through the woods, down to the shore, thinking as we walked, and now and then stopping to put thoughts into words.

Were our lives going to be different now? How would we *make* them different? We had to be careful. Removed from its familiar nest, the human organism instinctively starts building a new one, trying to make it conform to the same comfortable shape.

The enemy was inertia, the force that tries to keep things from changing, that keeps furniture arranged as it's always been, circling the TV, tables bearing the same magazines and books, clock set for the same wake-up time. For us, now, whatever we unconsciously yearned for must be resisted.

So chairs were turned toward the window, alarm reset, and

coffee table (an antique sled, runners and all) cleared; Jo's valid worry was me. Friends had anticipated it, jokingly predicting, "By the end of your first few months, there'll be a white line down the middle of the cabin." Would I become a *nureochiba*? Modern Japanese invented the usage (literally, "wet fallen leaves") to refer to retired husbands who, after retiring, hang around the house getting in the way. I made Jo a promise: no *nureochiba*, I.

Those first days at Moosewood, I made Jo another promise. Whatever I found to keep myself occupied, never again would I hold a consuming job that would take me away too often or for too long. I was an island dweller now; that was my profession. And I took it seriously. We both did.

We had plenty to do. Like Thoreau, I deemed myself "self-appointed inspector of snowstorms and rain-storms" and did my duty faithfully. Senses grew keen. From the tone of the gulls, screeching hungry dissonance, we could tell without seeing the water that the tide was out. With the wind right, we could divine the same truth from morning aromas, the pungent perfumes of exposed rockweed and dulse. We were learning to substitute senses. Sensorially deprived people were forced to do that. We were permitted to. That was part of our new profession.

What, then, about the message I got one day at the local post office while fetching our mail, when Warren, the jovial postal worker, told me there'd been a phone call for me that morning?

At the post office?

It was Fast Eddie, the resourceful fellow on the NBC assignment desk, who knew we'd gone backwoods but figured we'd show up sooner or later at the post office.

"Very enterprising of you," I told him. "But you didn't need to bother with the post office. We're in the phone book."

"Never thought of that," he said. What he wanted was this: Gene Autry, the old movie cowboy and longtime owner of the Los Angeles Angels baseball team, had just died. I had been the last person to interview him. So they wanted me to voice the obit piece they were going to air that night, which included clips from my interview. Could I get a flight to Boston immediately?

I could, I told him, but wouldn't. Thanks. We need to be here awhile. Settle into our new lives. Try me again in the spring.

Helping us unpack, new friend Frank playfully remarked on our infractions of Thoreauvian simplicity. "I thought you guys were quitting TV, big cities, fancy life. So Jack, why all the coats and ties?" Good question.

Out of styrofoam peanuts came a "boom box," a small stereo with radio and tape deck, selected because it could be powered by our stripped-down electrical system. "I'm not sure," teased Frank, "but best I remember, old Hank-Dave actually had to rough it at Walden without even mono."

A carton yielded kitchen things. "And I never did understand," he said, "how he could 'live deliberately' without an electric juicer and silver champagne flutes."

His playful gibes — as gibes often do — hit home. So much of what our moving van had brought from California were the trappings of the people we had been, not of those we wanted to be. So champagne flutes were shoved to a top shelf neither of us could reach without a step stool. The juicer stayed out, but shouldn't have; it eventually caused a midwinter "catastrophe." TV duds were retired to a popple branch slung between joists in the basement or were piled in a bag for the Seacoast Mission. In their place, jeans, boots, sweaters, and sweats took over the closet. New uniforms for new roles.

I sought to read more. An overworked mind craves exercise; it doesn't need to be coddled like a patient after surgery with insipid TV (especially viewed on our twelve-inch black-and-white, which experienced occasional flurries even in summer) or puerile bestsellers. Each hour we might be tempted to spend on Elmore Leonard, Danielle Steele, or Harold Robbins would be an hour not given to Emerson, Jefferson, or C. S. Lewis. We were no longer willing to make that sacrifice.

The local bookstore over in Bar Harbor special-ordered for me the thirteen-volume set of Thoreau's journals. Nailing leftover pieces of tongue-and-groove onto some of the horizontal timbers that reinforced our walls, I fashioned bookshelves to line the living room. Thoreau fit nicely. (Months later, one of the National Park people confessed she had come by to welcome us to the island and, not finding us home, had peeked through a window. Seeing Thoreau on the shelves, she decided we'd get along just fine.)

Other books found our shelves: nature guides to help us know the lives with which we would be sharing our new home; and to know the Maker of nature, works of Bible study and faith nourishment.

While hiking the island, stepping coastal stones, padding paths, climbing the peak, I found myself with a strange new abundance of scattered thoughts I felt a need to put down in writing. Years ago, I had tried to write a novel, but fiction had never seemed right for me. If I were moved to write, I decided, I would rather write truth.

The area provided a readership as well as subject matter. Soon I found myself volunteering to write a newsletter for a new Friends of Acadia group formed to support our neighbor, the national park.

I began committing myself to other neighborhood interests that my workload and the professional ethics of journalistic
impartiality had always ruled out in the past. There were fund-
raising efforts for the MDI Workshop that offered housing and
employment to the developmentally handicapped, and there were
benefits for a local church.

Also, there was time to begin to study photography at one of
the finest schools for that art, which happened to be just down the
coast: the Maine Photographic Workshops in the seaside village
of Rockport.

It seemed anachronistic, when everyone else was excited by the
coming of digital cameras and computerized photo-manipulation,
to be signing up for courses in old-fashioned view-camera work,
where the photographer sets up a clunky wooden camera, ducks
beneath a dark-cloth to examine his subject reversed and inverted
on a plate of ground glass. It seemed anachronistic but, to me,
seemed right, even predestined.

Carmel Highlands, California — Ansel's home perched on
the crest overlooking the sea. For photographers, this was Mecca,
Adams, the master. Master photographer, master photographic
teacher and innovator, master environmentalist, and, at one time,
almost master classical pianist.

Jo and I spent a week with him as I worked on a TV profile —
part of my journalism of self-indulgence.

What a gracious host he was, greeting us in western hat, plaid
shirt with bolo tie, and the warming wreath of a smile that seemed
constant over the next several days.

He wasn't shooting much in those days, but for our purpose, he would head out along the coast, not knowing what he might find. "Sometimes it seems I get to places just when God is ready to have somebody click the shutter." If this wasn't to be such a day, that was alright.

Back in the custom-built darkroom in his house, we watched him and an assistant laboring over a negative to draw from it the photograph Ansel had "previsualized." This was a crucial part of the creative process. He showed us a dupe negative of his most famous photograph, the one he called *Moonrise, Hernandez*. It was a magical scene he had spied while driving one evening along a dirt road in New Mexico. Yanking to a stop and clambering up onto the car roof with his camera and tripod, he knew the light was changing so rapidly that he'd have only one chance, so he guessed at exposure and snapped. His "guessing," of course, was the accumulated wisdom of many years, and he guessed right, and before he could load another plate for another exposure, the light had changed, leaving the scene useless. Even so, back in his darkroom, he had a lot of work to do. He had imagined the upper half of the frame, the evening sky, basically black, accentuating the full moon rising just below amid streamers of moonlit cloud above the village church. But seeing the negative, we could see that the upper half of the frame was not basically black (or clear, it being a negative). The effect of that dark upper sky was the creation of the darkroom. ("A photograph should not be just a record of what the photographer saw, but what he saw and what he *felt* about what he saw.")

If Ansel had printed that negative straight, no one would have paid a second glance. Let alone the fifty thousand dollars a single print of that work would one day command.

A bell rang. "Five o'clock," Ansel announced cheerily. "Cocktail time." He led us out of the darkroom and into the glowing warm light of the living room looking out on another dazzling sunset over the Pacific. Beside us was his grand piano; he had once thought of becoming a concert pianist, and some said he was good enough to do it. Time came, though, he had to make a choice. "I tried to keep both arts alive, but the camera won."

We won, I thought.

When his wife (since 1928!), Virginia, called us to dinner, we didn't talk much photography but for one question Mary Jo finally put to Ansel. She was seated across from him and asked simply, "Ansel, how many photographs do you figure you take before you get one that pleases you?" His reply was simply to raise his index finger and smile.

One day, to accommodate our crew, he gathered a hundred of his prints for them to shoot for our profile. As we spent much of the day going through those masterworks, carefully, admiringly, I thought about Christmas coming next week and what a wonderful and remindful gift it would be to present Mary Jo one of Ansel's photographs, autographed. I asked Mary Jo which was her favorite; by the end of the day she had chosen *Aspens, Northern New Mexico*, not one of Ansel's best known, certainly not one of his most expensive or one most likely to appreciate greatly. But we would appreciate it greatly. For one thing, it was the kind of scene, woodlands untrammeled, that the Guide of our lives would be leading us to one day.

Now at Moosewood, Ansel's *Aspens* hung on the wall of our cabin. He had recently died. I had started to immerse myself in studies at the Workshops under instructors including Ansel's former assistant, renowned photographer and master printer John Sexton.

For subject matter, I was blessed. All around us posed. At four thirty in the morning from the top of Cadillac Mountain, there was the splendor of the scarlet sun climbing the ladder of clouds over still-dark islands. Sixteen hours later, the setting sun inflamed the sea, three chairs on the rocky shore inviting the pensive to vespers. In between, there were rocks and rivulets, bridges and trails, smashing surf, sliding stream, fleeting shadow, the gleam of angelic birch, the Byzantine tangle of oak limbs, the track of a fox across a snowy meadow, the rising breath of sea smoke, the pale enveloping veil of fog — all of these challenging the photographer to fix them on film.

At the same time arose another challenge for one long given to working with words. Especially one who felt called to proclaim the new faith he was enjoying. I found that the same impulses which moved me to photograph a scene dared me to apprehend it, too, with language. To do this, I chose poetry, as far from journalism-speak as I could imagine. Where journalism talks down to people, poetry talks up. Where journalism uses too many words to say too little, poetry distills. Where journalism tries to be as precise as possible, poetry delights in ambiguity. Where journalism hurries, poetry lollygags.

I created poems for my favorite images, and before long a gallery in town was cutting special double-window mats to display photograph and poem side by side. I was thrilled when the gallery owner informed me they were selling well.

Eventually, my study at the Maine Photographic Workshops put me under the tutelage of Phil Trager, an oft-published photographer, who helped me turn my photographs and poems into a book, which I titled *Acadia: Visions and Verse*. Published by Downeast Books, it became Amazon.com's bestselling book in its category for that year.

At the same time, working with a new friend who, though a small-towner, was every bit as skilled a video cameraman as I had ever worked with in any big city, I started to write and narrate a series of videos about Acadia, the coast of Maine, the entire state. These were not journalism, nor did they pretend to be. (When I sent a copy of one to a TV friend in New York, he misunderstood my reason for sending it and replied, "Jack, it's lovely, but it's really much too slow for television." To which I replied, "Thanks. That's what we're going for.") They were gentle, reflective, adoring paeans to our new homeland. We provided them, as our contributions, to public television stations to run during pledge drives. We also produced at our own expense a new video for the Park Service, which was still running an archaic nineteen-year-old orientation film for park visitors and had no budget for a new one.

While I thus busily engaged myself, Jo happily disengaged herself, declining community obligation requests, the island an easy excuse. That is how she made time to return to her art, which, with her love of nature, brought her first to doing the illustrations for a new guide to be published on the birds of Acadia. Then, springing from those, she started doing full-sized bird pictures to be sold as prints and originals in a local gallery. (The day the gallery owner presented her with her first check for sales, she realized that that was the first time she had been paid for her work for thirty-five years, and that fact was far more important to her than the money.)

None of these were our accustomed occupations, but they occupied us.

Art is selfish. It is the ultimate consciousness expander, forcing us to perceive in new ways. We would never appreciate the texture of a tree trunk till we tried to depict it in paint. Never truly see the pattern of shadow and light on a forest floor till we tried to find the right f-stop. Never hear the surf till we searched for the music to say it. Art apprehends the world around us which otherwise simply flows by.

As artists, we followed paths to overlooks, explored copses, meandered meadows, focusing not on broad vistas but on tiny truths. With sketch pad or lenses or notebook to put down thoughts for verse, we happily labored to know this small place, this island, to develop a more profound familiarity with it than we had with any other place. Capturing not just a glade but each tree in the glade, noticing each birch-curl, each sprouting bud, aware of the deposits of acorn and cone onto pads of moss, discerning small movements of feather and fur — precious intimacies, gifts too often spurned. They were peaceful perambulations.

Mellow late autumn days snapped suddenly brittle and cold. On lowest low-tides, we set off to harvest the sea off the island's east end. We couldn't resist calling it Mussel Beach. The spit revealed by those unusually low tides very early in the morning, before sunrise, was made up of thousands of shells. In lashing winds and with quickly numbing hands, we prised the shells from their holds on rocks and each other, gathering a hod full for Jo to make into chowder or, better yet, array upon spinach on half shells embedded in rock salt in that adapted delicacy so appropriate to this place: mussels Rockefeller.

We'd heard the stories. How John D. Rockefeller Jr., after buying up vast tracts of Mount Desert Island, across the way, and constructing a fifty-mile network of carriage roads graced by magnificent granite bridges, then donating all to the federal government as the core of Acadia National Park, went on to purchase the western half of eighty-acre Bar Island and pass it to the park as well. And then, in the forties, when a certain Mr. Higgins, who owned the rest of the island, brought in loggers to clear-cut the eastern half, to scalp its peak and strip its slopes, his sawmills masticating great oaks and maples, Rockefeller, aghast at the plunder, sent an emissary to inquire urgently for what price Higgins would be willing to sell. A price was agreed upon, it appeared the deal was done, but Higgins, only belatedly determining the emissary's principal, bumped his price by five hundred dollars. Now, five hundred was a pittance to Rockefeller, but the thought of being jacked about he found unacceptable. The deal died, Higgins continued clear-cutting, and forty years later that meant two things to us: first, instead of dense old growth woods, we found a younger, more diverse, interesting, and penetrable forest; and second, the entire island did not belong to the national park. In gratitude, we hoisted mussels Rockefeller to the fabled millionaire's stinginess, without which we wouldn't be there.

We researched. How 375 million years ago, when seaweed was the highest form of plant life, Paleozoic sands and silt were pressed on the bottom of a sea to form the rocks that became our island. How centuries ago mainland Indians came to the shore for the sea's summer bounty and probably, we could speculate, trod these same paths across the island.

How on the arrival of white settlers in 1768, a certain Daniel Rodick took such a fancy to the place that before long, it would be commonly known as his — Rodick's Island. How his son, sea captain David, built the island's first home. How, in the War of 1812, as French and British naval ships battled across waters that ever after were called Frenchman's Bay, victims were carried ashore to the sheltering home on the island to heal or die. How generation after generation of Rodicks thereafter kept the house and worked the island—farming, smoking fish, breeding horses, hauling boats, selling bait, cutting flowers for the shops of Bar Harbor, raising pedigreed dogs.

What became of that old Rodick homestead? People who knew the island—the publisher whose tourist magazine recounted area history, the woman who was a one-person historical society, the man whose uncle once owned the island—didn't know, had never found a trace. So Jo and I went in pleasant pursuit of a past which wasn't our own but we wanted to adopt.

Down on the island's apron, no sign could be seen of Rodick's old fish shacks or smokehouse. Up in the meadow, the family's great barn was implied by an overgrown ramp and the ghostly, rectangular outline of its foundation in faded grass. But what of the house? From old photos, we had clues, but the woods had long since reclaimed the western prominence that once gave clear views to the sea. First popples and sumac, then moosewood and fir, then maple, spruce, and oak repopulated what people, eight decades earlier, had abandoned. We clawed through the thicket in search. It took two hours.

"Here." Jo spoke excitedly, inhaling the perfume of tiny white blossoms laid close to the ground. "It had to be somewhere near here."

The broad reach of lilies of the valley would not have grown wild, she reasoned; someone had planted them about the door-yard of a home. On hands and knees, we scrabbled beneath branches, through brush, and finally discovered a patch of damp, dark rocks, tumbled but still clearly deployed in a geometry that was not nature's. They edged a depression carved in the earth nearly two centuries earlier, the cellar hole of a structure that housed that most precious of things, a family's loving life.

We unearthed stories. On long-ignored pages in the basement of the town library, we came across the typewritten rompings and gigglings of a girl growing up on Bar Island in the early 1900s. It was Eugenia Rodick, old Daniel's great-great-granddaughter, looking back from her adult years to a childhood of swings beneath oak trees, pung rides, splashing dashes across a fast-covering bar, fish so abundant they wriggled between kids' wading toes, sun-warmed strawberries in a newly mown field, swallows darting about as the hay wagon rolled to the barn, Aunt Flora grafting apple trees while Uncle Charles read *Country Gentlemen*, stereopticon slides in the parlor, fried dough balls and bird stews in the kitchen, digging clams, spearing flounder, playful pups, nuzzling horses named Fencer and Molly, and silent strolls through sun-dappled woods beneath playful parasols of fern.

We collected these stories of her people in this place, frolicked among them ourselves, absorbed them. At this point, we had a ravenous hunger for perspective. Jo began a project of capturing in art, in delightfully nostalgic pencil sketches, the history of our island, researching that time, its fashions and fittings, and over the coming year completing seventy-eight delicate drawings to illustrate a book published a year later titled *Parasols of Fern*.

It was published by a local publisher, Acadia Press, which was run by the very same new friend Frank who had helped us pack away our things in the new house. The lesson in meeting new people proved to be the same in our lives now as it had been for a reporter at work: look beneath the surface.

On the surface, Frank Matter was a folksy, bearded innkeeper and publisher, full of yarns of Bar Harbor's halcyon days. Beneath that, though, was much more. After parochial school and four years of seminary, he had diverted from the priesthood to nuclear science (some diversion!), attending St. Louis University, where, nicknamed Prime Matter, he earned a BS in nuclear physics with minors in math and philosophy (intriguing blend). In those days of Vietnam, he joined the air force as a second lieutenant, was screened, granted highest security clearances, and assigned to a military unit so secret that the commander of the base in Nebraska where it was quartered in a windowless building didn't know what it was or did, although rumor said it was planning operations that never would be publicly acknowledged, functioning as a top-clearance think tank. (It was the unit called upon for advice when *Apollo 13* told Houston, "We have a problem.")

Leaving the military four years later, Frank earned a master's in business, went to work in private industry with computers in Lebanon, Pennsylvania, got married, got bored, and reached a crucial decision. It was 1977. He felt he had worked long enough with his brain and wanted, for a change, to work with his hands.

So he and his new wife picked up and moved to that part of the country she had enjoyed so much on vacations — Bar Harbor. With no place to stay, they pitched a tent in a national park campground and wondered what to do next. He spotted an ad in the local paper, saying something like, "Would you like a new life? Looking for a business of your own?" It was an ad for an old five-dollar-a-bed tourist house whose owner, losing money, wanted to sell.

Frank visited banks, a man with no local history and no job, wanting money to buy a run-down house which, even if it could be fashioned into a proper inn, since it was already late summer, near the end of the inn season, could not produce significant cash flow till next year. Yet here was this jobless man asking for money, and what was his address? A tent in Blackwoods Campground, and he couldn't even say which campsite because rangers made them move every week!

Give foresighted Bar Harbor bankers credit for giving him credit. He bought the forlorn property called Boscobel, and with his hands began transforming a low-end tourist house to a high-end hostelry, The Manor House Inn, on whose parlor coffee table we would find two magazines lying side by side: *Old House Journal* and *The Bulletin of the Atomic Scientist*. To most people, the juxtaposition meant nothing; to us, it epitomized the intriguing dichotomies of a new friend.

Norm Shaw, the round-faced, small-town lawyer who had handled our land purchase, might have made far more money had he unburdened himself of some scruples. But when you sit behind the same oak desk that two generations of forebears have sat behind in the same honorable practice, unscrupling isn't natural.

"I may go out poor," he confided in quiet moments, "but nobody's going to be able to say I was anything but honest." The first time we got a bill from him, for more than a year's worth of intermittent duties, we were surprised at how small it was. Two weeks later, another envelope arrived with an apologetic note saying his secretary had miscalculated, overcharging us, so enclosed was two hundred dollars. Don't tell the bar association, we thought; this man could lose his credentials. Norman P. Shaw was a lawyer who refunded!

There was something else about him that appealed, especially to a person like me, who all his life had followed but one career, displayed but one discernible talent. To a Jack of one trade, Norm, like so many people in Maine, was master of many. Sometimes, it was necessity that prompted diversity, a man or woman needing several abilities to survive in a stinting economy. Sometimes, it was just the flowering of many interests, the bountiful bouquet of human personality. So Norm Shaw, who had been Speedy Shaw, star athlete in school, became, at various times, lobsterman, customs agent, judge, officer of a savings and loan, and lawyer.

And master gardener. When time came to start our own garden, he waited till low tide, clattered his pickup across the bar, and rototilled our plot, promising that next week, he'd be back to spread manure. Spread manure? Once a lawyer, always a lawyer, I poked, and he poked right back that the proper verb for spreading manure, as you should know, Jack, is *broadcast*. Not taciturn, Lawyer Norm, a man who rarely spoke his religious beliefs but who lived them daily.

Tom and Sue Ingham, veterans of years of musical theater, New York and stock, sometimes on fringes, sometimes onstage, had slowly grown disenchanted with showbiz, or, perhaps it was fairer to say, had grown enchanted with another calling. Both of them (and two children) moved to Maine, where Mom and Pop enrolled at the Bangor Theological Seminary, and now the Reverend Susan Ingham would be our pastor at the Congregational Church of Bar Harbor and the Reverend Thomas Ingham had the church up the road in Ellsworth Falls. What great companions they would be on our own path in newfound faith.

Russ Wiggins was a man I first admired for his newspaper, which, like him, was mature, concerned, reasoned. There was probably no more literate weekly newspaper in the country than the *Ellsworth American*. But then, Russ Wiggins had the credentials. After more than sixty years as a newspaperman, ranging from small-town Minnesota to St. Paul to the *New York Times* to twenty years as managing editor and vice president of the *Washington Post*, in 1969 he had "retired" to a farm in coastal Maine, where one of his neighbors was that other renowned retiree of letters, E. B. White. Wiggins purchased the nearby weekly and, never considering this change of station a demotion nor his new constituents hicks, proceeded to attract a coterie of wise and articulate writers, men and women like him of many years and rich experience, and with them create a newspaper that was a blending of journalism, history, art, and philosophy. I had seen nothing like it. Entering the small storefront on Ellsworth's Main Street, you climbed two flights of stairs to find him pecking away at an old manual typewriter in the age of computers, an eighty-two-year-old with the glowing face and knowing eyes of an estimable grandfather — for a child or a town. You could picture him bouncing his grandchild, Ellsworth, Maine, on his knee, telling it stories while gently imparting the wisdom of timeless and timely decades.

I should mention also that before retiring to more work than he had done when he worked, James Russell Wiggins had served two years as the United States Ambassador to the United Nations. His concerns clearly outreached his grasp; his overview was broader than his view. While most local papers wrote editorials about school budgets and Fourth of July parades, he wrote as well of national fiscal policy, of AIDS as a symptom of moral decline, of lotteries as shameful exploitations of human weakness. He

quoted Franklin and recalled the lessons of Macaulay and de Toc-
queville. He did not talk down, never assuming that only those
of small minds lived in small towns nor that one's interests were
delimited by one's geography. His was a newspaper designed for
readers as eclectic, intellectually curious, and articulate as Russ
Wiggins himself. A splendid friend to find.

We were drawn to these people and others not because they
were famous or, as far as we knew, rich. Perhaps because some
had already negotiated their own life changes, had experienced
what we were experiencing. Perhaps because some represented
what we deemed the enviable small-town values of thrift, conge-
niality, and unalloyed integrity. We were seeking in new friends, I
guess, what we hoped to reveal in ourselves.

My father visited Moosewood. Having been recently wid-
owed, he appeared to us a different man, smaller, shrunken not
only by eighty-eight years but by grief, his skin turning transpar-
ent, his hearing growing dim and with it his interest, his blue eyes,
once bright with curiosity, now dulled except for flashes of pique
at the infirmities which limited him. Like Beethoven, he railed
against his afflictions.

Mary Jo's mom and dad came to Moosewood. Her dad, since
retiring, had suffered heart attack, stroke, ileitis, gallstones, arthritis of the back that for six months prevented him from either lying
down or standing erect, arthritis of the hands so bad that the fin-

gers were permanently swollen and gnarled and he could never again clench a fist, an eye dislodged from its socket in a bike-riding accident (he was in his seventies then; he held the eyeball with a hand till he got to the hospital, where it was reset, sight restored).

He tumbled off the seawall at our island, falling eight feet to sharp granite boulders below, agilely negotiating a complete backward somersault on the way to land on feet and buttocks, bruising a lot but miraculously breaking nothing, not even his glasses.

All those and more he had gone through, plus this: one day, while snorkeling with friends off the Dry Tortugas, he died. That's what navy doctors told him later, after a buddy snorkeling with him found him floating facedown, unmoving in the water, towed him back to the boat, did CPR while radioing the coast guard, whose helicopter ferried the unconscious body to a naval hospital at Key West, where, sometime the next day, he came back to life.

His reaction to these calamities was always the same: never for an instant doubting survival, he joked and pawed at the earth, eager to get going on the next adventure. Less than a month after the crippling spinal arthritis, he hopped on a grandson's saucer sled for a bone-jostling ride down a rocky sledding hill. Unable to clench those arthritic hands, he ordered the grips on his golf clubs tripled in girth to something he could clutch. Rather than railing against infirmities, he turned a joy-filled mind to matters that mattered. Saying grace at our table, he did not recite so much as exclaim an enthusiasm of gratitudes: "For the birds that woke us, the sun on the mountain over there, for having a chance to be with Josie and Jack, all of this is, it's ... it's ..." (if not articulate, he was unaffectedly sincere), "it's terrific." Invariably, he thanked God for "the work we were able to do this morning." That was twofold gratitude — for having work to do and, especially after all he had been through, for the ability still to do it.

We had scant weeks that first autumn to lay in and buck a winter's worth of firewood; that meant buying and learning a chainsaw. Never mechanically inclined, when the tide and the house's main drain closed at the same time, we were forced to enroll in necessity's crash course in plumbing, a stumbling seminar which, if nothing else, taught us that one should never — never again, that is — gape faceup at the main drain's basement cleanout while removing its cap. And certainly, once the gushing of sewerage begins, don't try to screw the cap back on. Above all, keep your mouth closed! Once we had finally stanched the gusher — or it had gushed itself out — Mary Jo, her face covered with effluence (to say it as nicely as I can), began laughing at my face, similarly defaced, and I started laughing at her, at both of us. Strange way to bond, but, hey, nobody promised this would be tidy. (With spring, we had a plumber come across to check out the sewer run, which was still balky from basement to septic tank. It was his father who had put in the system when the place was built. What the son found was a two-foot-long piece of two by four jammed into the pipe, debris and detritus backing up against it causing the blockage. He removed the board, cleaned out the gunk, closed up, and a week later his dad sent us a bill. Now, I should not have done this, I know, but the bank said it would be legal, and I knew it would be fun. To pay the plumbers' bill, I wrote a check with Magic Marker on the sewage-smeared board, packaged it up, and sent it. It was never cashed.)

Our animals had their own jobs. At six thirty one morning, we heard our Australian shepherd raising a row out toward the meadow. Yanking on Bean boots, I ran to find her yipping at the base of a small tree. (She was a small dog.) Her prey clung fearfully to fragile branches six feet up, staring wide-eyed with fright as she loosed her verbal assault. Oh, she was proud! Didn't her barking lips curl at the ends in demoniacal glee? After all, our other dog, Buford, a hundred ten pounds of hound, on his best day had treed only a twenty-pound coon. Our Aussie had done him ten times better! I felt sorry for her prey but had to struggle to keep from laughing as I undertook profuse apologies to the man, whose only enigmatic words as he leaped down and bolted away were, "In Washington, we learn to take dogs seriously." Huh?

Often in coming months, I thought of that scene, not of him but of her. Our little sheepdog, as they said in theater, had been cast against type, had played the role convincingly and loved it. Why not we? Why should Jo, because she was a woman, not enjoy the power tools I had bought for myself, rabbeting, routing, mitering, and dadoing picture frames, towel racks, fences, railings, medicine cabinet, and generally turning herself into a fair back-country woodworker? Or, studying a book from the library, learn dry rock laying to construct a garden wall? And if one could play against type, why not both? Daughter Julie was always too busy to make the hand-knit sweater I coveted, so why not learn for myself? If the woman in the craft store, when asked for a beginner's knitting book, responded, "Has *she* ever knit before?" the stereotyping was her problem, not mine.

There were crisp, juicy mornings of wild apples, of shaking eager fruit from old trees, filling backpack and buckets, then going inside to the warmth of the woodstove to puncture their cold skins — *popcrack! popcrack!* — to halve and kettle them. Then sweet afternoons of simmering and spicing, followed by evenings of canning the sauce. What satisfaction helping valiant trees, after so many decades, again fulfill purpose. "Moosewood Mellow," we labeled the jars of one batch, unspiced. "Orchard Sugar," another, mistakenly made too sweet. And "Rodick's Orchard Apple Sauce," we named the last batch, to honor those who had planted the trees a hundred years earlier.

On blustery fall days over the island, we watched gulls flying for fun. That must have been what they were doing. We would see them up there, wheeling in the wind, plummeting and soaring on unpowered wings, traveling but going nowhere, doing nothing, just flying, as if delighting in freedom and life. We felt like that too.

Or like otters. Over in town, a friend, returning home one evening, leaving his car at the foot of the hill to climb through an early snow to his house, was arrested by the sight of a lone otter out for a romp, waddling to the top of the driveway to smack itself down on its belly with its legs tucked in and slicker down the snowbank headfirst. Again and again, just playing. We felt like that too.

Play is not a waste of time, we decided. It may be that without a well-developed sense of play, a creative person can never reach his or her potential, for play walks hand in hand with joy, and creation without joy is as lifeless as life without creation is joyless.

Through all, though, philosophical as we might grow about island living, about the chores and responsibilities, challenges and obligations, we never forgot the overriding truth: we were here to enjoy. To enjoy the gifts God was granting us and, thus, enjoy God himself.

A storm came in October, and it, too, taught lessons. Radio voices quavered urgently: "astronomical high tides," driven by "a classic nor'easter," perhaps one of the "three biggest storms since 1912." We had no idea how big that might be.

We congratulated ourselves that we had thought to secure the canoe we had come to depend on high enough up the slope to be out of reach of the swollen waves — or so we thought, until we watched in horror as the surf clawed it down and dashed it against the rocks, where it capsized, breached, and swamped. We didn't know how foolish it was to wade in after it, how futile to try to drag a water-filled canoe back to shore — or anywhere other than where the surf wanted to take it. We'd just managed to loop a line around a thwart when we too were upended by crashing waves and then, regaining our feet, battered by the waterlogged canoe and bludgeoned flat once more.

Later, when those desperate, drowning moments finally softened in a blur of embarrassed satisfaction that we'd managed to secure the line to the canoe, we discovered we'd forgotten to tie the other end to anything fixed on the mainland. We had taken a foolhardy risk whose results could have been disastrous. By then, we could only conclude that, again, we were being watched over. And that storms like that happen to chasten us humans, to assert beyond argument the primacy of something other than ourselves.

12

AS PRISON
WAS MEANT
TO BE

Isn't it like being in prison, locked up by the tides, no freedom to come and go when you want?" It was a California friend on the phone that first autumn in Moosewood.

Locked up by the tides.

In a way, I thought, we were imprisoned by tides. Frenchman's Bay was our moat, the sun and moon our wardens. Only nature could raise or lower the drawbridge, and that was one of the beauties of islandness. No longer, at whim, could we run off to stores or a movie, or a church service, or freely to socialize in town. We were insulated. We did have the canoe or kayak or, eventually, a small boat for use in good weather, but for the most part, tides regulated us.

If, along most of the American coast, tides were inconsequential, at Bar Island the range between high and low tide ran about eleven vertical feet — eminently consequential.

Most people didn't understand. On the veranda of friend

Frank's inn over in town, two tourists sat rocking one morning at ten. When the innkeeper asked them cheerily what were their plans for the day, they said they heard the high tide was due at ten thirty, so in about fifteen minutes they were going to walk down to the shore and watch — apparently expecting an eleven-foot wall of water to thunder by on the dot.

Tourists would hike over to our island — *Bar Island*, I should say; we got quickly possessive — at low tide, wander about, lose track of time (or not know what time to keep track of), and when they returned to the end of the island where the dry causeway to town should be, it wasn't. They were stranded on a mostly deserted island that, suddenly, didn't seem as romantic as it had in Defoe. For one thing, they had no idea how long they would be stuck, or what to do. (Often, the answer was *us*, our phone, our hospitality, or our canoe, willingly proffered.)

If we returned from town just before the bar was due to start covering over with the waters of the incoming tide, Mary Jo and I often sat there to celebrate.

"We're an island again," she'd say with a great sigh of contentment.

An island speaks to you.

I am your universe now, a universe you can walk from end to end, can know, and if not wholly control, at least comprehend.

An island offers itself as a model for living unconnected, complete unto oneself. It's a deception, of course. Every island is connected: some covertly; ours, by its exposed gravel and shell bar at each low tide. People, too, need to be open to connections. Isolated? Not an island. Animals don't recognize the distinction; birds carry seeds across; storms that strike the mainland buffet islands indiscriminately. An island is not independent, self-sufficient.

Neither are people. But perhaps, on an island more than on mainland, we *try*. And maybe the trying is noble.

On a small island, nature is not something you see now and then, but something you live with every hour, every day. Live with and are part of. You come to accept that, as nature is the working of God, so are you. You come to know yourselves not as two people lost in a population of millions of human beings, the arrogantly dominant species on the planet, but as creatures equitably, inextricably intertwined with other creatures that are equally the work of the Creator.

The gravel bar to the island was exposed and traversable twice a day for two and a half hours before and two and a half hours after each low tide. Basically. Often we thought we had timed it right but had to wade the crossing nonetheless. What was the problem? We learned slowly and imperfectly: an impending eclipse could throw off the schedule; winds from the northwest could do it, heavy rains, the time of the year, whether high tides were extraordinarily high and lows unusually low — all those could warp the schedule. Sometimes, instead of five hours of dry causeway, we had three and a half. Sometimes — some rare times in winter, we were cautioned — the bar would cover with ice and not be free for *days*.

How can you live like that? friends wanted to know. Answer: contentedly.

Tides a problem? No more than an hour's commute on the Long Island Railroad, or rush-hour jams on the Ventura Freeway. Waiting for the waters of Frenchman's Bay to clear the bar was nothing compared with waiting for traffic to snail through the Callahan Tunnel, or for United Flight 141 to receive clearance at O'Hare. We're all bound by some schedule: commuter's timetable, employer's punch clock, kids' carpools — a schedule imposed or accepted, manmade or natural. The natural is most salubrious.

We tried our best to anticipate problems, to prepare for them, and tried not to fear them. We found comfort in the cautionary words of Peter telling us to be ready for "grief in all kinds of trials. These have come so that your faith — of greater worth than gold, which perishes even though refined by fire — may be proved genuine."

Being on an island, we knew that a medical emergency could be disastrous. At high tide, in rough seas, we couldn't get across with the outboard, and we surely couldn't paddle a kayak across. Perhaps a friendly lobsterman from town could help in an emergency, or the coast guard could dispatch a rescue helicopter, but in everyday bad weather or a predictable heavy storm, we were on our own. We each knew CPR; a first aid cupboard was stocked. Beyond that, we put ourselves in the hands that had placed us here.

One day in a dazzling display of mechanical ineptitude, I rammed a wide-bladed screwdriver through my hand, the meat between thumb and finger. The tide was coming in, the bar would be covered in an hour, and since it was three on a winter's afternoon and I didn't want to have to stay off-island until midnight, I thought maybe I wouldn't even bother going to the hospital. I couldn't paddle the kayak with that injured hand even if there hadn't been gale warnings posted. So I figured I would bandage it up and tough it out.

Jo figured otherwise.

Calling in to the little hospital's emergency room on the mainland, I implored the nurses to please have everything ready so we could start right away once I and the doctor arrived.

"Tide coming in?" the nurse asked. Locals understood.

The doctor worked fast: five stitches and done. I begged off the tetanus shot, promising to come back the next day, and raced the Jeep back to the foot of Bridge Street, jumped out, fought whipping winds to struggle into my parka with my one work-able hand, and started running out onto what remained of the bar. A hundred feet across, I came to water. I kept running as it rose. Ankle deep, calf deep, knee deep — I wasn't running any-more. Dark winter afternoon, twenty degrees, gale wind in my face and water to my thighs. Light-headed from the medication and the shock, I found myself in a comical nightmare — running, running, running, but every laboring step in slow, *slow* motion. I barely remember climbing from the sea at the beachhead of the island, only that suddenly it was much, much colder, wind whip-ping sodden trousers, but if I could make it the half mile up the lane, there'd be the smell of fir and fur — and warmth.

That time, it worked. Another time, a more serious emer-gency, a heart attack, whatever, it might not. We knew that, accepted that. Those who choose to live on islands choose to live with risk. Those who acknowledge their living with risk had bet-ter have strong and comforting faith.

A park ranger, aware of Mary Jo's love of birds, asked if she'd be willing to care for a crow that had been shot in the wing and couldn't fly. "He needs six weeks of cage rest," said the vet she consulted, "followed by six weeks of rest in a flight cage." *Cage rest* — Jo built a cage of wood and screen with a roost, and settled the bird in it as best she could. She fed it twice a day, watered it, and kept the family cats well away. She covered its cage at night and talked to it *a lot*. She named it Joe.

Watching Joe struggle to come to terms with his cage, I thought again of the question our California friend had posed: "Isn't it like being in prison?"

Yes. Moosewood was like prison, but as prison was meant to be. The Quakers invented the modern concept of prisons, calling them penitentiaries and intending them to serve as enforced retreats where penitents were removed from corrupting influences, given time for profound self-examination. Wasn't that just what we wanted? To be removed from corrupting influences and have time and a place to challenge ourselves, to undertake self-examination?

Los Angeles — Sirhan Bishara Sirhan was on his way to prison. His trial for the murder of Senator Robert F. Kennedy would be a formality. The smoking gun had been ripped from his hand amid a crowd of witnesses. The trial was a wearisome rehearsal of the mindless murder. Found guilty, Sirhan showed no emotion at the sentencing, almost as if it had nothing to do with him. And we fed our final reports and that dark episode at the end of a very dark year was over.

Almost.

NBC had made financial arrangements with Sirhan's lead defense attorney, Grant Cooper. Up to that point — from the assassination and arrest, through the arraignment and trial — no reporter had talked to Sirhan. Now, before he was removed from Los Angeles jail to prison, I would do the only interview with Bobby Kennedy's assassin.

Cooper had me visit Sirhan in his cell two days before the interview so we could get acquainted. A small, frail, swarthy man, Sirhan B. Sirhan was exceedingly respectful, softly voicing *yes, sir*'s and *no, sir*'s in almost every sentence he spoke. He seemed to be one of those people who wanted only to please and would be grieved if he were to give offense.

"Oh, yes, sir, I saw you back there during the trial. I'm glad to meet you."

His dark eyes did not avoid contact as he spoke. He did not seem nervous. As we were concluding our get-acquainted session, he made a small joke that I assumed he had used with many others.

"How would you prefer to be addressed as we do the interview?" I asked.

"You may call me by my first name, sir. Or, if you'd prefer, by my last."

The room was blackness with only a pool of blinding light in the center. Two chairs sat starkly in this light. It was an eerie setting into which jailers escorted the small man and put him in the seat facing the camera. He blinked, trying with difficulty to adjust his eyes to the lights. I took the chair facing him and, with no preamble, began.

"Sirhan, did you kill Robert Kennedy?"

His eyes were blinking nervously, his head jerking back and forth. "I'm sorry ..."

"Sorry that you killed — "

"I'm nervous. The lights. Can we go slower?"

The lights bothered him; perhaps, too, the abruptness of the questions. But I was of no mind to make him comfortable.

"Sirhan, do you know what the people of this country think of you?"

"I feel hated and I feel despised or something, but I honestly, sir, don't understand why."

"You killed Senator Robert F. Kennedy. Shot him down."

"I shot him."

"And he died."

"Yes, sir."

"You know that now?"

"I know it. I've been told that."

"You don't remember it?"

"I don't remember it. I don't know that I did it. And I know this sounds unbelievable to you, sir — I honestly, sir, don't care whether you believe it or not, because *I* believe it."

According to his journals, Sirhan at one time revered Robert Kennedy as "a saint," but when he heard the senator propose sending weapons to Israel, Sirhan, a Palestinian, had grown furious with him. I wanted to plumb the mystery of such a passionate reversal.

"On May 18th of this year, Senator Edward Kennedy wrote a letter saying that he believed your life should be spared. On May 18th of *last* year, Sirhan — you know what I'm getting at?"

"Yes, sir, I know."

"You were sitting writing in your notebook in your room in Pasadena, and the page is headed 'May 18th ...'"

"Nine forty-five."

"... and the words are, 'My determination to kill RFK is becoming more and more of an obsession,' and then you filled the page with 'Robert F. Kennedy must die … RFK must die … Robert F. Kennedy must be assassinated … Robert F. Kennedy must be assassinated before 5 June.' You were planning to kill Senator Kennedy."

"Only in my mind, sir."

"That's the only place you *can* plan."

"Not to do it physically. I never thought of doing it—I never—I can't—I don't see myself, sir, as doing it. I don't have the guts to do anything like that. They are—they are the writings of a maniac, sir."

"They are the writings of Sirhan Sirhan."

"Yes, sir, but they're not the writings of me now, sir."

"Well, if you were writing in your notebook now, what would you write about Robert F. Kennedy?"

There was a long pause before he answered. "To me, sir, he's still alive."

"You're playing with words."

"No, I'm not."

"But you do believe—"

"Oh, naturally, sir."

"You know that—"

"Yes, sir."

"That he is dead."

"Yes, sir."

"You know that you killed him."

"Yes, sir."

"Do you wish he were alive again?"

"Every morning when I get up, sir, I say I wish that son of a gun were alive so that I wouldn't have to be here now."

"Oh, that's why you wish he were alive, so that you wouldn't be in jail."

"No, I wish he were alive, sir, just to be president."

There had been much psychiatric evidence offered at the trial. I'd listened to it skeptically, and now I put the question for myself, eschewing medical terminology.

"Sirhan, are you in your right mind?"

"Well, I'm not mentally ill, sir, but I'm not perfect either."

"Sirhan, this is a question that I think the doctors asked you several times, and I'll ask you to see what your response is now. If you had three wishes, what would they be?"

"The first wish — I wish that Senator Kennedy was still alive. I wish that every day I've been here. The second one ... [long silence] that there should be peace in the Middle East. And ..."

He said no more. That was the last question and the last answer and, for Sirhan Bishara Sirhan, the last contact he would have with the world outside prison. That night, he was transferred to San Quentin.

Conspiracy theorists saw in Sirhan's eerie dissociation evidence that someone else must have plotted Robert Kennedy's assassination, that Sirhan had been only a brainwashed patsy, operating in a trance. I saw in his eyes something quite different, something all too ordinary: an empty man unable even to comprehend the concept of taking responsibility for his actions.

Who really killed Bobby Kennedy? According to Sirhan, it was the people of Israel, Jews generally, Kennedy himself, one might as well say all of humanity — except, of course, for the one man who pointed the gun and pulled the trigger.

At Moosewood, there was no way to duck responsibility. If the wood rack was empty, it was our fault. If tools were missing,

I was to blame. Should I trip on a root while hiking one of the national park's trails, I couldn't imagine suing the government for letting roots grow where people might trip on them. If I fall, it's my fault for not being attentive, for moving through life with my eyes closed, assuming someone else will catch me. Each step I take is my responsibility. If our lives together at Moosewood were not going to work out, it would be our fault. Being responsible — knowing that our happiness and well-being depended on what, with God's guidance, we decided and did — was the life sentence we willingly accepted in our island "penitentiary."

13

HERE'S TO YOU, HERE'S TO ME — STOP!

Even with only one other person around, I still made a point of finding a place at Moosewood where I could be alone with thoughts, with dreams, with prayer.

"When you pray," Matthew's gospel instructs, "go into your room, and when you have shut your door, pray to your Father who is in the secret place."

Our small home had no secret places, but I found a chair-sized rock halfway down the steep bank that led to the sea seventy feet below, and that became my secret place, my private, praying place. I would scramble down to what Josie called my Thinking Rock and settle myself on its welcoming slab, lean back against the moss of the hillside, listen to and smell the surf and gaze across at the rounded mountains of Acadia, and seal myself up in my own private cell of this "penitentiary." Even in a partnership as close as ours, where every pleasure, every memory begs to be shared and thereby become twice as pleasurable, a person needs privacy. Jo had her own secret place, hidden away in brush up near the island's peak. To these sanctuaries, we brought our idle thoughts, inexplicable ideas, resentments that should be allowed to fade away unspoken — and painful memories.

Sometimes, I thought — and prayed — about drinking.

I had never considered myself an alcoholic; alcoholics don't. I wasn't a stumbling drunk, a morning or desk-drawer drinker, not given to lost weekend binges. But for years I had poured vodka every evening and sometimes kept pouring, and there had been evenings (the surprise party on my fiftieth birthday comes to mind) I didn't remember as well as I should.

There were bursts of temper that fell on wife and sons. There were blurred freeway weavings when only a merciful providence spared me from wrecking my life and others'.

There were specific times I laughed about, mostly. (As alcoholics will do to keep from repenting.)

Acapulco — While I was doing a profile on author Harold Robbins at his villa on the Mexican coast, Robbins set out to prove he lived the kind of sybaritic lifestyle he storied in his novels by taking us on a long-night excursion through the nightlife of Acapulco, bringing along a retinue of beautiful people and calling forth bottles of chilled Dom Perignon at each stop along the route. At the fifth or sixth nightclub — this one noted for its particular clientele — Robbins hollered over at me, "Hey, don't you want to dance, Perkins?" I fuzzily took hold of the gorgeous gal he had arranged to sit next to me and weaved toward the floor when I heard Robbins shout out, "No, not with her!"

Springing from his seat he grabbed my hand, and through my Dom-dumbed fog I half realized I was in a transvestite nightclub in Acapulco, Mexico, dancing with Harold Robbins.

Oh, no. I wasn't an alcoholic.

Fairbanks — What about the night a cameraman, a producer, and I were introduced to Everclear? We first heard the word spoken by a rugged moose of a woman to the rugged moose of a man behind the bar in a seedy Fairbanks establishment. "Gimme an Everclear, hon, with a vodka back."

A vodka *back?* Whatever Everclear was, it must be *something* if you used vodka as a chaser. We tried it. We tried it again. And as I recall, again. After which I don't recall. Except that, deciding to leave before the others were ready, I headed out into the winter's night and started walking back to the motel a mile away. I walked along the edge of the road. I walked through the snow along the edge of the road. I walked through the snow along the edge of the road in my stocking feet. I had left my shoes back in the bar. I don't know why.

Next morning, our cameraman's pounding on my motel room door dragged me tortuously out of the fog that had passed for a night's sleep. He was asking me something through the door and seemed annoyingly loud and insistent. It was something about our producer.

"Hey, Jack, where's Mike?" he asked as I fumbled the door open.

"Mike?"

"I got a cab back from the bar last night, and Mike stayed and was going to drive back. But he's not here."

211

Mike's not here? Last night. The bar. Mike's not here. Moose woman. Snow. Where's Mike?

"Uhhhhhh, you know what?" I said, unscrambling thought-shards in my brain. "I think ... for some reason I think ... maybe ... he's in jail."

"*Jail?* Why would you think that?"

"I don't know. I mean I don't know how I know. But I'm pretty sure he is."

It was a frightful sight in that Fairbanks courtroom, the more frightening because of the ferocious stare with which our ragged, unshaven, and apparently unforgiving friend Mike fixed the two of us. Why? This wasn't our fault, was it?

Well ...

An hour or so after I had left the bar, he set out for the motel in the rental car, got pulled over by a cop, and was taken downtown to the drunk tank, where a couple of locals took turns vomiting on him. He wasn't exaggerating. We could smell it on his clothes.

The arresting officer was a good guy, though, and offered, when Mike couldn't raise me by phone, to go to the motel himself and track me down. The cop came to my door and knocked, called, pounded, yelled. No response. None.

So Mike spent a miserable night in the Fairbanks drunk tank because his buddy, Shoeless Jack, had been sandbagged. Everclear's fault, not mine.

I was not an alcoholic. I was not the type for it. Apart from a few colorful episodes, I walked (at times tipsily) the straight and narrow. I was a small-town boy at heart; I had a loving wife and happy children. Raucous parties and reckless scenes weren't in my character. I'd known some celebrated boozers, and I knew I wasn't in their league.

I had met a man whose name had once been William Beedle, though few people knew him by that. Few people knew very much of the truth about the man who had become William Holden.

Kenya — Mary Jo and I visited William Holden at his Mount Kenya Game Ranch, a wildlife preserve with captive-breeding programs for dozens of East African species and an animal orphanage nursing abandoned animals back to health.

Holden had never before permitted any press, any camera crews to intrude on this private side of his life (which by now had become the very core of his life), but he had made an exception for us — on one condition. He had given us the precise date we must arrive. It would have to be that week or never. Were we willing?

Willing? Eager, excited, and thrilled, we were. What a great story! What a great experience! Mary Jo, offered the opportunity to see African wildlife up close, needed no persuading to agree to come along, something she rarely did throughout my career.

He was waiting for us with ranch manager Don Hunt and Hunt's wife, Iris, at their house on the grounds. As an actor, William Holden never played too far from self — he was of that era when the movie-star presence spilled over into every on-screen role — and the first thing that struck us was the deep, instantly familiar voice, like that of a longtime friend.

He had just flown in from Hong Kong; we talked about that and our time living there, and then he began telling us what he had in mind for our crew to film in the coming days; he had the schedule worked out in detail, and his enthusiasm was infectious.

We were seated in the living room, Holden and Mary Jo on

a couch below a wide-open window, Hunt and me, my producer and crew scattered around the rest of the room. I had a small snapshot camera and raised it to catch Mary Jo on one end of the couch with the man she so admired at the other end, but before I could take the shot, with no warning and no sound, in through the open window bounded a full-grown cheetah! It landed on the couch and seated itself oh-so-decorously between Holden and Jo. Not at all nonplussed, Jo simply reached out and began petting the animal as my shutter snapped. I still have and love that photograph of a cheetah licking my wife's hand as she happily disregards one of her favorite movie stars in favor of a very pettable cat.

The cheetah's name was Batian, and he lived in the house. Or outside the house — whichever he chose. He was one of the many orphaned animals who had been nursed back to life on the ranch and, with no parent to teach him to hunt, had grown up almost as a house pet. Holden had slyly arranged for Mary Jo to sit in that spot, knowing Batian would soon make his usual entrance.

Holden was sixty-two at the time of our visit, his face no longer boyishly handsome but leathery, deeply creased. His drinking was no secret around the movie community — that he went off for days on binges, destroyed friendships. As we chatted with him, aside from animals, his favorite subject for conversation was the woman he considered his true love, actress Stephanie Powers. We didn't know it at the time, but she had recently given him an ultimatum: lose the bottle or lose her. In Kenya, that week in 1981, we never saw him drink anything more potent than coffee or Coke. He had made his choice.

He was a grand companion, an engaging storyteller. He didn't just *tell* his stories; he *acted* them. While we were filming part of our interview out on the club's patio one day with Mount Kenya as the backdrop, he responded to one of my serious questions by crossing his arms, putting a fist under his chin, and intently leaning forward as he delivered his answer in a solemn tone, his eyes locked onto mine. Leaning back then, he laughed. "Like that? That's my serious look." The man knew his craft.

Finally, we got to the ostensible reason Holden had invited us. Tracts adjacent to the preserve were quickly being developed as farms, encroaching on the habitat of the many giraffe herds that roamed these lands. Inevitably, farmers soon would start slaughtering herds they could not drive off. To prevent that, the Kenyan government had enlisted Holden's help in rounding up as many of the animals as possible and relocating them to safety.

We would set off on the Great Giraffe Roundup, he told us, "at one in the morning."

One in the morning?

Kenya speak. On the equator, the sun rises at six, the sun sets at six — every day, every season. So in the local language, Kiswahili, morning, *asubuhi*, begins at six. One in the morning means 7:00 a.m.

Lined up were four Land Rovers and two large trucks. The area picked for the hunt was a few kilometers away, which meant once again a spine-jamming ride in vehicles designed for utility, not comfort.

Holden and Don Hunt led the way in the first Rover, Hunt driving, with four native ranch hands in the back of the open vehicle specially rigged for this type of hunt. The driver was on the right in British fashion; over the lefthand passenger seat, cage work had been thickly padded to form, in effect, a cushioned donut at shoulder height above Holden. When the time came for him to stand, he would have only that protection.

Our camera vehicle came second, pursuing Holden's vehicle through choking dust clouds. The two other Rovers flanked the team for support, and the trucks, loaded with huge crates, stood by to transport captured animals back to the preserve.

"Over there, Don," Holden's voice comes over the wireless mike we had rigged in the lead vehicle. Our cameras capture Hunt furiously cranking the wheel as the Rover peels away at high speed toward a herd of giraffe they'd spotted grazing a few hundred yards off to the right. We swing around to follow.

Hunt accelerates to catch up with the alerted herd, and then, suddenly, "Hang on." The Rover lurches into a gully, springs up and out the other side, handlers clinging to the superstructure, Holden bouncing in his seat. The giraffes break and run. Hunt stomps on the accelerator. "How about the big one?" shouts Holden. We fall in behind a magnificent bull, fleeing at full speed. We're amazed at the speed of the seemingly ungainly animal. "A fast one," Don says.

"Very fast," Holden's famous baritone crackles over the radio.

From experience, Holden and Hunt know they don't dare run a giraffe full speed for much more than a minute and a half or its great heart, furiously pounding from both fright and flight, could burst. Their attempt to rescue it could kill it. Forty-five seconds have passed.

We're gaining. Fifty yards to close, when ahead, a deep dry wash. "Look out!" Braking and yanking the wheel, Hunt spins the Rover to the left, yaws it at an angle into the wash, then kicks up another dust cloud as he regains speed out the other side, shouting, "Damn! We've got to get him!"

Thirty seconds left. We're closing again, but will it be soon enough? The giraffe thinks he's running for his life; he may be running *from* it.

Twenty seconds, twenty yards to go.

"Up we go." Holden hoists himself from his seat, up through the donut. One of the ranch hands passes him a twelve-foot pole with a loop hanging from its outer end. He stretches it out as Hunt brings the Rover up on the giraffe's right flank.

Ten seconds.

Holden can almost reach the lasso over the animal's head. "Closer, Don," we hear him say with remarkable calm.

Carefully, Hunt edges in.

"Hold it; here goes!"

Holden reaches as far as he can, his sixty-two-year-old body thudding against the cushioned donut.

Five seconds.

And drops the loop perfectly over the animal's head, down the long neck.

"Got it!"

Hunt brakes, Holden keeps a firm grip as the Rover slows the giraffe's pace and they finally come to a stop together.

Flanking vehicles disgorge ranch hands who quickly throw their own loops of rope on the animal. Holden scampers up onto the bonnet of the Rover, hanging on as the giraffe lowers his great neck as though in submission but then, with one last effort of desperate defiance, jerks his head up, sending Holden crashing backward into the vehicle's windscreen.

"You okay, Bill?" Hunt's concerned voice over the radio.

"Yeah," Holden lies, struggling to catch the breath momentarily knocked out of him. "Is *he* okay?" The animal, he means. That's his priority. That's why a man his age puts himself through this kind of physical abuse: to make sure the animal they have just rescued, and all the others they will rescue in the coming days of their roundup, is okay.

I guess, in part, he was still playing macho man for the cameras. But I felt certain he would be here if there were no camera. He was doing this out of a profound and sincere desire to care for these forgotten animals.

At the end of the day, we were back at the Safari Club, our crew indulging in a few Tuskers (the local brew), Holden settling for a Coke, conspicuously on the wagon. It was as though he was proving himself again. To us and, indirectly, to someone else. Not just Stephanie Powers, off on a soundstage somewhere, but another dear, distant friend.

Ronald Reagan had been Holden's buddy for years. Not only had they been members of the exclusive brotherhood of movie stars; they had been activists together in the actors' union. When Ronnie married his beloved Nancy, the service was held in the living room of Bill's home in Toluca Lake. When the Reagans had their first child, Holden was the godfather.

This very week, back in the States, Ronald Reagan was being inaugurated President of the United States. On January 20, 1981, the day of his buddy's proudest success, Holden was chasing giraffe through choking clouds of African dust before a camera crew he had summoned.

We fit the puzzle together later, learning that Reagan's handlers had made sure Holden wasn't invited to the ceremonies, the galas. *He's a great friend, sure, Mr. President, but he's also a notorious drunk who could turn an historic event into a Hollywood-scale fiasco.*

So then, how could Holden, if someone asked why he'd "chosen" to skip his best friend's inauguration, explain his absence? He needed cover.

We were his cover — Mary Jo and I, our crew and producer,

and, oh, yes, that herd of giraffe that needed saving. That was why Holden was in Africa that week, why we had been called to join him, and why he was sitting there at the end of the first day's hunt drinking Coke. Emphatically, defiantly abstemious.

Could he keep it up? An alcoholic bent on quitting needs support. Holden had the support of his profession and his continuing successes in it. He had his devotion to helping the animals of Africa. He had the love of a caring woman. But one support form he did not have. AA and other twelve-step programs against addictions count on the support of a holy faith. The support of a higher power — God — which Holden lacked.

By the end of that year, he was dead. Discovered in his Santa Monica apartment three or four days after he had fallen in a drunken stupor, gashing open his head and bleeding out.

Some would say he died as he deserved. Cruel condemnation and not a judgment for people to make. Especially for me, guilty of the same sin, if not — yet — to the same degree.

Alone on my Thinking Rock, I accepted, with a mixture of shame and faith, that the time had come to face up to my own illusions and cover stories. I looked up the Bible passage where Paul cautioned believers in Ephesus, "Don't be drunk with wine, because that will ruin your life. Instead let the Holy Spirit fill and control you."

I had done a story in Long Beach, California, on the doctor who ran the alcoholism-recovery program at the naval hospital there. He was an authority on societal alcoholism, and at one point, he asked me if I thought I was an alcoholic. (A kindly colleague had put him up to it, I learned later.) No, oh, no, I insisted, though I don't think he believed me. He explained that drinking causes more problems than it solves; I already knew that. He explained that drinking brings people more torment than pleasure; I knew that. He asked me one decisive question: "Jack, can you tell me the last day you did not have a drink?"

Ouch! When would the time come for me, a rational being, to start acting rationally?

It came now, at Moosewood. There are only two convincing (if spurious) reasons to drink: to be sociable and to feel good. At Moosewood, alone on an island, sociability was not a high priority, and we already felt very good. Booze became splendidly superfluous. God's presence more than sufficed.

Mary Jo's adopted crow was recuperating well, ready to be transferred from her homemade cage to a "flight cage." Which, for us, meant our summer dining room, a sunroom, the one room we could close off. We rigged a pole diagonally across the room for Joe to perch on when he wasn't limbering his wings with short hops and flaps.

When, finally, the time came for his release, magic happened. The room was all glass on one side; Mary Jo slid open the outside door and waited. Joe dropped to the floor, stepped cautiously toward the open door, paused, looked around, paused, and finally hopped out onto the ground. Whereupon, almost instantly, came at least two dozen crows, swooping from trees all around, surrounding him and seeming to gather him up and escort him to the low branches of a fir tree fifty feet away. We watched him climb, limb by limb, to get higher in the tree. Then, satisfied with the altitude, he leaped off, powered the recovered wing, and flew away, joining the others because it was time for crows to roost for the night.

Next day, we saw him again. We knew it was he because the right wing still drooped. He flew down to the earth just outside the sunroom door, then took off, flew away, and we never saw him again.

You're welcome, Joe.

14

IT'S ALL
SOLAR POWER

Ooooh," squealed the clerk at the Sears out-
let when we told her that, yes, she heard right, we were going to
be living on that island year-round, including winter. "You guys
are gonna croak!"

Winter was already changing the town, our house, and us,
and in much the same ways. There was an affirmative withdraw-
ing, a reducing to essentials. Town boarded up restaurants and
shops. Of scores of summer dining places, only three were open
in winter; of shops, but a handful. Town, with summer tourists
gone, shrank.

In our house, the glassed-in sunroom which served for warm-
weather dining (or crow nursing) was closed off; its dining table
was moved into the main room close by the woodstove, an antique
feed bin replacing it in the sunroom to hold mittens, mufflers,
and gloves. The Shaker pegs which had borne decorative baskets
and clam hods were ready for parkas and hats in a foul-weather

entry, which Mainers call their mudroom. Skis stood in one corner, snowshoes in another. Down cellar, the wasted space created by cinder block walls supporting the weight of the rock chimney in the main room above became a storage niche for firewood, dimensioned to cradle two stacks of stove-length birch and oak, floor to ceiling—three quarters of a cord.

The house was prepared for the challenge. A couple of more cords were laid in and tarped outside. And, to our great surprise, that would be more than enough for the winter. The house had little insulation, open-stud walls allowing no fiberglass batting, only an inch of solid foam between the tongue-and-groove that formed our walls and the siding outside. But the house was built very tight, so tight Builder Vic had to cut a vent into an outer wall at one point to permit enough airflow for the woodstove to draw properly.

The house was ready for winter, and so, we thought, were we.

November's first snow was a mere dusting, a tease for us humans, a curiosity for California cats and dogs exuberantly dashing outside only to stop cold in their tracks, shake clotted paws, and lick at the ground, bewildered.

When the first tracking snow held, it told a story. Here he had come, our adventuresome old cat, Tramp, sauntering casually from the house up the lane toward the meadow. We could follow his tracks in the snow, closely spaced. But beside those were his pawprints returning the other way, spread in broad leaps and bounds, a cat running home like fury. Why? Fifty feet ahead we found the answer in other tracks from the opposite direction, milling about at this point, as though sniffing a new scent, a fresh possibility. These were the tracks of a hungry red fox. Tramp was prudent; city-raised, he had learned country real quick.

We too would learn. Winter is a time for learning. How to think about snow? TV weatherfolk apologize for it, their anchors chiding them for bringing bad news. And yes, snow can be an impediment if you have to shovel the driveway and scrape off the car before going to work; it's a bother if you must drive or walk. In a city, as soon as it falls, it's filthy. But on an island, it descends in joy and stays pristine. At Moosewood, each pine bough wore a drift of white; each spruce branch drooped low with welcome weight. The meadow was a jewel case of glittering gems; snow sparkled and brightened — brightened the day and us.

The sun also warmed, doubly when mirrored by reflecting snow so that even when temperatures of deepest winter fell to twenty below, if the day was bright and the ground snow-covered, we could let the woodstove — our only heat — go out by midmorning and not relight it until evening. For us, snow was welcomed and appreciated.

There was something else about snow at Moosewood. Nature balanced accounts. It took away color, then gave some back. Depriving us of flowers and fall leaves and blanketing the world in white, it sent sweeping flecks of intense color — redpolls flashing scarlet, pine siskins glinting gold. In great wheeling masses they came to delight us in the woods and at our feeders, gifting us with the privilege of their dependence and reminding us that all things are relative. While many Mainers whimpered to escape winter's cold by fleeing to Florida, redpolls, denizens of arctic tundras, escaped there for here. We were their winter getaway; Maine, their Florida. The lesson of perspective.

Snow did cause a problem with our solar panels, but as the Bible writings of James instruct, that problem produced a challenge, and the challenge yielded a joy. The problem was that

225

solar panels blanketed with snow don't produce electricity to store in the battery banks down in the basement to power our little house, a house that was "green" decades before green was in. The challenge was to get those panels up on the roof cleaned off. If it was going to be a day of heavy cloud when there'd be little or no insolation anyhow, we could put matters off. Accordingly, we didn't have to consider climbing precariously up to the roof until the day was sunny. Then, having positioned the ladder from the outside deck up to that part of the roof onto which we had fixed special grab rails, one of us (we took turns, one climbing as the other rooted the ladder) carefully ascended with broom and ice scraper — and found the most magnificent vista spread before us.

The rounded white mountaintops in the park, snowplows scraping streets over in town, dump trucks beep-beep-beeping out the town pier to deep-six loads of snow into the bay. Perhaps, if it was an especially cold day, the rising exhalations of mist from icy waters — *sea smoke*, it is called — wafting in the sunlight while, all along our island, trees with puffy white branches and, occasionally flitting among them, those sparkles of brilliant color.

One icy November morning as we were walking across the bar to town for supplies, we came across another astonishing demonstration of the power hidden within nature, and of how often we walk through the world oblivious to our surroundings. Bundled in parkas, wool pants, and boots, we stood in the bitter cold for minutes taking in a most peculiar sight.

At a shallow place in the bar there was a boulder several feet in diameter. Balanced atop it now, as if placed there by some immense hand, was a slab of ice twelve feet across and three feet thick. How had the ice gotten there? Floated down from the upper bay after a late-season thaw, we reasoned. But how had such an irregular chunk of ice come to perch, as the tide went out, so precisely on that rock? That question puzzled us all the away across the bar and into town, where we picked up mail at the post office and then walked to Don's Shop'n Save to fill our backpacks with a week's groceries. But even as we walked the supermarket aisles, part of us was pondering that mystery of nature.

It was only as we were headed back home, back across the bar, parka hoods drawn tight around faces now as we walked directly into the wind, that the solution occurred to us. As is often the case when we can't figure the answer to a question, it was because we were asking the wrong question. Think of it. We had traveled this bar on foot or by Jeep a hundred times, but we realized only now that we had never seen that boulder itself before today. Ice or no ice, it hadn't *been* there before.

So the correct question was not how did the ice get there, but how did the *boulder* get there? And to that, the answer had to be: the ice had brought it. The invisible, supernatural hand we had instinctively introduced into the equation wasn't invisible at all; it was there before us, in plain sight. That large ice chunk — it would have been much larger when it first broke loose somewhere up-bay — had grasped the uppermost tip of the rock in an immensely powerful grip, lifted it as the tide rose, and carried it all the way here, where at last the boulder had bottomed out on the bar. All day the sun had been at work softening the ice slab's grip and calving away pieces, and when the next tide came in — when we'd be cozily at home — the last of it would float away silent and unobserved, leaving its cargo, the rock, behind.

As awesome as this event seemed to us, we knew it was but a trivial demonstration of what had happened on a tremendously larger scale fifteen thousand years ago. In those days, Ice Age glaciers—frozen mountains floating on a skim of water—had carried rocks the size of trucks and houses hundreds of miles to deposit them wherever the sun chose to have them released. Today geologists call such anomalies "glacial erratics." We had seen some over in the park. Now a sample of what had occurred over geologic time happened here in one November night, a teasing model of God's work through nature.

Catastrophe struck Moosewood at 10:21 on a drizzly winter's morning. Jo had been making an orange cake, using that electric juicer we shouldn't have brought, when suddenly—how to say it?—the house went berserk. Our idiosyncratic electrical system always had a mind of its own, and suddenly that mind snapped. Not only did the juicer die; lights everywhere in the house on that dark day began crazed oscillation—*onoffonoffonoff*—flailing in apoplectic seizure. Was something going to blow? In ignorance, we were terrified. I raced to the basement, threw all the master switches I could find until blessed calm was restored. But now we had no power. What had happened? What to do? What to learn?

It was not until the next day—agonized hours later—that finally we reached our solar engineer, Sunny Dave, and he could try, from long distance, to diagnose. Only then did we understand how close to disaster we had come.

"Catastrophic fuse," he said laconically. "Never happened before. More'n a hundred systems, I never had that devil go. Started to think I was wasting my time putting it in."

His darkly nicknamed "catastrophic fuse" was the system's

ultimate defense against terminal insult. Something in our system had gone drastically awry, causing a ferocious burst of power to charge toward the battery bank. Only the blowing of that catastrophic fuse — *a three-hundred-amp fuse!* — had saved it. Otherwise, "Batteries would've fried. Total meltdown."

Over the phone, Dave told us how to rig a patch. Temporarily, until he could get here to sort things out, things got back to normal.

We thought of ourselves at Moosewood as exceptional because our electricity was derived directly from the sun. But as people so often do, we overstated our specialness. Not only we but everyone depends on the sun for power. Wood, coal, and oil are nothing but deposited and transformed plants that somehow turn sunlight into living matter — photosynthesis. Both wind power and tidal power are solar power. Our fuel, our warmth, and the ultimate source of all food is the sun.

Winter blues (SAD, scientists call it — seasonal affective disorder) emerge from insufficient direct exposure to sunlight. Even sunlight filtered through windows is less than effectual, the glass absorbing crucial ultraviolet rays. The cure requires either fitting the home or workplace with expensive full-spectrum artificial lights or going outside to be closer to the sun.

We hiked, cross-country skied, snowshoed, enjoyed the beauties of sunny days even in dead winter. We were not sad.

Though, now and then, bemused.

As I was readying to leave the house early one morning to make the tide and get to an airport for a flight down to New York, we discovered that the inverter had failed. That meant that, though we had plenty of DC power stored in the batteries, it could not be converted into the AC needed to run the deep-well submersible pump. With no functioning pump, we had no water. And I was leaving Mary Jo for a day there in the cabin in the snow on the island.

Good luck, dear.

I was able to get a call through to her from New York so that as I began the speech I had come to deliver, I could say, "I have just spoken to my wife on the snowy island in Maine where we live. Our water system has failed, and as we spoke, she had a bucket of snow on top of the woodstove, melting it to get enough water to wash her face for the day. That's why I say to you now, with more meaning than the trite phrase usually conveys, 'Ladies and gentlemen, I am really glad to be here.'"

Approaching the holidays one day, we found that the backup propane generator wouldn't generate. Or (though we didn't know this at the time) it generated, but the control system misrouted its power so we didn't get it.

We really didn't get it. What was it this time? We still had limited power, the energy stored in the battery bank, but weather forecasts warned of several more days of prolonged gloom. If there was going to be little sunlight to recharge the batteries soon and the generator refused to charge them, then what? In a few days, lights would fail. We'd have no lights, no electric pump, so no water, and this in the middle of winter.

Anxiously, I began fumbling with the new multimeter Dave had encouraged me to buy, testing continuities, fuses, switches, voltages through circuits. In the three-contact outlet into which the battery charger was plugged, depending on which poles I measured, I read 122, 36, or 12 volts. What did that mean? Why? Ignorance stopped me.

Dave's service reported he was out of town for several days; sorry, they didn't know where. The fellow down in Camden who used to work for him had moved away. Local electricians we called up in Bar Harbor would be happy to take a look, but, unfamiliar with the system, would be leery to do anything with it.

Whereupon, the phone conked. With no wired phone lines to the island, and cell phones not yet a factor, we were trying to operate with a standard home cordless phone across the water to an antenna atop a friend's house, stretching the signal to its limits. Erratic in recent days, the phone now succumbed to static and died. Next day, still dead.

So now we had no phone, half an electrical system fading in dingy weather toward nothing, and the only man who could save it, save us, away and unreachable.

Happy holidays.

I cursed, then cursed some more, imprecations as unfocused as they were profane, raising my voice to make sure that the fury of my frustration was heard. "Why are we here?"

Snowing heavily. Could we rent a backup generator? Could we get it here? Could I figure how to rig it into the system if we did?

"Why don't we get out of here?" I shouted.

Heresy. Jo looked perplexed. Was I serious?

"If we want to live a deprived existence, surrounded by the hulks of burned-out buildings," I said, looking out at the rock walls of the old foundation, "why don't we just pack up and move to the South Bronx?" I bellowed in a voice too strident to be credible, and, of course, I wasn't serious, not wholly. I wanted to make sure she knew that. I wanted to make sure *I* knew that.

Calm down! She didn't say it, didn't have to. Her manner conveyed the message. We would manage. Somehow, we would manage. We had faith now; we had God.

Faith, I thought, and flashed on a line in the Bible that had intrigued me. In the gospel of Mark, Jesus was begged to drive evil spirits from a young boy whose father added, "If you can." And Jesus replied that anything is possible for those who believe, and the father with exceeding humility cried out, "I do believe, but help me overcome my unbelief."

That's where I was at this very moment: crying out! My profane imprecations had been my anguished confession that, yes, though by this time in our new Moosewood lives I did believe, truly I did, still mixed with that belief was a countervailing quotient of unbelief. *Please, dear Lord, help me, too, overcome my unbelief!*

Jo was right. We could handle this. Already frugal with power, we'd be niggardly. Instead of burning power for Turkey Day football on TV, we'd play our own games; out came dice cups and Trivial Pursuit. As the radio reported how "miserable it is this afternoon," we pulled on jackets for a ski.

Snow clinging to branches softened sounds, creating in a birch glade along the lane the arching hush of what Jo had named her White Cathedral. Our prayers in the cathedral that Thanksgiving Day were sincere: we were grateful for blessings that around us abounded, but also, we had to admit, for problems. James had said as much in the Bible. Problems are testings, and testings are always to be welcomed. It was the wisdom that had buttressed me as I awaited the birth of our first child, that without testing there can never be proving—or improving. I guess, had we spoken such thoughts aloud this day, they would have sounded corny, but in Jo's White Cathedral, thoughts did not need voice.

15

WHAT DID
BRANDO WANT?

Our first Moosewood winter raged on. It was cold; we were cold. We had few visitors and, able to get out little, saw few people, but heard from some.

Call them Christmas friends; the term is not derogation. It is to such people you reach out at that time of loving. That's what Christmas cards should be for, not to wish a spongy "Happy Holidays." Those are cards designed to offend no one and, so doing, honor no One. We wanted Christ in Christmas.

And, yes, we appreciated cards that included pictures of friends and their families and plenty of news, the annual family logbook, catching us up with everyone.

The greeting we sent was a burlesque, the cover a photograph of us about to partake of our Christmas fowl, except that the festive board was the picnic table on our deck outside, both the ground and the tabletop wearing a clean foot of new snow, the turkey platter and lighted candles teetering coldly atop it. The picture made several friends' refrigerator doors, which pleased us. We wished to be remembered, not missed, as we strove not to miss, but remember.

Our sons flew in for Christmas, Mark returning from his cabin in Canada, Eric on break from college in Malibu, that much of the family together to celebrate an old-fashioned holiday made modern with a rented video camera taping the trek into snowy woods for the tree.

Which should it be? Red spruce, white pine, balsam fir? Many remarks on the audio about how much this or that one would cost on the lot in LA.

Snowball throwing, exuberant grown-up kids climbing trees, dogs romping beneath. Then dragging the seven-foot spruce triumphantly to the house, painting ornaments and frosting cookies and catching it all on videotape, which, after Christmas, we would take to grandparents in Florida.

The rest of the year, apart, we shared letters or phone calls. Plenty of snapshots crossed country. In a sense, we communicated more intimately a continent apart than some families do in the same house. It reinforced for us the truth that family wholeness and change need not be contradictions. Change, well arranged, can bring families closer together, even if no longer proximate. It might also lead us to accept that the full realization of us lies not in us as part of them. Nor does the full realization of them lie in them through us. We learned not to "miss" family.

It was upon returning from our quick winter trip to Florida that we discovered a heavy dump of snow on the island, snow so deep that the Jeep, trying to climb up the lane to the meadow, quickly bellied out. We had to back it down again to the end of the island and leave it there while we walked through the night the last several hundred yards to the house.

At first, up the lane through the woods, bending and climbing toward the meadow, all went well. Then, out in the open, things changed. The snow there had been exposed to sunlight for days, thawing then refreezing until there was now a substantial crust on top of two to three feet of snow. Trying to walk it, we found that sometimes it supported our weight (even as we hefted our awkward suitcases), but sometimes a foot cracked through and sank into the depths of the snow. Every fourth or fifth footfall we sank up to our crotches or waists, and we never knew which footfall it would be. Having sunk, we then had to struggle back up and out and on.

It took half an hour to plod through moonlight to our dark, cold, and seemingly unwelcoming house, and what we didn't realize (good that we didn't) was that this was just the beginning.

Should we hire someone to plow us out? No, with this much snow it would take a front-end loader eight or ten hours, several hundred dollars' expense, just to rid ourselves of snow that probably would be gone on its own by next week. That's what everyone said. When next week it wasn't gone, we thought, surely, next week.

Wrong. Moosewood was snowbound for the next *two and a half months*. And it was not terrible.

We snowshoed or skied to the end of the island where the Jeep was parked, and from there made our way to anywhere, assuming we wanted to leave. Which, increasingly in those weeks, we did not. We were content being at home. At expensive ski resorts, people pay extra to be able to ski to their door; at Moosewood, it was free. If for two and a half months we couldn't take trash to the town dump, that simply meant that if we found we needed a piece of paper we had thrown away weeks earlier, it could still be excavated from the mounting pile of plastic bags in the basement.

It was a strange time, about to get even stranger.

Late afternoon in the frozen heart of winter meant it was already dark outside the cabin. I had begun fixing dinner. Mary Jo and I were reading when the phone rang, a call from a man I had never met, never talked to, had no reason to expect ever to hear from.

"Jack?" the voice started.

"Yes."

"Do you know who this is, Jack?"

And I did. That's the damnable thing about it. I did. I instantly knew. I just didn't understand.

"This is Marlon."

I had never met him, but he could rightly assume that I knew him; everyone did, and the voice confirmed the identity. It wasn't the cotton-wads-in-mouth menace-mutter of *Godfather*. It wasn't the agonized "Stell-ah! Stell-ah!" or the mumbling "I could have been *somebody*. I could have been a contender." But I never doubted who the pinched nasal voice that filtered through our jerry-rigged phone system belonged to. I didn't know why it *would* be, but it definitely *was* Brando. Why was Marlon Brando calling me?

I can't say, even now. Not because it is a secret but because though we talked for more than an hour, I never did understand why he had called. Nor did I ask how he had found me. I assumed Brando, being Brando, could find anyone.

One of the great films about the Vietnam War was Francis Ford Coppola's *Apocalypse Now*, in which Brando played a putatively insane renegade special forces officer. How appropriate, I thought now as I tried to parse his lengthy, largely indecipherable phone call. He talked a lot about Vietnam, about my work there back in the sixties (he knew of that), and about the war itself, what he thought of America's involvement. What did I think about it? I'd start to answer, but he'd keep right on talking, giving me more of his thoughts.

"How can we keep from getting involved in things like that?" he wanted to know.

"Well, Marlon — "

"Jack, I'll tell you what I think."

And on. He had given the subject a lot of thought. He thought lengthily and talked logorrheically.

Was the man — in the phrase my mother used to use — a bit tetched? Or, in the simpler word Mary Jo chose as we discussed the strange call later over dinner, drunk? Paranoid, certainly, living up there in his mansion atop Mulholland Drive, and given his extreme celebrity, even notoriety, and the slanderous public accounts of his life and his family, paranoia might be appropriate. Still, why me? Why — drunk, drugged, or sober — had he chosen to reach out to a guy he didn't know, living on an island in Maine, to talk about Vietnam?

South Vietnam was a deception from the beginning, from the day men inscribed arbitrary lines on meaningless maps until its inevitable dissolution. America's role in the debacle was compounded of arrogance and innocence. Arrogantly we believed that we needed to "save democracy" where it had never existed, and innocently we believed that we could.

It was a war of dishonesty. Saigon deceived Washington;

Washington deceived itself and tried to deceive America. In the end, Vietnam served as the unmaking of a nation's pride, self-confidence, and clarity, but at the same time served as the making of a young correspondent's pride, self-confidence, and clarity.

What the war did not do for me was instill or strengthen faith. Sometimes war can do that. It didn't with me — as Brando's call got me reflecting — because I wouldn't let it. I was young, thirty-one, and already not just a foreign correspondent but a war correspondent and full of myself for that. He who is full of himself cannot be filled by God.

Even in combat?

My first battle experience was out in Hua Nghia province west of Saigon. It was the first time American troops moved into the fringes of the Mekong Delta, a potentially treacherous incursion. My cameraman was Vo Huynh, NBC's senior Vietnam cameraman and a man who knew the country and the war better than anyone I would ever meet.

Going in on one of the first helicopter assault waves, Huynh pointed knowingly. "See over there, those trees? That's where the VC are. Small arms, machine guns."

How did he know? How could he know?

"Because that's where they were three years ago when the Arvin [Army of the Republic of Viet Nam] came here, so that's where they'll be now." He had not only wandered the country the length of this war seeing, filming, and learning; he remembered! We didn't move.

Rifle fire rattled from the tree line, just where he had pointed; machine guns erupted, peppering incoming choppers as they had three years before. Twin-rotor Chinook helicopters rumbled in to set down vehicles for the Americans, but, seeing them, Huynh shook his head. "Wrong place." The choppers sank to their axles in marsh.

As the first company moved out from the LZ, Huynh cautioned, "We wait. VC will ambush." The sound confirmed it, fusillades of fire taking Americans by surprise.

When the ambushed unit called back for medics, Huynh again said, "Not yet. Now they have snipers waiting along the trail for medics." And in a few screeching shots and mournful ricochets, we heard that too.

"Let's go, Jack. Now it's okay," and we moved out. Nervously. Knowing how the enemy planted poisoned punji sticks and mines, I was frightened just to walk through jungle or fields. Once, upon hearing gunfire beside us and a GI saying, "Charlie's closing in on our right," I trembled inside and out. When I realized that he didn't mean Charlie as in Victor Charlie, VC, but our own Charlie company, I felt foolish, very foolish — and very relieved. This is not something I talked about then. Or anytime until now. Brando's call unearthed the emotion.

I was scared. Did I pray? No. A few years before, at the height of the Cuban Missile Crisis, when the world seemed to hang in the balance and our first son was being born, I had tried to pray, and perhaps that praying worked or perhaps it was coincidence that the crisis was soon swept away. Still, when that crisis passed, so did my perceived need of prayer. Now, a few years later, I shied from the impulse to pray out here in a war zone partly because it would be a cliché — "battlefield conversion," "foxhole faith." I spurned clichés. To pray would require either hypocrisy or honest commitment. I disdained hypocrisy and still lacked commitment.

Fearfully, then, I moved forward as fearlessly Huynh captured the raw meat of battle, the frantic and furious. After a couple of hours, he said, "We can go now."

Though relieved, I questioned. Shouldn't we stay? It's quiet now, but shouldn't we keep on and see?

"No need," he assured. "The place we just passed was where VC put on the big fight last time, and if they're not going to do it there now, then it's over. They've gone. We can leave; won't miss a thing."

The troops of the 173rd Airborne stayed and continued the operation for several more days, but never again had significant contact.

The story we sent back with the film Huynh had shot got cabled praise from NBC New York, the cable saying, "SET NEW STANDARD COMBAT COVERAGE."

Without my having to pray.

Brando was still talking; I was still recalling.

Maybe sometimes, instead of waiting for prayer, God sends guidance through other people. Josephine worked in our office, a lovely young Vietnamese woman, graceful in her *ao dai*, the flowing, long Vietnamese dress, but also a person with keen sensitivities and instincts I quickly came to trust. It was she who scouted around town to find me, the new bureau chief, an apartment on the second floor of the old building at 104 Tu-Do Street.

Tu-Do was the notorious street lined with bars full of too-young Vietnamese girls, thirteen- or fourteen-year-old children, painted, cheap-perfumed, rouged and sheathed in tight silk, pitiably telling half-drunk GIs, "I love you too much, Joe. You buy me drink?" That I knew.

What I didn't know when Josephine led me to my new digs was that the apartments upstairs in the building were occupied by the girls who worked downstairs. My place, I learned, was the only one that wasn't. But had been. Which is why at one in the morning on my first night in residence, I heard a relentless pounding on my door and an American voice insistently demanding, "Suzie, you in there? Suzie, it's me, Hank. It's your lover boy. Suzie. Suzie!" I gave him my deepest bass voice, grunting, "Hey, guy. I ain't Suzie!"

Whether Josephine had even indirect channels to the Viet Cong was a matter of frequent speculation (as it was about all the local staff). Maybe she was clairvoyant. Did she have hunches or information? Whichever, I owe my life to one of them.

On June 15, 1965, as her new boss, I invited Josephine out to dinner to celebrate her anniversary with the company and suggested we take in the famous My Canh floating restaurant down on the river. I'd never been there but heard good things.

"When?" she asked dubiously.

"I figured tonight, whatever time you say."

Her look was cautionary, but I did not understand. "Is there a problem?" I asked.

"Could we go somewhere else?" she wondered. "Not My Canh tonight." She said no more. And I gave it no more thought.

We went out to Cholon, the Chinese part of town, for some always-welcome sweet-and-sour soup and spicy orange chicken. We dined early, which meant we were back downtown by shortly after eight, just in time to hear thundering explosions. It sounded like down by the river — one massive burst followed maybe thirty seconds later by another cluster of smaller explosions. Soon flames and smoke rose in the southern sky. Racing to check it out,

I found one of our cameramen already there, getting film of the My Canh floating restaurant being consumed by flames, dozens of bodies strewn on the street and sidewalks around it. The first explosion had been a bomb driven directly into the restaurant. The subsequent blasts had been claymore mines spraying deadly shrapnel at the poor souls fleeing the scene.

"Poor souls" who would have included me but for Josephine's instincts, insights, or — could it have been? — inside information. Angel or spy, I did not know. That was the way of the war.

One of the paratroopers' biggest ops, a job several days in the planning, was the talk of the Tu-Do bars the night before it was launched. The morning it began, when I left my apartment in combat gear at 4:30 a.m., I was asked by the doorman if I was going out on the big operation with the 173rd that day.

Several hours later, it was little surprise that, having arrived at their objective — a notorious Viet Cong redoubt which for months had been crawling with a VC regiment — the masses of American soldiers found only an old man (whom they took prisoner), a thatched hut (which they burned), and four water buffalo (which they shot).

Let it not be said that the whole ungainly and presumably secret operation, with its lumbering movements of armor and artillery the day before, with sixty helicopters gathered from bases around the country to lift in four thousand soldiers, with jet fighters sent up to provide prelanding air strikes and continuing cover, and with a flight of B-52s called in from Guam to soften up the target area, that all this had not come as a murderous surprise to those buffalo!

Cynical I grew in Vietnam. Skeptical I was trained to be, but before long, my soul soured with cynicism. How could we, a Christian nation founded on faith, have come to this? What did it say of us? What did it say of Christianity?

As is often the case, answers to such questions were found not in big things but in small.

The marines staged a big thing. Actually, a battle had been going on around Chu Lai for many weeks, but between Arvin and VC. When the American marines arrived, it became an operation of superlatives: our first amphibious assault of the war; its largest battle; its costliest; and in the number of enemy destroyed—probably an entire regiment—its most successful. It was all these things to be cabled home for front pages the next day, dramatized for the weekly newsmagazines, transcribed years from now from unit logbooks into official histories. It was all these big things, but for me, it was one little thing, a moment, that would mean the most and come closest to addressing my questions about God's hand.

The battle was over, the mortars, recoilless rifles, and AR-15s stilled, most of the warriors departed. Only a few of us—my cameraman and I and a small group of GIs—remained when, slowly, cautiously, timidly, people began to emerge: the people of the hamlet of Van Truong, who, as the fighting began, had hidden away underground, directly beneath the battlefield for many hours and then many days. Now, from their tunnels and pits, caves and bunkers, they surfaced, blinking into the light, crawling out to reclaim whatever of their lives might be left, for however long they might be permitted to live them.

How long had they been down there, in the blackness and damp? Maybe weeks, we were told. Long enough that they had outstayed the meager supplies of food they had taken down with them. When it was gone and they had nothing left, still they stayed.

Children felt it first. They sobbed with the hunger. They cried, and their parents tried to still their crying. Some parents cried too. But stayed.

They heard the shooting above, and the bombs. There was a war right over them, and they heard it. They stayed. Hungry or not, they remained in their holes. They waited. Finally, when there were no more war sounds, a few of them dared to move toward an entrance tunnel to look out. What they saw first was a face looking back at them, a face with a big nose and blue eyes. They could go up.

The marines standing around the entrance to that tunnel did not count how many people came out, but suddenly the hamlet had its people again. It was a scene never to forget: the people of Van Truong coming home. One man in particular I focused on, and so did several of the marines. One frail man with, in his arms, his baby daughter. The mother? No sign.

The baby was naked, a tiny girl. Father wore peasants' clothing, black pajamas, no shoes. His face was tightly drawn, cheeks pinched, eyes hollow, their whites dimmed as though the walnut stain of his face had run. He was weak; hunger had ravaged him and, for a while, his daughter, his precious tiny daughter. She was perhaps six months old. It didn't matter anymore. Cradled in his arms as he climbed up out of the hole, she was tiny and brown and dead, yet he held her, tenderly, with a father's love, as though she still lived.

A marine saw him and pulled from his field pack a box of C-rations. He opened the first can — "Lima Beans and Ham in Juices," it said — and handed it to the man. Digging in with the plastic spoon, the man ate eagerly, voraciously but awkwardly, for he used only one hand, his other arm clinging to his baby, her face against his cheek as he ate. Lima beans and ham, then crackers and cheese spread, then sliced peaches followed by a disc of sweet milk chocolate. He ate, holding his baby as though perhaps somehow the nourishment might flow from his body back into hers. He held her.

Wordlessly, a young marine unstrapped his poncho, unrolled it and offered it. The man understood. This soldier's cloth was to be his daughter's shroud; the shallow hole another marine was scratching in the sandy soil with his trenching tool, her grave. The father watched the digging, noted the shape, the tiny size. When it was ready, he gently wrapped his daughter in the poncho and lowered her slowly into the grave, kneeling to arrange the sad bundle so that her face should be up toward the heavens. He rose. He stepped back. The marine replaced the soil. And then, standing over the small dirt mound, he came erect, bowed his head, and softly spoke a prayer. I did nothing; I just stood there. And to this day, I hate that I just stood there.

It was over. The marines left. We all left. The villagers went back to their huts, those who still lived, whose huts still stood. Perhaps one day the Viet Cong would return, or perhaps it would be government soldiers, but no doubt somebody would come again to do war in this place. And the people of Van Truong once again would go underground, as once again warriors heedlessly trudged over a small mound of soil where, under the hot, yellow sun, grasses had just begun to recover.

Will men never pound swords into plowshares and learn war no more?

Mary Jo walked over to ask me if she should take over the dinner as, clearly, I was still tethered to the phone, though she hadn't heard me talking for many minutes. She raised an eyebrow as a question. I grabbed the notepad and scribbled "Marlon Brando," held it up for her. She rolled her eyes and walked off. Dinner would wait.

Brando rambled. When finally, after most of an hour, he wound down, having made no coherent point that I'd been able to decipher, he told me I should give him a call if I had any more thoughts on the matter. *What* matter? How could I call him? What number? The instructions he gave were arcane, Gordian. Did I have a paper and pen? Okay. Whenever I wanted to reach him, I was to call the number he was about to give me. *Don't try to reach him any other way.* I wouldn't get through. Too many people try. He had to protect himself. But I should call this special number and someone would answer. Not him. He couldn't risk answering his own phone. Nor should I ask the person who did answer if I could talk to Marlon. I'd be cut off instantly, and no call from my number would ever again be accepted. Instead, I should ask the person who answered for Doctor Tim. I would be asked my name. I should say I was Doctor Tim's mother and had just gotten a call from Jack Perkins, and then give my phone number. Then, and only then, Brando would call me back. We could talk again. There was more he wanted to say about Vietnam.

The main point I got out of that conversation with Brando: that even here at Moosewood, isolated, insulated, insolated, there was no escape. Anyone could reach us — those we knew, those we didn't know but were glad to hear from, and those we didn't know and would feel no loss should we not hear from them again.

But I did hear from Brando again awhile later. As before, he was loquacious and puzzling, but this time I could partly understand what he was talking about. It was an idea he had to do an hour-long TV program to expose the nation to his ideas about something or other; I never was clear on that. His reason for calling me was to propose that he and I do the program together. (I was hosting A&E's *Biography* at the time.) What was my price? he wanted to know. What would it cost him to get me to do the program with him?

"I don't know, Marlon," I said, balking. "What would it entail? What would you see me doing?" Mainly, I gathered, he wanted me to interview him. So he could let the world know what he felt it needed to know. So what was my price?

"Marlon, I can't really say. I don't have a set price," I said, hemming and hawing. (I hated negotiating, and did it badly.)

"Everyone has a price," he insisted. And then he told me about a film he didn't want to do, so he'd told the producer he'd only do it for six mil, figuring that would discourage the guy on the whole idea. Instead, the producer *gave* him the six million! He got his price even when he didn't want it.

"So what's your price, Jack?"

I could stall no longer. "Six mil?" I joked.

"Jack, Jack," he chastised, "you're not Brando."

That call ended with no agreement, partly because I never did understand what his project was about or what I would be required to do, and partly because I never could "set my price."

Some months later, I learned his fallback position. With much publicity and fanfare, full-page ads, and the rest, he took over the full hour of *Larry King Live*. And at the end of the show, he got up, stepped over, and kissed King smack on the lips.

Six mil would have been about right.

Moosewood kept us busy. Simply to get warm, to cut, stack, carry, and set firewood, to see to basics like fueling and trimming wicks on kerosene lamps, to figure out and maintain the enigmatic electrical system — in other words, to provide heat, light, and energy, which people in other lives took for granted as we always had — in winter, Moosewood demanded heavily of our time and effort. In winter, when less is given, more had to be earned. More than we even yet knew.

A California friend was curious. He'd heard that Maine was having an unusually harsh winter.

Yes, we told him, we were. There was a stretch of eleven days and nights that the snow didn't stop falling. When it did, here came the coldest Maine cold: nights twenty below, days that never broke zero. Nonetheless, long johns, turtlenecks, sweaters, and wool pants availed by day, and flannel pajamas, down quilt, and fortitude by night.

Our friend wanted details. "So how cold does it get?"

"Oh, not bad," I said sanguinely. "This morning, for example, it was forty-two ..."

"Forty-two? Hell, that's not bad," he said, dismissing any pretense of sympathy.

Until I added, "... in the bedroom."

The woodstove's heat did not reach our bedroom, nor did we want it to. In the little great room (a pleasing paradox), first thing in the morning, the temperature was, perhaps, fifty. Whoever got up first (and it would be both disingenuous and cowardly not to admit right here that it was usually Mary Jo) would recharge the fire, and by breakfast it would be sixty-five. In our previous homes, even that would have been uncomfortable, or previous *we's* would have thought it so. Here we accepted it as normal. In a room warmed by woodstove, at times you will chill, at times perspire, but always you will be aware. That's not a bad way to live.

There is a special comfort to wood heat. It derives partly from the ritual of puttering — laying the fire, coaxing it to life, adjusting damper and flue to keep the burn steady — partly from the mellow, warming aura of the stove that draws one to it on the coldest of days.

And beyond the quality of the heat itself is the comforting fact that you have *earned* it. Directly. You bucked the wood, hauled it in, set the fire, nursed it, nourished it with kindling (small bundles of pin-cherry tangle you harvested from the woods), weaned it to logs which you faithfully renewed. *You* did it. In most of life, the link is not so direct. In most homes, heat cycles on, cycles off at a thermostat's command, burning natural gas siphoned from wells in Oklahoma, dispatched, without our awareness, through cross-country pipelines to our house to take flame in a furnace we might see once a year when filters need changing or maybe not even then. We pay a gas bill at the end of the month but pay it with money, and that is not really *paying*. We may have worked for the money, but it's not the same. There is an indirection there that blurs reality.

It didn't used to be this way. People used to know what things were worth. Now they know what things *cost*.

In the warmth of our morning woodstove, Jo and I, gathering for breakfast, smiled at how we were rediscovering breakfast foods we used to hate. Hot cereals with old-time names like Maypo, Maltex, Wheatena. Those were cereals moms gave kids before clipping mittens to jacket cuffs, buckling galoshes, and sending them schoolward with cautions about not removing their hats until they were all the way inside the cloakroom. Those were the foods forced upon us. Now we were adults, free to choose, but also free to rethink old rejections, and *surprise*, hot Maltex was *good*!

Sometime after breakfast, the timing dictated by that day's tide schedule, we'd set off on what we called our Tennyson trip — Crossing the Bar. Challenging. By now the upper bay was thick of ice. Floes drifted down, crunching upon each other as they reached the bar, often piling up at its end until, even with most of the bar exposed, there were giant stairsteps of ice four feet high.

We carried a pickaxe in the back of the Jeep to chop our way across, but when the ice floes got too high, even with chopping we couldn't make it through. For a month, we could cross only on foot: a half-mile ski from the house to the end of the island, then another half-mile walk across the bar. While trees sheltered us on the island, for ten minutes on the bar, we were totally exposed. Ten degrees below with a thirty-five-mile-an-hour wind straight in the face brings tears; if skin isn't covered, it first tingles, then bites.

A visit to town let us collect whatever supplies we needed back on the island. These could be loaded into backpacks; that was no problem, though, I'll confess, we wished we'd had the foresight last fall to stock up on the fifty-pound bags of dog food and kitty litter. But, on the other hand, having purchased a plastic sled for such burdens, we had a sled to ride for fun.

One day, sledding dog food home, our big guy, the lab/bloodhound mix, Buford, found us at the end of the island and let me tie the sled rope to his collar. I got a memorable snapshot of him sledding his new bag of food to the house.

Tramp the cat couldn't tow his kitty litter but would make the effort to crawl out from his favorite napping place underneath the woodstove and hop into a lap and purr.

Jo would head to her crafts, busily filleting every pair of blue jeans our family had worn for the past twenty years, braiding the strips of denim to create an amazing, multihued heirloom rug. In the small spare bedroom-become-den, on a laptop computer suckled on 12 volts DC, I began stitching together the pages of the journal of our journey so far.

Then, together in the great room, huddling hard by the woodstove, the two of us shared meals and books and ideas that warmed. The Bible was open on a table, not banished to a shelf. My first, disgruntled impression on arriving home on that snow-deep night was wrong, very wrong. In winter's grip, this house was not unwelcoming. Being snowbound was not onerous.

More onerous were questions of friends back west intent on knowing, "So what are you guys doing with all your time?"

They didn't want our answers, I was convinced; they wanted to hear that we were suffering and maybe even rethinking our foolish decision to escape all that they, back there, still cherished. We weren't.

What were we doing? Surviving. Surviving had become our occupation. A fine one, if demanding. Maine essayist E. B. White had expressed it with down-east conciseness: "Just to live in New England in winter," he allowed, "is a full-time job."

16

BLESSEDLY SILENT SPRING

If spring came but once in a century, instead of once a year,
or burst forth with the sound of an earthquake, and not in
silence, what wonder and expectation there would be in all
hearts to behold the miraculous change!

— H. W. Longfellow (from Maine)

No rumble or belching of earthquake ushered spring into Moosewood. There were shad.

The little shadbush or serviceberry tree — inconspicuous and unnoticed most the year — was the first plant to show itself, bursting forth in brilliant white blossoms around the edge of the meadow, stars alone on the stage of the new spring.

Soon, though, the old apple trees made their entrance, their tiny pink and white flowers not just lighting the scene along the dirt road but perfuming the warming air. Walking their way was a sensual joy. Six months earlier, we had lovingly preserved some of the fruit of those trees in glass jars of homemade applesauce and apple butter. Now we wished we could somehow bottle that perfume.

Trees in flower mean sap is flowing, so next time over in town, we made our way to the local True Value to pick up some equipment. Back home, we picked out a few of our maple trees and even a couple of the birch, inserted sharp V-shaped devices into their trunks, hung buckets on them, and waited patiently as their life-juices began drip-drip-dripping. We knew we wouldn't have the patience, nor did we have the paraphernalia or expertise, to boil the maple sap down to syrup (a thirty-three to one reduction, we had been told). Nor would we ever make birch beer. But we didn't need to. Some of the great naturalists standing there on the home-rigged bookshelves of our little cabin had better ideas. *Take it and drink. As is.* That was their advice. So instead of going through the rigors of distillation, we simply refrigerated the birch sap and maple juice to preserve them, and then started each morning by drinking what, more than any tonic we could have purchased, was the perfect elixir, a very essence of life. We could *feel* it. (Or imagine it?) Downing a healthy draft, we were imbibing the bracing liquor of life, feeling the God-given rebirth that each year is the promise of spring.

When Fast Eddie, the NBC assignment editor, had contacted me back in the fall soon after we'd arrived wondering if I'd do an obit piece on Gene Autry, I had told him no, but told him to try me again in the spring.

This time the call came directly to our house. "Jack? We've got a story we'd love you to do. It seems right up your alley."

This was Tuesday. They wanted a story for the *NBC Nightly News* on Friday. It was to be a story about outsiders who were being recruited to help repopulate a distant Maine island. I knew the island and knew the story.

What I didn't know was whether I really wanted to go back, even in a limited way, to TV reporting. I had to test myself. I accepted.

Thursday, the day of the shoot, I could feel the familiar process beginning again, though this time with delightful twists. Leaving the house early in the morning to "go to work" meant paddling away in a kayak, getting a few feet offshore, remembering, turning around, paddling back to where Jo was standing on a rock, leaning down to kiss me goodbye. Then off again into the sunrise, marveling that this way of working must be as good as it gets.

The rest of the day brought back the comfortable, problem-plagued routine of TV work: rendezvousing with the camera crew and producer from Boston, scrounging transportation in a small fishing village, ferrying an hour offshore while plotting the story (about a tiny community shriveling toward extinction coming up with the idea of offering free land and homes to anyone willing to move to the bleak island and settle there), landing at a creaky dock, hauling cases of equipment, watching the cameraman set up and shoot, introducing ourselves to people and explaining what we were doing and when it would be on, checking facts, probing the interview subjects for their feelings, and looking for the right ways of expressing what this was all about. When we shot the standupper, it was my first time before a camera in almost a year, but it felt completely comfortable. Then, with the story in the can, an overnight in a local motel and a quick flight to Boston.

Friday morning. Editor waiting at the NBC bureau, story to

be written and cut, New York show producers consulted, air time allotted, more time fought for, technical snags, editing gear breakdown, start again, running late, fast lunch, back to editing, record the narration, change the narration, record it again, and where's that shot of the church with the flowers waving in the foreground?

The internal machinery worked. Untested for months, the gears and wheels meshed and turned. After the story aired as the closer on that night's show, it was nice to be complimented by several folks there in Boston but also by phone by a few other old colleagues. And then the executive producer of the show called from New York to say, "Really good to have you back, Jack," and that threw me, really threw me. *Back?* Was I back? Did I *want* to be back?

I could have caught a late flight for Maine. The tide wouldn't be right when I got to Bar Harbor, but I had my kayak waiting in town. Still, that would mean paddling across to the island in the dark, and I was already tired. And needed to think. So instead I checked into a hotel in Cambridge and spent the evening walking the streets around Harvard, checking out quaint shops Jo would love to browse, and then, after dinner alone (always the worst part of traveling), I returned to the hotel.

Whereupon two things happened. First, Jo called to tell me that her dad, who was visiting us, had taken a terrible, somersaulting tumble from the top of our seawall to the jagged rocks eight feet below, and Jo, alone, had had to help him crawl up the hill to the house, get him painfully into the Jeep, and ferry him across to the hospital, where he was patched up and sent achingly back to Moosewood. "You should have been there," she said with a weary laugh. Yes, I *should* have been there.

Second, the hotel's automated fire alarm system went wild,

and four times in the night, sirens squealed through bedroom loudspeakers as an electronic doomsayer commanded sleepwalking travelers outside. Four times! Four false alarms! Virtually no sleep. Terrible night.

Or looking at it another way, miraculous night. I was given by providential blessing precisely what I needed — a sleepless night through which to ponder and pray.

I prayed for guidance and reflected on the feeling of being back in harness. I had enjoyed it, no doubt. Shooting the story had been fun, writing the script satisfying as always, being flattered afterward deeply warming. I was impressed by the quality of the craftsmen I worked with. I guess, all those years I'd been in the midst of it, I had taken that for granted, but to work again among such skilled people was a privilege. Yes, I *had* enjoyed it.

Still, I realized something else, something telling and pivotal: I didn't *need* it. Working TV didn't burn in me anymore the way it used to. I'd been happy to be on camera again, but I'd be just as happy watching someone else do it. And, after all, what a fitting last piece to do for NBC: that simple story about people leaving old lives behind to move to a small Maine island to start anew.

I was finished with the news business! Before leaving Boston that morning, I called Mary Jo to tell her. We celebrated that night.

What a coincidence that only a few weeks later I got a call from another former colleague who reported that she, too, was finished with the news business. Only in her case, the decision had not been hers. She was my friend Kirstie, a news anchor I had worked with in Los Angeles. Now she told of how, on the very week her *Four O'Clock News* for the first time ever hit number one in the ratings, on the very day she went to the studio to tape promos thanking Los Angeles for making the show number one, on the very afternoon of her triumph, she was fired! GE had bought NBC and brought in efficiency experts determined to make the production of TV news as cost-effective as the making of sixty-watt bulbs or toasters. People were being fired or bought out. Great chunks of the corporate body were being hacked away, and what remained bled.

Would I really miss the business? *That* business?

Maybe on occasion I would want to do something on TV in the future, but not much. And certainly not the same things I had done before, because that wouldn't teach me anything. Nor would I want to do anything that would take me away from Moosewood either too frequently or for too long. For me, our new lives at Moosewood as they'd evolved that fall and winter were close to ideal.

For her part, Jo was joyfully committed to finishing six dozen color illustrations for field guides to the birds of Acadia National Park and the state of Maine, due to come out that summer — her first published work! Also, she had done those pencil sketches of our predecessors on the island for another book to come, and was beginning other jobs as well. Her pride in her achievement was a thrill I delighted in sharing.

Spring cleaning, that year, wasn't so much about cleaning the house; we'd barely had the leisure time to let it get messy. But we did want to spruce up ourselves in our new lives. One afternoon, I sat down and wrote two lists. On the first, I set down lessons we had learned so far:

Lesson: More than ever before, we need patience. (The man who waits for no tides gets wet.)

Lesson: Problems cannot keep us from being happy.

Lesson: The Skeptic's Creed ("You won't believe it until you see it") is backward. Moosewood has taught the reverse: you won't see it (or hear it) until you believe it. Until you believe there is a heaven beneath your feet as well as over your head, you won't bother to look down to admire an intricate collage of fallen leaves, or the skittering among the mosses of insects in their miniature world. Until you believe that those who preceded you still have something to say, you won't listen for the echoes of their voices. Until you believe that birds are the grace notes of God's symphony, you won't listen for the song of the unseen hermit thrush.

Lesson: Being islanders does not mean being hermits. Some people — big city bustlers and climbers — consider us kooks, but we know better. What we are is fortunate people who have found ways to synchronize our wants and our needs. Jo's crafts and my writing and photography are pleasures; our pleasures are now our vocations. Hiking, kayaking, skiing, snowshoeing are enjoyments. Enjoyments have become necessities.

Lesson: Thoreau knows us. On the wall of my office hangs a plaque with his line, "This curious world which we inhabit is more wonderful than it is convenient; more beautiful than it is useful; it is more to be admired and enjoyed than used."

Thoreau's words always seemed felicitous, but never more than now, after we'd weathered the stress of a winter at Moosewood. It is not easy to live on an island in a sometimes inhospitable climate, removed from family, friends, and urban opportunities. Not *convenient*, but wonderful! Our life is not notably useful, withdrawn to ourselves and our interests, holding no real jobs, producing no steady product. Not *useful*, but beautiful! Federal law and Park Service rules strictly forbid us to clear woods, build onto the house, rent rooms, or open a business, but none of that matters because we understand that the island is more to be admired and enjoyed than put to what some consider a more practical use.

Lesson: We don't have it made, but with God's help, we are making it.

Those were lessons I inscribed on our first springtime list.

We had spent two and a half months snowbound, going at one point several days without electricity, refrigeration, or running water. We carried drinking water over from the mainland, flushed with seawater, used kerosene lamps and candles, put perishables in snowbanks, and suffered inconvenience, true, but nothing more. Many necessities aren't necessary.

Living in Hong Kong in the sixties, there were many times that our apartment had running water only four hours every third day. Hong Kong was still a British colony, but its water supply came by pipeline from China, which arbitrarily shut off the valves from time to time like a landlord trying to get rid of a tenant. On the days you had water, you canceled all appointments, ran home, bathed, and then began filling the tub again, plus every container you had — pots, pans, jugs, bottles, water heaters — to make it through the next three days. And you know what? It wasn't unbearable. We got along fine without running water.

At Moosewood, now, we drew a second list, this of things we didn't need:

To make a living. That's a singular blessing. If you don't have to work to make a living, you can work to make a life.

As much money as we thought. Money is not what it was, does not mean what it meant or do what it once seemed to do. It (and the flaunting of it) is no longer the measure of success.

So many clothes. In cities, it's easy to admire people who wear clothes well and shop for clothes knowledgeably. But around here, people dress less deliberately. *GQ's* photographers aren't expected here soon (though *National Geographic's* have been here). In a city, one wears clothes as a way to stand out. Here, people try to fit in. There's no fever to rise above the crowd where there is no crowd. Consequently, it's harder, much harder, here to identify social or professional status. A lawyer dresses like a lobsterman, a waitress like a bank officer, and even former defense secretary Caspar Weinberger forgoes the pin-striped suit when he totes grocery bags from Don's Shop'n Save to his little tan Plymouth in the lot. Khakis or jeans, turtles or T's, flannels, sweaters, sneakers, and moccasins — we need no more and, with limited closet space, shop parsimoniously. Feel the urge to buy a new coat? First, give an old one away.

Masks. Too often, life seems a masquerade ball. Everyone knows everyone else is wearing a mask, but there's a tacit agreement that I won't rip off yours if you won't rip off mine. We've ripped off our own.

Contracts. Whatever work either of us chooses, if prior agreements are required, a handshake will do. Too many times I signed contracts swearing to things I knew weren't true, or didn't understand, or never expected to be required to abide by. Too many times hypocrisy was codified and I swore to it. If I can avoid it, never again.

The news. We have a radio and four TV channels on our little black-and-white. A friend from LA, appalled that we did not get a Sunday paper delivered, suggested, "You could pay a kid to bring one across." Yes, we could. But why? Sunday papers are important to some people, a way of filling time on that day originally left open so that church and family might be attended to. That was before merchants, responding to a demand that they themselves created, lobbied for repeal of archaic blue laws and called employees in on Sundays. Sports clamped onto Sunday TV schedules where *Omnibus* once had set a standard for excellence. Church attendance declined, and people, lolling at home, hefted twenty-pound papers into bed and spent the day smearing their fingers with newsprint. It's become a cozy and familiar ritual — but *why*? Sunday papers are bra ads, computer sales, and typhoons in Bangladesh. Not our idea of news. Sunday morning newscasts lead with stories like, "The secretary of state is flying back from Geneva today after meeting with ..." A person flying is news? Not since Kitty Hawk. At Moosewood, big news is finding a pink lady's slipper, or having the bald eagle perch on the oak limb out front. We read a small-town weekly, which is to journalism what New England town meetings are to democracy — a more intimate, maybe more meaningful experience. It tells the people of a town about each other: who died, who won the spelling bee, what the council plans on taxes, how a six-year-old pulled a thirty-two-inch togue out of Tunk Pond — none of this of global moment, but our lives are not globally momentous. Our lives, arranged right, are about fishing holes and taxes, winning spelling bees and dying. The rest of it, what is generally thought of as news, puts one in mind of another line from Thoreau: "To a philosopher all news, as it is called, is gossip and they who edit or read it are old women over their tea."

A big house. Moosewood is fifteen hundred square feet. Some visitors find it small. We find it small. Some think that a deficiency. We think it cozy. Friends, a childless couple in Bar Harbor, have a comfortable mountaintop home of six thousand square feet. Good for them! Unless you're the Sultan of Brunei in your twenty-five-hundred-room palace, someone always has a larger house than you, and a faster car, and earns more, and has broader fame, greater power, a wife more richly attired, sons and daughters more successful — and more hair!

Success. Not if measured by income, ratings, or recognition. There was delicious irony in an item I discovered in the College of the Atlantic library one day. Back in the daily TV years, I had been delighted to discover an entry under my name in *Who's Who in America.* Now the small college library had the latest edition, so for old time's sake — for vanity's sake — I looked myself up. No listing anymore for Jack Perkins.

Gone were the days of celebrity. Oh, still, now and then there was recognition, and I enjoyed it. But I started asking myself, Is that enough? Is it enough to experience celebrity and just enjoy it? God had given me talents. But for what purpose? I knew what Jesus in the Gospels taught about people who were given talents and wasted them. (Yes, he was speaking of units of currency, but the idea fit nonetheless.) What a sin to be given talents by God and not use them to glorify God. If I was looking forward to purpose in my new life, this was the key.

The poetry I was writing to accompany my photography began to show a difference. Remember the simple shad, that unpretentious little tree that only for a short while in early spring comes to blazing white blossom, the first harbinger of the season? For my photograph of a shining shad came this:

Am I willing to learn from a tree?
A tree that is small and so commonly drear

That it goes hardly noticed for most of the year?
Now what, pray, can that say to me?

Well, look at it now in the spring,
At this moment with all of its blossoms alight
For a brief burst of glory, its pride shining bright
In a singular, spring-ular fling.

There are people this tree can define
Feeling small, without purpose, unnoticed each day.
Don't they know that with God's light within, even they
Like the shad, for a moment, can shine?

For a photograph of the old foundation wall surrounding Moosewood:

We humans, trusting Genesis
Presume dominion over all
So, wresting rocks from nature's hold
Where stream or glacier let them fall
We call them ours
And build a wall

The wall says: This belongs to us
A proof of Man's supremacy
Here people rule and order reigns
And shall until eternity
Such be our thoughts
Our vanity

But truth to tell we'll soon be gone;
Then who will walk the paths we trod?
And when they find our futile wall,
Will they perhaps believe it odd
How we confused ourselves with God?

266

Or that white birch glade Mary Jo had come to think of as her White Cathedral? I was thinking of that holy place when I accompanied a photograph of birch trunks with this verse:

Think of Acadia's woods as a church
Each spruce, a steeple
We hikers its people
Its angels, those heavenly birch
See them gleaming angelically white
Glowing, enrobed in all that is right

Trees as angels? The doubter doubts
Am I being awfully naive?
No, I'm convinced that birches are angels
But only for those who believe

Try this: Inscribe a heartfelt prayer
On some fallen bark of birch
If you believe, you might find that prayer
*   answered*
Next time you come here to church

Of all the works in my first book of photography and poetry inspired by this early, revelatory time at Moosewood, I think the apotheosis of the state of my faith is the poem that accompanied a picture of Bass Harbor Light, the lighthouse surmounting a rock cliff. It is titled simply "Faith."

Granite ascending, rising from granite
Steel upon brick upon stone
I see this scene, this symbol of certainty
Thinking: Can I be alone
In puzzling why we squander our trust

On the seemingly certain; and why
We believe that a scene's being seen makes it so?
Why should we? We see the sky
Or think that we see it. It spreads overhead
Cerulean blue, we could swear
But that's an illusion; the sky is not blue
The sky is not really there
We're certain we see it. We're wrong, so be it
Credulity has us undone
Believe in the seen? Maybe we shouldn't
Instead, believe in the un-

Unseen — the love that peopled those towers
And still attracts from afar
People loving themselves for loving lighthouses
As were and as they are.

Unseen — the faith that keepers clutched,
Unwilling to contravene.
For "Faith," the Book said,
   "is the substance of things hoped for,
The evidence of things not seen."
Jesus told Thomas, who only when seeing
Finally felt relieved
"Blessed are they that have not seen,"
      He told him
"Have not seen and yet have believed."

Invincible Invisibles
The God we place above
That sky we only think we see
Up there. And faith. And love.

Those three are certain enough for me.
Henceforth this is my plan:
Believe much more in what I can't see,
Much less in what I can.

17

ASPARAGUS
AND THE
LILY PATCH

Where spring had budded, summer bloomed; the promises spring had made, summer colorfully kept.

We had come a long way, Jo and I. But to what end? We had smashed the vessels of old lives and turned new, had emptied our selves and begun to restock, but why? If simply for novelty, something to do, it was wasted. There had to be a more fundamental reason for the changes we had undertaken, and we needed to make specific that reason.

Knowing reasons isn't always easy. The journey to Truth, I had learned years before, can be long and vexing.

Into Africa — "I need you on this trip, Jack," insisted Father Bud, his call catching me in my NBC office in LA.

Father Elwood Keisser, Paulist priest, one of the holiest men I would ever meet, large of body, mind, and spirit, was a noble man and a dedicated servant of God. His churchly assignment was to spread the faith, and he used television and movies to do it.

"Tell me, Bud."

He had invited three Hollywood stars to go to Africa with him to see the blighted lands of starvation, and he wanted NBC to bring a TV crew to do a documentary about the trip, to raise awareness in the States and raise money for continuing relief work.

"You've got to come."

"Except for one thing," I demurred, though I should have known the demurrer was futile.

"What's that?"

"Bud, I'll be honest. I don't want to see it."

"See what?"

"The hunger, the suffering. It's a powerful story, I know, journalistically compelling, but on a personal level, I'm simply afraid that if I were to see it, I would never be able to stop seeing it."

"Jack, I'll promise you something. Promise you two things. I promise that, to be sure, you will never stop seeing it. But I promise as well that you'll never want to. God will see to that."

The flight was eternal. Across a continent, across an ocean, through a day and then a night we droned to reach a new continent and a new day, though those, too, would be but way stops. There was plenty of time to meet our traveling companions.

Patty Duke Astin. Patty Duke. When was it, years ago, I had waited, a teenage admirer, at a Broadway stage door to see the child who had just brought me to tears, the brilliant young actress who, along with Anne Bancroft, had spun tragedy into triumph in the play "The Miracle Worker"? Patty Duke was a child with a talent already adult.

Now she was still rather short like the child star she had been, but full-figured, married to actor John Astin, and mother of three. Her real first name was Anna. She preferred that.

She was curled around in her airline seat, already dressed for Africa — fatigue pants, baggy T-shirt, and new canvas hiking boots. She did not need defacing makeup. On Broadway as the blind child Helen Keller, Patty's eyes had appeared appropriately lifeless. Anna's lived brightly. As Helen Keller, Patty could see and hear only by touching. Anna was still a toucher. Talking to you, she reached out and stroked; laughing with you, she patted; engrossed, she gripped.

"I had to do this," she said intensely. "I have little idea what we're getting into except that Bud says we can help."

"Are you ready for what you're going to find?" I asked.

"I've read the briefing sheets. I've seen the statistics. And, no, you're right. I'm not ready."

"Not ready to find yourself holding a baby in your arms, knowing that in two or three days, he'll be dead, and you'll be somewhere else?"

Her soft eyes melted. "I know if it happens, I'll do it, I'll have to, and God will give me the strength." She squeezed.

In the row ahead sat Dick Van Patten, like Anna a childhood star come up in the business for decades, light comedy, always the likeable chap, most famously in the family TV series *Fight Is Enough*.

"When Bud asked me, first asked me, I really didn't want to do it. Really, really didn't. Not that I had anything else to do. Our series was shut down; I had time off. But I just didn't feel right about doing this, ya know?"

I knew because I had been told: Van Patten was terrified of flying. More than once in his career he had turned down jobs to avoid having to fly. Yet here he was on what threatened to be a nightmare series of flights for one with such fear.

"I went home after telling Bud no and figured I'd forget about it. It was the weekend, and we always play a lot of tennis." His eyes crinkle-smiled as he talked. "But the funny thing was I couldn't get it out of my mind. All that Saturday and then Sunday, even while playing tennis, I couldn't stop thinking about what Bud had said, how badly he needed me, and I'd turned him down. It really bothered me. Something really strong, you know, told me I'd made a mistake and I had to go on that trip. So I called and told him, 'Okay, I'm in.'"

The third of Father Bud's enlistees was LeVar Burton. With a gleaming black face alive with both youth and the joy of being youthful, he was a child of his generation, unfettered by ineptitude or uncertainty. A couple of years earlier, he had come out of USC drama school to play Kunta Kinte in the iconic TV miniseries *Roots*. But though having convincingly portrayed that African progenitor, in fact, he had never been to the root-ground of Africa. This would be the first time.

A flight attendant brought our menus. This was the first of many times we would feel this same irony, so let me describe it. We were enduring this two-day flight to visit people who go longer than that between meals. And our menu was an embarrassing abundance, from caviar to *pate de canard*; from chateaubriand complemented by sauce Perigeux with truffles, to frog legs Provencale, to lobster Thermidor in a mustard-flavored bechamel sauce, to duck with mangoes and brandy, to ...

Human beings — brothers, sisters, cousins, strangers — were starving in the darkness as we straddled the black flanks of this night, and our greatest problem up here was to choose between chateaubriand and frog legs, and which wines would we like?

Our tickets for this flight cost $4,925 each. Could the people we were going to meet comprehend that?

In Somalia, according to our briefing sheets, the average income was $110 dollars a year. If the average Somali began earning at birth, he would have to work for forty-four years to pay for one of our tickets.

Life expectancy in Somalia was forty-one years.

Anna was bleary, her face as rumpled as her khakis. Dick was scraggly, unshaven, the eyes still ready to crinkle-smile, but the rest of him finding no reason to. Only LeVar, with youth, still looked fresh as we approached the first stop. A place none of us — until preparing for this trip — had ever heard of. Tickets and baggage tags read Nouakchott. Capital of Mauritania.

The local Catholic Relief Services field agent, a Frenchman named Jacques, loaded us into minicars and a van and drove us to a small hotel which was mean and dusty like everything else along the dirt streets of Nouakchott. Anna, in her room, found a cockroach the size of her fist. Dick discovered a plumbing mix-up: the toilet in his room, instead of disposing, delivered; his room stank of strangers' urine.

Hardly pausing, we were loaded into pickup trucks for the ride to a refugee camp.

To describe such a place, I need to reach beyond words like

wretched, putrid, fetid, diseased and somehow get you to picture ramshackle tumbles of scrap metal balanced on cardboard
enclosing a five-by-ten-foot home inside which eight people,
rarely fewer, haplessly huddle; you must see choking clouds of
dust and bugs, must smell the stench which blankets those hovels
like despair. This awful scene extended as far as could be seen —
horizonless horror.

With one oasis. As we entered the metal gates into the compound of the Catholic Relief Services' feeding station, we knew:
this was it.

Here was a baby lying in the scoop of a rough metal merchants' scale while a caring nurse recorded numbers (again,
reduce horror to statistics; make it bearable). Five kilos, we heard
her report the baby's weight. About eleven pounds. The child was
a year and a half!

Here was an older child, maybe three, in Jacques's arms as
he explained to his visitors how the child's black hair had turned
reddish-blond from malnutrition.

Neither Dick, who was usually voluble, nor Anna or LeVar
said much. Anna touched. Her small hand reached out to caress
the orange hair that was not just unsightly but probably a fatal
symptom, and to soothe the brow of the baby crying in the scale,
the child too fragile for a future. LeVar took to his arms a tearful,
snuffling tyke with giant eyes surrounded by sores, sores swarmed
over by incessant flies; he held the baby and talked to it, knowing
that it knew no more of his language than he did of its distress.

Only Dick, in these first moments, seemed withdrawn, ill
at ease. He balked, overwhelmed. Then he too asked by gesture
to hold a mother's child. And he cradled it in his arms, kissing
the baby's head until suddenly, and rather awkwardly, I saw him

shift the baby to his other side, cradling it in the other direction, and I understood why. He had been in show business all his life, constantly in front of cameras, and he knew his angles. As first positioned, holding the baby, his left hand and wrist were closest to our camera, prominently displaying his gold Rolex. What a terrible image: Hollywood star holding starving baby while wearing a ten-thousand-dollar watch. That's why he had shifted the baby to his other arm and gotten the watch out of sight. In fact, next time I looked, he had removed it altogether. Not insincere but keenly aware. Of what he had, and what they had not.

For many days there would be those awful contradictions. There seemed an unbridgeable chasm. We witnessed the pitiable state of their lives, and pitied, then headed back to our hotels and full-course dinners. How could we do that? How could we eat knowing they were not? How could we sleep in comfort when they had none? I asked Father Bud.

"Jack, we do what we can with what we are given. And what we are given most abundantly, our little group, are compassion and caring, yes, but also the means to reach millions and millions of people who may also be found to be compassionate. Those people will be drawn to LeVar and Anna and Dick. They will listen to them and pay attention to what they are experiencing here. And you and your crew will make that possible. That is what we can do, and it is not insignificant. Don't underestimate the gifts we are given or can give."

The meal Catholic Relief Services workers patiently taught refugee women to prepare from their meager rations was austere indeed. Mix bulgur and soy grits with water, add cooking oil; that was it. For today and tomorrow and the next day, that was it. For whatever days they were in this desolate camp in this perfidious life, that was it. It was a diet designed to stave off the worst of malnutrition's ravages. Nothing more.

The meal Catholic Relief Services prepared for us that same evening was a white-cloth, china-and-crystal banquet in a garden restaurant under the stars of a tropical African evening, course following course, wine replacing wine, an extravagant indulgence. Those of us who just arrived from America joined Jacques and other relief workers in Mauritania for banter, companionship, and reciprocal admiration. It was a splendid evening.

It was awful! Monstrously inappropriate!

I was almost blinded by fatigue, questions burning in my bleary mind like embers in a charcoal cooking fire. Why weren't we the ones hunkering there fixing soy grits, bulgur, and oil? And why weren't they at the groaning board laid with cloth, china, and crystal, selecting among proffered main course options?

Our meal kept coming.

I couldn't take it. This wining and dining ourselves in self-congratulatory excess sickened me. Excusing myself, I left the banquet room, walked out onto the sandy floor of the desert, looked up at the brilliant stars in the deep-black sky, and wept.

Exhaustion! Of course, it must be the fatigue.

It wasn't the fatigue. I stood there shaking my head and muttering softly to the unhearing night, "You don't celebrate a starvation tour with a banquet!"

Everywhere we traveled in Africa those weeks, from Mauritania through Senegal over to Kenya, up to Djibouti, down to Turkana, one truth, more than anything, surprised us. There was hunger, awful hunger, and poverty, and to see flies sucking at a child's open sores, the child too weak with starvation to brush them away, made the throat clench, the eyes avert. Dying should not be a spectator sport; that kind of dying hurts all who see it and cannot help. Yet even in the midst of that, where there was the least justification for joy, we found joy in abundance.

Not once in our travels did we walk into a slum or refugee camp that we were not greeted joyfully, especially by children. Children universally have that right — not only to be joyful but to show it. So Dick, walking among hovels, always had both hands filled with kids' hands, children's faces turned up to reflect the famous crinkle-smile they had never seen on TV. LeVar, again the student, would be off trying to learn the language, sitting on a heap of debris with new friends gathered round, sharing gestures and pidgin words, laughing with the attempt to bridge a gap so wide. Anna would not try to learn a new language, because she and the children she met already shared one: she touched them, and they touched her. Oh, they touched her.

In Djibouti, at Ali Sabieh refugee camp, hours from anything, Dick brought back vaudeville, doing the same slapstick routine over and over, standing next to the Jeep facing the crowd of grinning kids, waving goodbye, saying, "Well, so long; I've got to go now," turning as though to leave, running smack into the Jeep, slapping its side to make it sound like his face hit it, then reeling dizzily and falling to raucous laughter as kids insisted he do it again. At Balbala, a slum in Djibouti, a young girl's face lit with gleaming happiness because, whether she understood the words or not, she realized that LeVar was telling her she was beautiful. Or in Turkana, tribal lands in northwest Kenya, where the worst droughts had brought the most widespread starvation, where so many people were dying there wasn't the time or the strength to bury them all, yet those who survived, given music, any music at all, would begin hop-dancing and keep at it for hours. It made bizarre pictures, they with broad smiles on their shining black faces, pogoing to frenzied music while a few yards away on the parched earth lay skulls and bones that recently had been parents, siblings, spouses, friends.

"This is outrageous," said LeVar, joining the dancing.

"Outrageous good or outrageous bad?"

"Outrageous great."

What did they know, all these people who, by material standards, had no right to be happy, yet were? What did they know that we did not?

There was a moment on the border of Senegal that enthralled me. We had to wait a few hours for the siesta to end so Immigration would check us in. So we found shade and took to chatting with children. I had packed a dozen bandannas, all colors. One was rolled and tied around my forehead as a sweatband, one was in a hip pocket for mopping. Kids gestured their wonderment at that colorful rope around my forehead. I whipped off the rolled bandanna and unfurled it as a magician might produce his colorful silk. They cheered. I waved the bandanna around, then ceremoniously laid it over the extended index finger of my left hand, incanted what to them must have seemed appropriately mysterious mumbo jumbo, and whipped it off, at the same time folding my finger into my fist and loudly proclaiming the magical finger's disappearance. Some of them laughed; some stared with such puzzlement I wasn't sure if they just didn't get it or didn't care or, perhaps, really feared that my finger was gone. But then one of the girls stepped forward with shy hesitation and said something that I didn't understand. She held out her hand for the bandanna. I wondered if she had a trick to show me. I gave it to her. Whereupon, she turned and ran back through the kids to the women standing behind, and they all started to giggle and gabble, passing the bandanna from one to the other, each inspecting it and giggling some more till it got back to the girl, who carefully folded it and rolled it just as I had done that morning and, with a pride so great she beamed, tied it around her own forehead.

As I took the other cloth from my pocket, intending to replace my sweatband, the kids surged forward. I lost that one. I went back to the truck to rummage through my bag to find others to distribute. Red, pink, blue, orange, black, green — they all went. (Save two for the rest of the trip.) And still there were kids who had got none. Naturally those were the shyest kids who had not been bold enough or tough enough to push to the front or thrust their arms the farthest. Someday, supposedly, the meek will inherit the earth, but until then, they miss a lot.

One of the meek who lost out was a boy, maybe ten. Sweet face, black hair, dark eyes, he wore no shirt, no shoes, only shorts of the same indeterminate color as the dirt and the houses hereabouts. He stayed on after I had waved all the others off with exaggerated gestures of pretended truculence. They all saw through the bluster but played with it. This lad, though, had a more serious purpose. His voice was hesitant. "Mister ... I ... spee ... Engish."

Mandinke and Fulani were the languages of Senegal. But this fellow had learned a bit of English and wanted to practice. He began slowly, methodically crafting questions for me to elicit conversation. Where I from? Where I go? What my name? Each time I answered, which meant I had understood him, he smiled proudly. We talked for a long time. I didn't always understand him; he didn't always understand me. But we both understood that the wanting to understand was what counted. As the time came to leave — siesta was over; the Immigration shack was open now — I reached into my pack to pull out one of the last two bandannas for him, but he stopped me with a question.

"Mister ... you have ... book? Engish book? You ... give?"

He watched for my reaction. When my response was a nodding smile, he laughed. There were four books in my pack, but was any of them right? Imagine him trying to track the labyrinthine plot of a Robert Ludlum spy novel, or follow the paranoid non sequiturs of Woody Allen, or decipher the lowercase codes of e.e. cummings. Ah, but the fourth book was perfect. Simple words and short sentences would be easy for him to read, and it was an American author who had cared about Africa. At least one of the short stories in the paperback was about Africa. A hungry young lad on the border of Senegal could improve his English with the help of Hemingway transporting him to *The Snows of Kilimanjaro*.

He took the book in his hands gently, with quiet reverence, then suddenly turned and ran in excitement. He didn't thank me. He didn't have to.

In Kakuma, northwest Kenya, one little girl being fed the routine gruel had such a bad case of dysentery that it passed right through her, and she sat in a puddle of her own waste, crying. A nun picked her up by the shoulders and moved her to a dry spot, but still she cried. So the nun picked her up again, this time putting her arm under the child's bare, wet, and dirty bottom to cuddle and comfort her. Father Bud turned to Anna. "That's Christianity," he said. She did not reply, but five minutes later I saw her doing the same thing.

Later, able to hold her composure no longer, she looked up to heaven and cried, "Why? Why, God, do you let this happen?"

Father Bud was walking beside her. "Anna, maybe it's to challenge us to do something about it. Perhaps human suffering is not so much a problem requiring a solution as a mystery requiring a presence, the loving presence of God."

We felt it. At Moosewood, we felt that loving Presence and cherished it.

So many, we knew, do not. The Swiss psychiatrist Carl Jung reported that most of his patients over thirty-five were found to be suffering from the unfulfilled desire to find a religious outlook on life. Failing to find it, he reported, caused much of the discontent and mental illness of his time. Is our time different?

Thomas Jefferson generally refused to discuss religion with his children, not wanting to influence their searching, but he did give them this advice: "Question with boldness even the existence of a god." He reasoned that if there is a God, then it is he who implanted in the human brain the capacity to doubt, so it would insult him if that brain were not thus exercised.

Questioning is good. Does the Bible reveal more about human longings than godly realities?

Should we think of the Bible as the voice of a parent addressing a growing child? To the baby, a parent speaks sternly with unarguable commands (No! Don't do that! Come here!), but to an older child, he moderates tone, increasingly appealing to reason, until, finally accepting the offspring's maturity, the wise parent backs off, from then on offering suggestions and counsel only when asked. Is that how we should think of the Bible, as God, in the Old Testament, addressing humankind in its infancy with stern commands (Thou shalt! Thou shalt not!), then, in New Testament days, addressing a maturing people with explanations and appeals to reason; until, now, God has backed off, allowing us to live our lives with only suggestions and counsel when asked, and the suggestions are not written as mandates, and the counsel is rarely requested and even more rarely heeded. Is that how to think of the Bible?

What of the classic paintings of a white-bearded male God, enthroned and towering? Should not those be understood as mere metaphors, people's frail strivings to comprehend the incomprehensible? If some concepts are too elusive to be expressed as anything but metaphor, what metaphor, then, should we choose for God?

However profane it might seem to you, I think of asparagus.

Again, it was Jung, writing about "the wisdom of the unconscious," who proposed that the unconscious resides not solely within the individual but somehow also *beyond* the individual. Think of it this way: One day we are suddenly aware that we know something we have no reason to know, no apparent way of knowing. Perhaps it is a fact, perhaps a relationship between facts, perhaps a seeming memory of something we never experienced, yet we know it. How? Some adopt theories of multiple lives; they were here before, they think; that's why something unfamiliar seems familiar. Others come to believe in paranormal powers, in psychics and seers and ESP; that's how they "know" what they could not know. Jung, for his part, pictured rhizomes.

At Moosewood that summer, we knew rhizomes. The asparagus that Lawyer Norm had put in for us the summer before was sprouting nicely through the seaweed cover he had said would nourish it. Asparagus is propagated by underground rhizomes from one sprouting to the next.

The lilies of the valley Mary Jo had discovered at the site of the old Rodick family home also spread by way of rhizomes. The rhizome is where the plant's life permanently exists. It sustains that part of the plant that is aboveground; the plant aboveground is the rhizome's expression.

As the rhizome is to the plant, the unconscious might be to the individual person.

That analogy, in itself, doesn't explain the phenomenon of "unknowns" known, until we understand another truth about rhizomes. A single rhizome can service many plants. If we dug up that ancient patch of lilies of the valley, we would discover many stalks rising from the same underground root-source. All those individuals shared and were nurtured by the same rhizome. And if individual plants can share the same rhizome, Jung wondered, is it possible that individual people somehow share the same unconscious? His work on that idea brought him to his theory of the collective unconscious. Each person's unconscious, it proposed, comprises both a personal precinct and an area shared with others, perhaps with his community, with his race, perhaps with the rest of mankind. That portion shared, Jung believed, is that vast pool of sense and impulse, instinct and memory, that is the collective unconscious, the single rhizome sustaining the entire lily patch.

If that's how it is with plant life, I thought, standing in the asparagus patch, might it be that way with us? What is vital and continuing and essential in us lies unseen, even unknown, something beyond ourselves to which we are connected in ways that even we, its immediate and temporary realizations, may not recognize. It is, at once, the source of our connectedness and the thrust of our continuity. Through it we share with other beings, and through it we extend our own being to others. By its power, Jung believed, we inherit the wisdom of the experience of our ancestors without ourselves having the personal experience.

So what is this source of connectedness, this thrust of continuity, this power by which we may know what we do not know?

(I felt myself back in the stacks now, back in the College of Wooster library boning up for next week's speech tournament. Only in this case, studying the volumes on our own makeshift bookshelves at Moosewood, and not for a trophy but for the prize of a godly life.)

Jung called it the collective unconscious, but Jung felt constrained to use scientific terms. I came to think the matter too important to be left to scientists. Came to believe that the collective unconscious is that part of God that is within each of us. That that is the rhizome beneath the whole lily patch, the cloning continuity, which projects itself through us across space and time, giving us our best crack at immortality.

Nor, I found, is the idea original. The ancient Greek philosopher Heracleitus wrote about *Logos*. There is no simple, singular translation into English for the Greek word *Logos*, but here is how Heracleitus used it. Considering the seeming orderliness of the universe about him, he assumed a force that must be responsible for that order and called it *Logos*, or the Way, or reason, analogous to the reasoning power of man. Indeed, he theorized, man's soul is itself a part of this Logos. And this Logos is in some part and in some manner God. This was Heracleitus of Ephesus in the fifth century BC.

Jews believe that a transcendent God provides continuing guidance and inspiration for his people through Wisdom, Word, and Torah (Law). Wisdom, it is said, is itself the presence of God. Word (and *word*, used in this sense, is one translation of *Logos*) in Hebrew thought is more than just something said; it has inherent power to effect. Thus, we find the prophet Isaiah quoting God: "For as the rain comes down, and the snow from heaven, and do not return there, but water the earth, and make it bring forth and bud, that it may give seed to the sower and bread to the eater, so shall My word be that goes forth from My mouth, it shall not return to Me void, but it shall accomplish what I please, and it shall prosper in the thing for which I sent it."

God's Word (*Logos*) is not mere utterance but, if accepted and employed by people, can effect change, in Judaic belief.

It took a trip over to town, again to the college library, to track down the man who had finally synthesized both Greek and Jew. He was Philo Judaeus of Alexandria, himself both Greek and Jew, a contemporary of Jesus, and known to historians today as "the first theologian." To Philo, God is the ultimate, essential Being, so great and indescribable that humans can only know *that* he is, not *what* he is. Any descriptor limits, and humans cannot limit God. This much, though, they can know: that a lofty and indescribable God acts upon people not directly but indirectly through a mediating essence or force. All individual human ideas are comprehended in this one highest and broadest Idea. It is the connection between God and his people. Where Jews speak of a host of mediating beings called angels, and Greeks have *diamones*, Philo believed that all of these are linked to that divine reason that creates and guides the world and through which God reveals himself to people through their souls, which are part of God. This is how

Philo believed, and his belief is not inconsequential. Renowned historian Will Durant thought Philo's *Logos* to be "one of the most influential ideas in the history of thought."

In 1841, renowned preacher-turned-philosopher, Unitarian-become-Transcendentalist Ralph Waldo Emerson published his first set of essays, and in the first paragraph of the first of those laid forth this stunning proposition: "There is one mind common to all individual men. Every man is an inlet to the same and to all of the same ... What Plato has thought, he may think; what a saint has felt, he may feel; what at any time has befallen any man, he can understand. Who hath access to this universal mind is a party to all that is or can be done, for this is the only and sovereign agent."

One universal mind? Is it God? Or at least our God link? Emerson preferred in those days to speak rather of nature.

More than a century later, Dr. M. Scott Peck came to the question and did not shrink. Conceding that while it could never be proved, one hypothesis for him was persuasive. "To put it plainly," he wrote, "our unconscious is God, God within us."

All these speculations and contentions our Moosewood bookshelves or college library stacks embraced. All these thinkers through all these times, grappling with puzzlements like ours, groping for the same comfort of comprehension. Each of these, our intellectual forebears, discovering in his own way in his own time that special insight, that *gnosis*, that Word, that *Logos*, that godly unconscious which we, in our own way and time, were discovering for ourselves on a small island off the coast of Maine.

The collective unconscious that guides us is God.

Our purpose in finding Moosewood was to find God. Our purpose thereafter would be to make ourselves ever more godly.

Let me put it another way, begging your indulgence as I do,

because I need to use language not customary in my lexicon. It is the profanity of the whiners of the world, firing barrages of blasphemy in all directions, cursing, as they say it, *the God-damned government*. Or *my God-damned boss*. Or their *God-damned wasted life*.

Desperately they need an anagram.

God is a loving God, we are told, an understanding God, a forgiving God. But he is also a demanding God, making demands on us for at least five thousand years, since the day he handed Moses that list of demands we call the Ten Commandments. Those demands spell out precisely what his believers must and must not do. Jesus added two more demands: "You must love the Lord your God with all your heart, all your soul, and all your mind; and love your neighbor as yourself."

Those are the demands God laid down. We — whiners and shiners alike — need to heed those demands. The structure and propelling force of our lives should be a faithful adherence to those God-demands.

And there's the new anagram: lives will be fulfilled and sanctified only when *God-damned* lives become *God-demand* lives.

Learning that lesson, we are to model it, becoming a beacon that others can follow. That's our job. It's a big job! God doesn't give us small ones.

18

LOOSE ENDS

It is time to gather loose ends. Not that there is anything wrong with loose ends. I have spoken before of my admiration of the great American composer Charles Ives. His symphonies, so complex and layered, strike some ears as ragged tangles of loose musical ends. And at first listen, they are. But masterfully woven together, those loose ends make majestic music. Similarly, our lives themselves are bundles of loose ends, random strands, dangling before us, waiting for us to weave them into our own symphonies.

We've come a long way. In early chapters, we thought of the changing of our lives as important for itself — the very act salutary. We didn't, at first, realize that the course and impetus of our change were directed not by chance but by the Holy Spirit. Later, we realized that change by itself isn't enough; rather the dimensions and nature of the change are what count. Now we understand that ultimate success is measured only by how close our change brings us to holiness. Aspiring to live and act in accordance with the godly impulses of the Collective Unconscious, the Holy Spirit, should be our goal at Moosewood, and for the rest of our lives — God, through the Spirit, moving us closer to God.

At Moosewood that summer, one moment marked for us the final resolving. It was a moment that may lose import in the telling. It may not mean to you what it meant to us. Maybe you not only had to be *there*; you had to be *we*, to have gone through what we had gone through, made the changes, surmounted the testings, harbored the doubts, asked the questions, perceived the intimations of answers, and, most of all, been open to the interpreted wisdom of the commonplace.

A balky sliding door. The door from the living room to the deck outside had grown so recalcitrant that at times it couldn't be opened at all. My meager mechanical skills availed not. Friends, advisers in matters like these, failed. The door, we joked resignedly, had become our Nautilus machine. Since it was only getting worse, we sought professional help. A rescuer named Chuck arrived from the local building supply yard, a gentle, soft-spoken man who knew well his specialties, and his specialties, we discovered, were two. Monday through Friday he did windows. In a half hour, he had removed the improper shim that had pressured the lintel, and our glass door, for the first time ever, could be slid with one finger. That was Chuck's weekday expertise. On Sundays, he was a preacher, pastor of a small church over in Manset, Maine. In a sense, he had just come to that calling recently; in a sense, he had schooled for it years before, but there'd been problems.

Graduated from Princeton Divinity School, he was called to a church in Massachusetts to undertake the life of parish pastor. But it didn't work, for what seemed an understandable reason. The very first time, as he stepped before the congregation to begin a service, he fainted. The second time, same thing. And the third and the fourth. "God was nudging me, I figured, saying, 'I don't want you here, at least not yet.' I didn't know why."

He moved to northern Maine and, giving up expectations of preaching, found a job in building supplies where he worked several years until a Bible passage triggered his next epiphany. "How can they call on him to save them unless they believe in him? And how can they believe in him if they have never heard about him? And how can they hear about him unless someone tells them?"

The passage is from Romans, the epistle of that great life-changer Saul/Paul, and it persuaded Chuck that he was needed to tell others of the Jesus who had saved him and could save them too. With that insight and the renewed commitment it spawned, he moved again, to our area, where he found both a building supplies job and a church. And this time around did not faint.

Pastor Chuck's epistle epiphany resonated in us. He knew, he said, he had made the right choice; we knew the same thing of ours. He knew, he said, his path was directed by God. We knew that ours had been as well.

In the narrowest sense, what got fixed that day at Moosewood was a sliding door. In the broader sense, it was we. And here I use the word *fix* not in the sense of repairing what's broken but in the sense of cementing what's changed. Does it seem I am reading too much into the story? Am I guilty of excessive exegesis? Not if the exegesis served us. If, in the telling, the tale rings hollow, perhaps that's because such moments are meant to be experienced, not explained.

To which I would add just one thing more — make of this what you will. Pastor Chuck's proper name — I tell it now to tie up this final loose end — was Charles Ives.

19

FOREVER?

We lived at Moosewood for thirteen years. Why did it end?

The airline that flew from Boston to Bar Harbor often swept over the little town of Bar Harbor, which meant they flew directly over Bar Island. On one such flight, I was looking down at Moosewood as the PA voice came on saying, "We hope you'll have a pleasant day here in Maine or wherever your final destination may be."

Was Moosewood our final destination? At that moment, we thought yes, most certainly it was. We were blissfully content with our new lives, delighted in the knowledge that at the dawn of the twentieth century, most of the blooms in the flower shops of Bar Harbor had been grown on our island, and that Bar Harbor used to be named Eden. Which meant we were living in the garden of Eden, and why should we ever want that to change?

One answer, of course, is that minds can change. To deny that would be to deny the very concept of life changes such as ours.

If we could make a dramatic change in direction once, we might choose to do it again. The challenges next time surely would be different, but the inevitable anxieties would be fewer because we had passed this way before.

One day in town, having pizza at Epi's, we spotted an elderly woman whose sprightly eyes belied the wrinkles of her weathered face, whose keenness contradicted her white hair. Seeing Helen Nearing like that, we reflected on how her husband, Scott, at age seventy, had thought himself mystically "touched on the shoulder" and informed he had "another twenty years of service." He didn't doubt. So they celebrated that certainty by moving to Cape Rosier, Maine, the two of them, to start *Living the Good Life* all over, building a stone house, tilling fields, growing food, thinking, writing, and serving as philosopher-exemplars for countless aspirants to a back-to-basics lifestyle who would follow. Scott lived to be a hundred, dying in 1984. Now Helen, though still appearing to enjoy vitality, was telling friends she felt sapped. She repeated a line from Trotsky: "Old Age is the most surprising thing that happens to a person." She recalled, "It didn't happen to Scott till he was ninety-five," adding ruefully, "I'm only eighty-five." She was writing one last book: *Loving and Leaving the Good Life*, then, reluctantly but affirmatively, she planned to depart their famous homestead, moving back — moving on — to the Netherlands, her family's homeland.

Conditions change. For us, living at Moosewood demanded vigor and health. Should either diminish, the island might no longer seem hospitable. Or should our sons need us, or should ... There were manifold imponderables. We too might, one day, feel compelled to move on. Moosewood might *not* be our final destination. We accepted that. When friends asked had we "really moved there forever," we thought of Mount Rushmore and dinosaur digs and the ambiguity of that word, *forever*, and replied with a literal truth that also was open to interpretation, "We're here for good."

Sometimes, the worst thing that could happen is the best thing that could happen. We heard several cases that made this point as we continued to enjoy and learn from Moosewood.

I wrote earlier about Kirstie, the young anchorwoman who had been fired from her Los Angeles job the very week her broadcast had finally risen to number one in the ratings. She came to visit us at Moosewood, she, her husband, and their baby. It was a beautiful week, but she said she was anxious to get back to the coast because she had accepted an anchor job at another LA station, a job she had taken, I sensed, more for career continuity than from conviction. Each day they were with us, she and her husband seemed more and more intrigued by our experience. We were happy to have these good friends visit and so eager to evangelize our life change that we bubbled endlessly about everything we had experienced and discovered that winter, things that would have sounded absurdly trivial to a major-market news anchorwoman.

A year later, we got a letter from them. Fifteen years younger than we but "inspired by you and what you did," Kirstie and her husband had decided to leave the pressure cooker of big-city TV and make their own break. They had bought a house in a small town in northern California, and though they weren't sure what they would do, what would become of them, even what would happen the next week, they were determined to find out.

A few months later, they sent a clipping from a northern California paper that recounted how this former anchorwoman from Los Angeles was inaugurating a local news program on a small TV station in Salinas. Her husband, a former network producer, would be the fledgling station's news director. The two of them, making such drastic changes in their lives, such dramatic downscaling, claimed they were following the example of friends they had visited in Maine.

Another friend visited Moosewood. It was Mauri, who, looking at us and our new lives, was reminded of the Texas lawyer she had profiled as a TV producer: he who had come up with the theory of "left-turn people," those who one day get up, get dressed, climb in the car, back out the driveway, and instead of turning right to head to work as usual, turn left and never look back. A month after her visit, Mauri wrote to report she had been offered a good job in Washington, D.C., but was thinking of turning it down. She and her husband, she said, were "still thinking of the tide. It captivated us. To live so dependent on the sea and so tied to the sea must be full of wonder. It is that connection with real life that we want to find in our spot."

And then there was John. The day after he was fired from his job of many years at KNBC, the *Los Angeles Times* headlined the story: "Sacking 'The Best Reporter' in Town." John and his wife were good friends of ours. After Jo and I moved to Maine, whenever their own travels brought them near, we rendezvoused. Now, hearing his bad news, I dashed off the one letter he wasn't expecting. "Dear John: Heard the news. We're delighted."

It was his turn, I told him. Maybe it didn't start out as his choice, to be sure, but now he had a wonderful opportunity to turn bad news into good. He had done what he had done for so long and so well, now there was no need to do it again. He had nothing left to prove in that particular line of work. Other stations, no doubt, would be after him, but maybe it was time to move on. Anything, everything is possible.

I was disappointed a few weeks later to hear that John had accepted a new job that, to me, sounded like the same job in a different place. But several mornings later I got a phone call from him. There was almost a tremble in John's voice. He wanted us to be the first ones to know. Had we heard about the new job he had taken? We had? Well, he had started work at Channel 13 the day before, but when he got home, he was unsettled and unsure. He sat down, he said, and read the letter from Moosewood again and again.

"It didn't say anything I didn't know, I guess, but for some reason I had to be told. It really is time to change, see what else I can do." So as soon as he hung up from us, he said, he was going to go to the new job, see the new boss, and quit.

Two days later when we talked again, he had just come home from his first flying lesson.

"Always wanted to, but never had time," he said with a new enthusiasm in his voice.

This was becoming contagious.

299

Then Scott Craig came calling. After being best friends in high school, Scott and I had gone our separate ways — separate but parallel; he had become one of the preeminent producers of television documentaries, working out of Chicago. He came to our island one summer weekend for business — a TV series for the HGTV network that sought to depict drastic life changes some people had made while seeking, as the series title put it, *The Good Life.*

The half-hour profile Scott and his crew crafted about Jo and me and our new lives was the finest thing ever done by anybody about us; the most flattering, certainly, but also the most honest and insightful. Each time the program was rebroadcast, there came to us a new flurry of letters, phone calls, and even visits to the Bar Harbor area by people motivated by that show, infected by the contagious enthusiasm we expressed. Some were pondering or puzzling their own change and wanted tips, ideas, guidance, or just encouragement. Some told us they had never considered doing such a thing before, but after seeing the program had decided they ought at least think about it. What did *we* think?

What we thought was that, just as it had been a challenge for us to change our lives, now it was a scary challenge for us to be considered models for others. But we accepted it with genuine enthusiasm. Yes, we told them, it's a big decision, their own decision, but it's worth seriously considering. It *can* be done.

What was not to be enthusiastic about? The best things we had in our lives at that moment, we owed to finding Moosewood. As we approached the tenth anniversary of our move, we considered. What were we enjoying most? What was most gratifying, most meaningful in our lives? What pursuits and achievements brought us closest to the holy? The list gleamed.

A few years after taking up residence at Moosewood, expecting little or no further work in TV, I was contacted by folks at the A&E Television Network who asked if I would like to host a new series of documentaries. It would require not much more than dropping down to New York now and then to tape several programs, then return home. I said I'd give it a try.

In the next few years, I learned to appreciate not only the warm camaraderie of a new group of friends but the highly professional and successful programs they produced. It was an honor to represent them as the on-camera face and voice for their programs, and if there were those in the audience who mistakenly believed I was responsible for the whole production, I was not eager to correct them.

As the work with A&E evolved into hosting specials like Boston Pops Fourth of July concerts and holiday programs, and then joining Peter Graves to present the network's five-night-a-week signature series *Biography*, I found myself reaching a new generation of viewers, few of whom remembered me from my NBC years.

I was working far less than I had worked back then, but to acquaintances it appeared I was fully employed. "How do you get any time to spend on that island you talk about?" they asked. The answer, of course, was that if the work had taken me away from Moosewood for more than a few days now and then, I wouldn't have been doing it. Never again, I had promised, would work determine our lives. But this way, I again had a hand in a different aspect of a business I still enjoyed without unbalancing our carefully chartered new lives. It was ideal. I never expected it, never planned it, never could have conceived it. And it never would have happened had we not found Moosewood.

I also was enjoying doing the videos of Maine with colleagues Jeff Dobbs and Bing Miller. I admired their work as much as the work of network TV professionals.

My still photographs of the glories of Acadia were selling well over in town at the Spruce Grove Gallery — prints, prints with accompanying poetry, photographic note cards, plus the book I had produced, *Acadia: Visions and Verse*.

Mary Jo's art also sold well at the gallery. Our book, *Parasols of Fern*, recounting the frolicking lives of kids on the island decades before, was doing well. Published by a small regional press (the story was small and regional; it seemed appropriate), the book was generously received and soon went into a second printing. It was distributed only in our area, but because so many tourists come to our area each year, we received kind letters and reviews from all parts of the country. A great satisfaction for Jo came when a distant relative of the kids she had depicted showed her a photograph of the boys, whom Jo had drawn from her imagination. Not only did they look almost exactly as she had drawn them, one of them was wearing precisely the same straw hat she had imagined.

Our greatest satisfaction with that book, of course, was that we had worked on it together. Or, as I informed our younger son upon completion of the book, it was the first thing his mother and I had collaborated on since him.

All of these — the books, the art, the photography and poetry, the videos, the "full-time" TV job requiring just a few days a month — we counted among what most fulfilled us those days. These were blessings that derived from God. We believed that; we *knew* that. And knew too that we never would have found them had we not found Moosewood.

As the years passed, bringing us peace and fulfillment, time did not stand still. We grew older. A skin cancer was surgically removed from my forehead — gouged out — just three days before I was due on camera for a Fourth of July Boston Pops concert on the Esplanade. Forewarned, a makeup artist was prepared to spackle and cover so five million viewers weren't aware of it.

Prostate cancer came the next year, and while a urologist was doing his thorough workups for a radical prostatectomy, he discovered an unrelated tumor on my right kidney. Had that kidney cancer not been caught then, it likely would not have been discovered until it became symptomatic, and that could have been too late.

Someone told me I was lucky. No, I replied, luck had nothing to do with it.

Recuperating from the removal of the prostate and awaiting the removal of the kidney, I was due once again for another July Fourth broadcast with the Boston Pops.

Boston — The annual charity auction was coming up, and I persuaded a friend, the PR woman Kim Smedvig (wife of renowned trumpeter Rolf and later Mrs. James Taylor), to stay on the phone with me while I bid on the one item I eagerly wanted to win — a chance to heed Buckskin Bill's good counsel and, for a change, make my own oompahs. Sort of.

The item was a onetime opportunity to conduct the venerable

Pops at one of its Symphony Hall concerts — in fact, conduct the Pops' most famous performance number, Sousa's "Stars and Stripes Forever." As I anxiously clung to the phone in our rec room in Tarzana, California, listening over the radio, I found myself locked in a bidding war with someone on the East Coast. He would top my bid for the conducting gig, Kim would come back on, report to me, and I'd have to decide whether to raise him or fold. Mary Jo was completely supportive, knowing one of my lifelong fantasies was to conduct an orchestra. She'd gotten used to watching me conduct music on the radio or stereo, waving a pencil and shaking my imaginary mane at the unseen orchestra. She knew this auction was the only way a self-respecting orchestra would let me point a baton at it.

It took most of three hours before Kim reported to me that, when I'd raised the bid to $2,500, my adversary had dropped out and the prize was mine. It was a lot of money, it was for a good cause, and I was giddy with the thrill.

For a few hours.

The next morning a woman identifying herself as a reporter for the Quincy, Massachusetts, *Patriot-Ledger* phoned my NBC office, asking, "Mr. Perkins, are you intending to conduct the Pops for a TV story?"

"Oh, no, this is strictly personal. No cameras. Just something I have always dreamed of doing."

"Do you know who you beat out in the auction last evening?"

"*Whom* I beat out?" I said, correcting. "No, I don't."

It had been a couple in New Jersey, she told me. They had been hoping to win the conducting opportunity for their ninety-eight-year-old father, who was in a nursing home. At one time, long ago, he had played in John Philip Sousa's band, and this was to have been his last chance to relive such an affirming time of his life. And, oh, yes, the old gentleman's name was — of all things — McNamara!

"I'll get back to you," I told the reporter.

I placed an urgent call to the BSO. "Kim, we've got a problem."

"We sure do," she agreed as I briefed her.

I don't recall whose idea it was, but between us we agreed on a solution. I would yield the prize to Mr. McNamara and pay the difference between his family's highest offer and my winning bid, and then the next year, I could pay my bid and have the conducting honors for myself.

Joe McNamara was wheeled onto the stage at Symphony Hall in Boston one spring evening that year. NBC, alerted by me to a good story, covered his conducting debut with the BSO (temporarily McNamara's band) for the next morning's *Today Show*. All was well.

The following year, I flew to Boston with my family and found my way backstage at Symphony Hall to join old friends of the orchestra and conductor John Williams, with whom I had done several stories over the years. They were all very helpful. John wryly assured me, "There's nothing to it; all you have to do is go out there and, when they start playing, you start waving. When they stop, you stop. Turn, take a bow. That's all there is to it." Thanks, John.

One of the orchestra members stopped me as I was about to go onstage and added, "Remember, Jack, the orchestra is the only animal with its horns in the back and its behind out front."

I went out front.

Seen from the stage, the main floor of Symphony Hall as it's set up for Pops is a panorama of tables filled with snacks and drinks, and chairs filled with people in a buoyant (and I hoped forgiving) mood. The air is charged with light, and polite applause rises as a stranger strides onstage, all in red (tie), white (shoes, pants, shirt), and blue (blazer).

Then you step up onto the podium, take a deep breath, give a downbeat, and feel the explosive rush of a magnificent orchestra thundering into life.

I didn't completely deceive myself. I knew the orchestra had played the Sousa piece hundreds, even thousands, of times and didn't need me out there. The piece was so woven into their genes that they probably would perform just as well with no director.

On the other hand, what if I actually were leading it? Could I bring everything to an instant stop the way John Williams no doubt could? Or would it be a train wreck?

I decided I'd try a little test. I had rehearsed a hundred times before a mirror with the score in front of me and the BSO recording of the piece on the player. I was ready. So at one point where I thought it might be appropriate, I retarded the beat of my baton just enough to see if the musicians would retard as well. It worked. They followed my direction. I really was conducting them!

I confess, about then I let my ego get the best of me. Two-thirds of the way through the performance there erupted from the audience behind me a swell of cheers and applause, and of course I thought it was for me. They recognized what a terrific job I was doing. Most civilian guest conductors wouldn't know the time signatures of the piece as well as I did, or know the proper way to mark the beat with the baton. I wasn't just waving a stick up there. I knew what I was doing. I wondered if this roar behind me is what a standing "O" feels like, but I didn't dare look around.

Later, watching the video, I realized this was the place where a huge American flag was unfurled above me, filling the upper half of the proscenium.

I whipped the baton to the conclusion, the orchestra bursting the final crescendo and the audience erupting in even more applause. Generously, I motioned the players to rise and share "my" ovation and, following their conductor's lead, they rose. I was one happy "behind out front" savoring a live audience response, something TV newscasters seldom experience, then headed, reluctantly, to the wings and backstage.

Ah, but I was still in demand. Kim found me, saying she wanted me to meet someone special. What admirer could this be? She led me to a parlor where, in a wheelchair, clutching his woolen lap robe against the air-conditioned chill, sat none other than Mr. Joseph McNamara. I told him what a great pleasure it was to meet him at last. How happy I was that he was there. His only response, as he fixed me with rheumy eyes, was to say with the blunt candor the old can get away with, "You didn't come to see *me* conduct. I came to see *you*."

For ten years, I had the joy of cohosting the *Pops Goes the Fourth* broadcasts across the nation from Boston's Esplanade beside the Charles River. I also cohosted with Mary Richardson of WCVB the annual *Holiday at Pops* program at Christmastime. It was at one of those concerts that I was asked (and didn't have to be asked twice) to narrate the orchestra's playing of "The Night before Christmas." As conductor Keith Lockhart was kind enough to announce to the audience, I dedicated my contribution to the program to Miss Annie Jo Perkins, our just-born first grandchild.

The Fourth broadcasts were the more spectacular, of course. A third of a million people gathered on the Esplanade in a festive, picnicking mood, the cannon batteries standing ready for the finale. After Mary and I finished our opening remarks from the apron of the stage, a phalanx of Boston's finest escorted me through the crush of people to climb to the roof of the eight-story Emerson College dorm building at 100 Beacon Street, a perfect catbird seat from which to take it all in. I stood on a platform in front of our camera, surrounded on three sides by the many VIPs invited to take in the show from here, as in front of me, below me, was that undulating sea of people. From here I hosted the rest of the program, stepping in front of the camera to reset the scene, introduce the orchestra's next number, toss to commercials. The concert ended with Tchaikovsky's *1812 Overture*, the military artillery unit at river's edge firing its battery in practiced synchronization with the score while church bells rang on cue. It was a grand performance every time. I had never — and still haven't — done any work on the air as exciting, as gratifying, as *fun* as those ten years of Boston's *Fourth*.

This year, though, my waiting time between surgeries was especially memorable. The prostate operation had not — it turned out — left me quite as "dry" as had been hoped and expected. There was temporarily at least some incontinence. Without dwelling on things, let me simply say that I shall never forget the secret feeling of standing at the edge of the roof of 100 Beacon Street in Boston, hundreds of thousands of people spread before me, millions more watching me on television, none of them ever to know that as I stood there speaking with ease and glib profundity, *I was peeing my pants.*

With all that — the surgeries, their aftermath, and clouded health prospects — it became clear to Jo and me that the time had come in our lives that it would be prudent to have medical care more readily available than it was from the island, bound by tides and more than an hour's drive to the nearest major hospital. So far, in thirteen years, there'd been four rush trips to an emergency room. Each time luckily happened at low tide. We were pushing it.

Our thirteen years at Moosewood had been — in so many ways — the best of our lives. Years that had transformed us, bringing us closer toward holiness. But there were good years still ahead, and when we come to a fork in the road, we have to make a decision. Change, we had learned, is not necessarily to be shunned.

We had spent some vacation time in southwest Florida, where Jo's parents hosted us many times and where we were comfortably familiar. We found a house on one of Florida's islands, an island quite different from Bar Island, but an island nonetheless. We moved there.*

---

* What we did not know, as we headed that summer to Florida, was that — in the greatest irony — out in western Maine there was a tragic roadside accident late one afternoon. It happened along Route 5, the very road that sixteen years earlier we had traveled on the first leg of what became our Maine lives, going to meet the Horrible Man. On this day, that wholly unhorrible man suffered a horrible accident. Run down by a careless driver in a minivan, Stephen King was almost killed, injured so badly that the first police reports his devastated wife, Tabitha, heard claimed he had been killed. That was wrong, but the diagnoses of collapsed lung, smashed hip, multiply fractured legs, and excruciating pain were not. He endured five operations in ten days, followed by continuing consultations and treatment from pain authorities at Duke, but never again was able to live painlessly. Especially in the cold of winter did the pain torment.

So they chose to escape it. This devoted Maine couple, who had always eschewed the lives they might have had in the capitals of glamour and wealth, began their seasonal escape to an island off the west coast of Florida. Stephen and Tabitha, who years before had unwittingly helped kindle our new lives, now began living their new seasonal lives a mile up the road

We moved there. How simple a sentence for such a complicated change. We began the dispersal of goods, determined to see it not as painful but joyful. We invited Maine friends to come and take whatever they wanted of the furniture and fixings. For dear friends who years before had gotten us interested in antiques but recently had run into financial straits, we invited their daughters as a surprise to their parents to drive a rental truck from Cape Cod to Maine and deliver to them several antique pieces, some of which we originally had acquired from their family. Our gift of remembrance and affection.

Finally, the day came. As we left the little house for the last time, driving away across the meadow, past the yawning oak, along the blackberries, the outline in the grass where a barn had once stood, down through Mary Jo's White Cathedral to the end of the island and across the bar, putting Moosewood and our Moosewood lives behind us, did we go with regrets?

No. Not regrets. We chose not to miss Moosewood but always, always to cherish the memories of our little house and our time there, the new lives and new selves it helped us create. The godliness it let us find and express. We would not *miss*, and yet even today I do not write these words with dry eyes.

The National Park Service people had long coveted our piece of Bar Island to incorporate into Acadia. We sold Moosewood to them. A few months later, one of the park people called

---

from us. Talk about tying loose ends.

One Florida winter's day, I was telling them about one of their new neighbors, who had an extravagant collection of classic cars — McClarens, Ferraris, Lamborghinis, a gull-winged Mercedes (of which only twenty-five were made, at two mil a copy) — and he'd accrued so many that he bought the oversized house next door and gutted it to make it into an extra multilevel garage.

Steve turned to Tabitha and joked, "I guess we just don't have the hang of this bein' rich thing yet."

to ask for our approval of their plans for Moosewood. The call was unnecessary but very considerate, and I thanked them for thinking of us. Their intention, they said, was to tear down our house. What would we think about that? Jo and I had talked about it already, so I told them there was nothing we would like more. It would be right for our twelve acres to revert to nature and for the complete island to be preserved. But we did make one request.

"Please don't let them take down the rock walls and chimneys of the old place from a hundred years ago," I begged the park representative. "Those should remain. As for the rest, it's up to you."

At that time, the Park Service didn't have the money for the demolition and removal, and so years dragged on with nothing done. Friends who wandered over to the island reported back that Moosewood was aging, and not gracefully. The buildings had been uncared for, the property overgrown with trees and bushes and vines. This, we told them, was supposed to happen, nature reclaiming what belongs to it. Though we went to another part of Maine each year to see friends, and I returned to shoot for a new visitors' video for the park, Mary Jo and I made it a point never to return to the island. We wanted to remember it the way we'd left it, the way we'd lived in it.

And now, all these years later, came a friend's call. Thanking him and hanging up, I went in to tell Jo.

"Joey, that was Jeff. He says it's finally happened."

"Moosewood?" She knew.

"They left the walls of the old place, but they've completely removed everything of ours."

"Moosewood gone," she repeated quietly, expressionless.

"Yes," I said, making myself believe it. And again, softly, "Yes."

I knew it was true. At the same time, I knew that in a way it was not true. That place we used to own still, today, owns us.

In our hearts, in our souls, in the blessed recall of our God-demand minds, we will always find Moosewood, find God.